D0987294

NOV 1 9 2018

The 1933 Chicago World's Fair

The 1933 Chicago World's Fair

A CENTURY OF PROGRESS

Cheryl R. Ganz

UNIVERSITY OF ILLINOIS PRESS

URBANA AND CHICAGO

Library of Congress Cataloging-in-Publication Data
Ganz, Cheryl.
The 1933 Chicago World's Fair : century of progress /
    Cheryl R. Ganz.
p.   cm.
Includes bibliographical references and index.
ISBN-13 978-0-252-03357-5 (cloth : alk. paper)
ISBN-10 0-252-03357-4 (cloth : alk. paper)
1. Century of Progress International Exposition
    (1933–34 : Chicago, Ill.)—History. I. Title.
  T501.B1G356   2008
907.4'77311—dc22   2008006403

Uncredited images are from the author's collection.

This book is dedicated to
Donald and Daryl Johnson,
Eloise DeYoung,
and Terry Sheahan,
for extraordinary guidance
and support,
and in memory of P. Felix Ganz,
Helene Kern, Beatrice Ganz,
and Patricia Haines.

CONTENTS

ACKNOWLEDGMENTS

For twenty-five years I lived along Chicago's lakefront with a thirty-third-floor view overlooking the site of the 1933–34 Chicago world's fair. I found inspiration in the city, its skyline, and its people every day. Perry Duis, Richard John, and Margaret Strobel have each provided me with guidance, encouragement, and support, challenging and changing my thinking and my writing as I worked on this book. Susan Levine and John D'Emilio broadened my horizons with their insights. For additional intellectual support and encouragement I thank Michael Alexander, Eric Arnesen, Manfred Bauer, Jen Boyle, Dorothy Crombie, Tom Crouch, Pete Daniel, Ron Davies, Roberta Feldman, Kathy Franz, Jim Hill, Melvin Holli, Thomas Hughes, Anne Meis Knupfer, Dieter Leder, Mike Leiderman, Miriam Levin, Ted Light, Sonya Michel, Don and Margit Naden, Bessie Neal, Sean M. O'Connor, Rick Rann, Christopher Reed, Leo Schelbert, Lisa Schrenk, Todd Shuman, John Staudenmaier, Gordon Vaeth, Linda Van Puyenbroeck, Lynn Weiner, and especially Bonnie Campbell Lilienfeld and Art Molella.

I am indebted to those who extended financial assistance. The University of Illinois at Chicago (UIC), the UIC History Department, the UIC Gender and Women's Studies Program, and the Jane Addams Hull-House Museum supported my research through fellowships, assistantships, and travel grants. It was inspirational to work one year in Jane Addams's office at Hull-House. The UIC Dean's Scholar Fellowship allowed me to use the Jefferson Room at the Library of Congress as my research cubicle, which was truly historian heaven. A fellowship at the National Museum of American History, Smithsonian Institution, was a research dream come true. The Lemelson Center at the National Museum of American History and the Illinois Historic Preservation Agency further supported my research travels. The UIC Graduate College, the UIC Graduate Student Council, the Midwest Art History Society, the Society for the History of Technology, and the Business History Conference supported travel to present my research at conferences in the United States, France, Germany, and Mexico. The Folger Shakespeare Library provided repeated access to housing in a setting with dynamic scholars. Most recently, Allen Kane of the Smithsonian Institution's National Postal Museum has supported my study.

I am grateful to those scholars who have researched international expositions and the 1933–34 Chicago world's fair, A Century of Progress, as well as those who have written inspiring works on related topics and important themes, especially John E. Findling, Thomas Hughes, Lenox Lohr, Roland Marchand, David F. Noble, Ruth Oldenziel, Robert W. Rydell, Lisa Diane Schrenk, and John M. Staudenmaier.

The thrill of the hunt in an archive can be matched only by the dedication of outstanding resource specialists who surpass their job descriptions to assist the researcher. I am especially grateful to Patricia Bakunas, Mary Ann Bamberger, Carmen De Leon, Julia Hendry, and the entire staff at the Special Collections Department of the University Library at the University of Illinois at Chicago for unearthing many, many files and for making me feel like one of the family. Ana Ortiz in Interlibrary Loans at the University Library continued to amaze me when she filled my requests for obscure publications. John Fleckner, Venessa Broussard Simmons, and the staff at the Archives Center of the National Museum of American History of the Smithsonian Institution ensured my research would be productive and pleasurable. Cecilia Wertheimer gave me access to precious materials at the Bureau of Engraving and Printing. Mary Wilke, Center for Research Libraries at the University of Chicago, compiled a useful source list of the libraries' collections. I am very grateful to Lesley Martin, who pointed out important collections and negotiated my entrée to unprocessed files from the Sally Rand papers at the Chicago History Museum.

I am thankful to many others who shared images from their collections or archives to supplement the ephemera from my own collection, including Jim Adams, Barbara S. Evans, Linda Goes, Bud Graske, Norine McSweeney Murphy, Joan Reisig, and Gordon Vaeth. Howard and Betty Bauman were family friends, but only after their deaths did I learn from their daughter Barbara that Howard, a talented amateur photographer, had taken many wonderful photographs at the fair. I am grateful to Roger, Barbara, Tom, Bill, Carolyn, Nancy, and their families for making them available, and to Tom's son, Sam, who scanned the original negatives.

It was a joy to work with the University of Illinois Press, and I especially appreciate the support and professionalism of Joan Catapano, Associate Director and Editor in Chief; Copenhaver Cumpston, Art Director; and Carol Betts, Associate Editor.

Underlying the professional assistance has been the unflagging loyalty of my family and friends. My parents, Donald and Daryl Johnson, not only modeled the work ethic and passion needed to sustain me in this mission but provided a writing environment on Washington Island, Wisconsin, that included Dad's fresh-caught fish and Mom's home cooking. Dan Portincaso gave me a tour of the Chicago Woman's Club building (now owned by Columbia College). I am especially grateful to Barb Rykaczewski for her assistance in researching biographical information. My dear friend Patricia Haines did not live to see me finish my work, but she picked up mail, watered plants, and gave me sustenance as I researched this book. William Asher and Theresa Pfister served as my sounding boards for all kinds of issues. Eloise DeYoung proofread every draft of every chapter as I wrote my manuscript.

She opened the world of grammar and syntax to me in new ways. Terry Sheahan joined me as my copy editor, writing coach, and intellectual sparring partner. Both a cheerleader and disciplinarian, she got me to the finish line. She shared my vision and helped bring it to life. My late husband, Felix, would have been so proud of my accomplishments. His voice was with me every step of the way. These and many other special people have inspired me and enriched my life immeasurably. Thank you.

The 1933 Chicago World's Fair

INTRODUCTION

In 1833 Chicago was a tiny backwoods settlement on the western frontier.[1] By 1933 it had become the nation's transportation hub, an industrial and meat-processing giant, and the fourth-largest city in the world, surpassed only by New York, London, and Tokyo.[2] The Great Depression's staggering blows, however, cast much of its industrial labor force into desperate idleness. Further, a well-deserved reputation for underworld crime and political scandal plagued the city.

Chicago's centennial year, 1933, saw one-fourth of the nation's labor force out of work. Well over one-third of all banks had closed their doors. In the previous November exasperated voters had voiced their desire for change by electing Franklin D. Roosevelt, offering him the opportunity to initiate the "new deal for the American people" that he had pledged in Chicago when he accepted the presidential nomination.[3] Across the Atlantic, response to unemployment and inflation paved the way for totalitarian regimes. Adolf Hitler had assumed full power in Germany, and Benito Mussolini had tightened his grasp on Italy. The National Socialists, popularly referred to as Nazis, had established the Gestapo and built the Dachau concentration camp. The continuing decline of the economy brought unprecedented suffering to the United States and Europe. Recovery seemed remote.

A small group of visionary civic and business leaders, including Charles and Rufus Dawes and Lenox R. Lohr, boldly planned to celebrate Chicago's hundred years of remarkable expansion and development by staging a world's fair, despite the warnings of cynics who predicted a financial fiasco. Fair organizers' futuristic plans for what came to be called A Century of Progress championed corporate capitalism, the very culprit that many Americans blamed for their economic woes. Not unlike Roosevelt's New Deal programs, a fair would, the planners predicted, counter the Depression's insidious economic and psychological impact by giving Chicago and its labor force a financial shot in the arm. Like Roosevelt's later Work Projects Administration, it would create much-needed jobs and stir hope that conditions would soon improve. It would also offer Depression-weary visitors an escape from disheartening daily lives. Fairgoers would carry their optimism home to unnumbered beleaguered communities across the nation and world. At the same time, a dazzling exposition would display Chicago as a creative, robust city, thus redeeming its reputation as a crime-riddled metropolis. Indeed, the fair would be a privately organized New Deal.

Chicago had hosted a world's fair in 1893, the World's Columbian Exposition. The exposition's enduring icons—the Ferris Wheel, a technological wonder, and Little Egypt, the exotic belly dancer—still evoked vivid memories for all who had attended. The international exhibition had showcased Chicago as an industrial leader with visions of urban grandeur even while it venerated tradition and the past. Championed by local business leaders, the 1893 exposition's classical architecture and conventional accouterments clearly expressed this mindset. Though financed in small part by private donations from luminaries such as the real-estate mogul Potter Palmer, the fair relied heavily on federal, state, and municipal grants for its funding.

In a significant break with the Columbian Exposition and all earlier fairs, the 1933 exposition reflected the business-military-engineering model fundamental to the professional careers of its primary organizers, Rufus and Charles Dawes and Lenox R. Lohr. This trio drew from their national networks to fill key leadership roles, including directors, and they enrolled nationally prominent advisers from the fields of science and technology. They and their team created a civil-military enterprise—a world's fair that reinvented the concept of international expositions. Unlike previous fairs, private funding rather than government support financed Chicago's 1933 fair. Also unlike previous fairs, which featured competitive, individually staged industrial exhibits to illustrate progress, Chicago's 1933 fair achieved that same end by using *cooperative* scientific and technological exhibits housed in thematic halls or corporate pavilions. Exhibits also emphasized science and technology's application to everyday life, leading viewers to imagine a better future.

Fair organizers innovatively approached the 1933 Chicago world's fair as an engineering project that celebrated the second industrial revolution. Their control of organization and operations enabled them to host a mammoth exhibition with spectacular educational exhibits from the various disciplines of science as well as to create an atmosphere of entertainment that attracted families, individuals, and conventioneers from throughout the United States during the economic crisis. The architecture and public spaces from which fair organizers operated and from which their planning for technological advances could be showcased illuminated further the influence of military, corporate, and university models. Through such means as the appointment of expert advisers and the selection of a theme that highlighted the idea of progress and what it entailed, they defined the western, masculine perspective of technology and exhibited it at A Century of Progress.[4]

Those former military leaders who conceptualized Chicago's 1933 fair also severed ties with the past philosophically by displacing humankind from its nuclear position as progress's prime mover. The World War had shattered their faith in humankind's ability to direct social advancement, whether through religion, education, the state, a free market, or social conflict. This conventional belief about progress and what pushes it had shaped modern civilization's understanding of history since at least the Enlightenment. Though ideas about the meaning of progress and what drives it have differed radically, all acknowledged humankind's dynamic role in civilization's gradual climb toward a more perfect world.

Fair organizers, influenced by the war and early twentieth-century distrust of humankind's capacity to produce a better world, replaced orthodox views with their belief that progress rides on the swell of technological innovation. Their belief limited humankind's role in world progress to consumerism. In the fair's robot-dominated *Fountain of Science* they boldly expressed their philosophy that science and technology, independent of human agency, drive progress, a philosophy succinctly articulated in the fair's theme, "Science Finds, Industry Applies, Man Conforms."[5] Further, those who organized Chicago's 1933 fair identified the population's material desires as key to technological innovation and a higher standard of living. By insisting that exhibits demonstrate ways in which technology improves daily life, they spoke to an economically depressed population's most fundamental notions of progress.

Beyond their break with conventional views of progress, fair organizers took another, significant step away from those who had promoted earlier fairs: they ingeniously used the very *idea* of progress as a tool to generate optimism. To communicate their message, they daringly underscored the fair's modern, streamlined, and colorful architecture, using radically new materials and building techniques to capture attention. Again, they severed ties with the Beaux-Arts tradition used at the 1893 exposition. Futuristic exhibits in both fair-sponsored halls and corporate-sponsored pavilions emphasized efficiency and accessibility while directing the fairgoer's gaze toward a better future.

The idea of progress drew together disparate voices for the very brief time that A Century of Progress glowed along Chicago's Lake Michigan shoreline. Though in many ways fair organizers sought inclusivity and saw themselves as facilitators bringing together various corporations and individuals, their elevation of science and technology as the engines of progress did not harmonize with the life experiences of all fair participants. Not all those who struggled for space and a voice at Chicago's 1933 exposition had abandoned old notions of progress that included social justice, recognition of ethnic and gender-related accomplishments, and personal freedom. A handful of exceptional individuals representing African Americans, socialites, ethnic populations and foreign nations, and groups of working women—fan dancer Sally Rand being the most successful financially as well as the most infamous of the latter—met obstacles but ultimately introduced personal, social definitions of progress and thereby influenced the ways the fair took shape. They found ways to resist and navigate in order to participate, to redefine power relationships, and to celebrate their own values and goals. Women from different classes and races found their own organizational strategies and public spaces from which to exert control and promote a vision, whether they be from the trustee dining room or the Midway entertainment zone. At the same time, Germany and Italy used air technology to display their reclaimed military prowess, firing fierce emotions among their American constituents.

The idea for a fair could flourish only in a political and social climate that opened a window on hope and opportunity. Fair organizers sought to generate optimism in a city beaten down by economic woes, but they also sought to redeem Chicago's unsavory reputation, drilled into imaginations worldwide by events such as the St. Valentine's Day Massacre, and thus to attract more financial and industrial wealth to the city. When confronted with the idea for a fair, Chicago reform politicians saw an opportunity to recreate the city's image in the proposed exposition and they supported the initiative.

The story of the 1933 world's fair is the story of Chicago's pride and its legendary "I Will" spirit to succeed despite adversity.[6] It is the story of a generation of successful business entrepreneurs who had been victorious in the Great War in Europe and now sought to leave a legacy that promoted their city, its culture, and its opportunities. These leaders articulated their modernist vision through art, architecture, advertising, and industrial design. The origins of this aesthetic can be traced to military, engineering, and corporate prototypes for a model drawn from organizations or sectors of society dominated by men. During the era of the rapid growth in scale of American businesses and the rise of the use of scientific organizational methods, engineers moved in large numbers from professional engineering into business management.[7] At the same time, they assumed "a special social responsibility to protect progress and to insure that technological change led to human benefit through the use of scientific advancements and industrial innovations for the masses in everyday life."[8] Finally, Chicago's 1933 fair is the story of nations, ethnic groups, and classes of women expressing their own ideas of progress.

A Century of Progress mirrored national and international developments, interests, and concerns: Its planning and organizational structure reflected the demand for greater efficiency within business management that marked the post–World War I period. Germany's and Italy's participation at the fair forecast their sinister political and military agendas. Attempts by Chicago courts to censor Sally Rand signaled a broader attempt to monitor public morality as Prohibition ended. The conflict over women's representation at the fair further articulated the ebbing of the women's movement. The African American community's thrust to reclaim its own history while commanding respect underlaid the National De Saible Memorial Society's insistence that Chicago acknowledge its first citizen. Finally, society's increasing consumerism directed fair management's insistence that exhibits highlight technology's practical application.

The fair ultimately attracted a paid attendance of more than thirty-nine million, the largest of any world's fair to that time. Its legacy included a distinctively new notion of progress for a world traumatized by the economic crisis of the

Great Depression. The new deal for progress in 1933 Chicago emerged from a world's fair that promoted optimism embedded in scientific, technological, and democratic ideals. Perhaps because the 1933 fair was a temporary research and development project run through private enterprise, it has not received the recognition that government-sponsored Depression-era projects such as the Tennessee Valley Authority have received. Not only did it succeed financially in troubled economic times, its timely staging had a major impact on the social and cultural life in Chicago and the nation. Like government-sponsored projects, it provided employment and offered hope and ideas that brought many Americans one step closer to a better life.

1

Sally Rand
and the Midway

The idea of someone dancing with ostrich feathers appealed to me. . . .
My mother . . . hurried me past the packed pavilion, but I managed to
see one of the pictures out front, and there Sally had turned around, fan
dropped, and was showing her big peach-colored bottom. I felt I had
seen something of importance . . . . It was part of the century of progress
and I was happy to be part of it too, to have seen the future in Sally's
bare bottom.

—Donald Richie

Years after glimpsing the poster showing Sally Rand's bottom, Donald
Richie remembered the exhilaration he felt as a nine-year-old when he and his
mother escaped their cheerless daily life in Lima, Ohio, by visiting A Century
of Progress.[1] His aunt had given them the money for the train ride to Chicago.
Despite the passage of years, recollections of the fair's magic never slipped
away . . . the Sky Ride, the Hall of Transportation, exhibits of Kraft cheese
and flashy new cars and Pabst's Blue Ribbon Beer. Relaxing in a Midway café,
he recalled, his mother hummed "The Isle of Capri" while "looking so different from the way she looked around the house." From the Sky Ride view
of downtown Chicago, Richie rhapsodized, he beheld the "whole progressive
century laid under [him] like a map."[2]

Millions of fairgoers returned to communities across the nation and shared
similar feelings of buoyancy and hope for the future with their neighbors. Almost all remembered the scandalous fan dancer Sally Rand. In Rand they saw
both "the most beautiful woman in the world," as Cecil B. DeMille referred
to her, and a woman determined to succeed despite obstacles presented by
the Great Depression and the nation's court system.[3] They wanted to reclaim
that determination for themselves.

John S. Van Gilder, a businessman from Knoxville, Tennessee, found in the fair both commercial inspiration and his opportunity to behold the glorious Sally Rand. Daily headlines announced increasingly grim economic news, and as vice president of McClung wholesale hardware, Van Gilder needed inspiration. When a photo of Rand, the rags-to-riches showgirl, performing her fantastic new bubble dance caught his eye, he made up his mind. He would go to the international exposition to see Rand perform, and touring the fair's exhibits would give him a sales advantage. Further, he would try to get one of Rand's four-foot balloons as a souvenir. His excitement soared. The thought of the fair and Rand's bubble made him feel light, optimistic. Like Donald Richie and his mother, Van Gilder sought an escape from the daily doldrums of the Depression era.

Van Gilder made the trip. He enthusiastically reported back to his traveling salesmen that the exposition was an education in tomorrow's uses of electricity, paint, construction, merchandise, and entertainment. "Any merchant visiting the Fair cannot help but come back home a BETTER MERCHANT!!"[4] While there, he visited hardware exhibits and had a private tour of the lagoon fountain's waterworks. He even enjoyed the honor of pushing the button to start its colored light show. But nothing he saw or did those three days compared to the few magical moments of watching Sally Rand perform her bubble dance on an outdoor stage.

With the dramatic opening of Rand's dance, all Van Gilder's thoughts of the outside world evaporated. Strains of soft music, semidarkness, and the parting draperies set the stage for a blue spotlight that pinpointed Rand and her iridescent balloon. Her nude body, covered in white greasepaint, appeared statuesque. Van Gilder recalled Rand's entrancing performance: "With all the grace of a woodland nymph, she toyed and danced around and played with and tossed into the air her transparent soap bubble. Somehow, one felt as though secretly watching some little woodland creature at play in the moonlight."[5]

Van Gilder arranged a backstage meeting with Rand to request that special souvenir, one of her luminescent bubbles. A gracious Rand, wrapped in a silk kimono, shook Van Gilder's hand. Hearing his request, she apologized that because of the high cost to produce the special balloons, she could not part with one. Instead she gave her admirer an autographed photograph of herself posing with the bubble, another for his Rotary Club, and sealed the moment with a kiss. The next day Van Gilder sent her roses with a note expressing how she made life in the world more delightful.

For John S. Van Gilder and many, many others who attended A Century of Progress, Rand's rise from poverty embodied optimism and faith in progress. Clearly, she captured the spirit and significance of the 1933–34 Chicago world's fair. At the same time, her ingenuity, daring, and independence spoke provocatively to changing notions of women and sexuality, something only time and perspective would reveal.

The Sensational Sally Rand

Harriet Helen Beck wanted to make it big in show business. It was in her blood. She had run away from her mountain home in Elkton, Missouri, at age fourteen, determined to join a carnival. She had been around the country some since then—Kansas City, New York, Chicago, Hollywood. One could even say she had enjoyed a bit of success, performing in the circus, vaudeville, nightclubs, and even bits in silent movies. But she hadn't really made her mark. And in 1933 times were tough. Family radio programs had cut into vaudeville's audiences, and theaters countrywide had reduced the number of contracts they made with traveling troupes. Good-paying jobs for a showgirl were few.

Her life having recently scraped some low points, the ambitious Beck hungrily sought contacts and a venue. An astute self-promoter, she knew she must market herself, and she needed a new twist, something sensational. She found the twist that spring in her risqué and thoroughly captivating fan dance. Believing she had something salable, she needed only an audience. "I realized from the outset," she recalled in 1935, "that 90 percent of the merchandise that is sold in this country is sold to women. In my case, that presented obvious difficulties."[6] No ingénue in the business world, she understood the maxim "the quickest way to get ahead in any industry is to present the product to the largest possible number of persons."[7] Chicago's glorious world's fair offered the perfect stage. Her fortunes were about to change. Twenty-nine-year-old Harriet Helen Beck—a.k.a. Sally Rand—would take Chicago by storm.

Finding an "in" proved difficult. She approached contacts such as Charlie Weber, a county commissioner who operated a beer concession at the fair's "Streets of Paris," but she ran into dead ends. "I've used up every friend and connection I've got in Chicago," she complained to her employer, Ed Callahan, "but they [world's fair commissioners] refuse to see me."[8] Callahan had hired Rand at the city's Paramount Club. Hardened by uncertainty and disappointment, both valued creative thinking and tenacity. Together they schemed.

Accounts differ as to exactly how Sally Rand landed her notorious and extremely lucrative position at the fair's Streets of Paris concession.[9] One thing is consistent in each account, however: an uninvited and scantily robed Rand crashed the exposition's posh preopening party riding a white horse. It's not clear who put Rand up to the stunt. After all, Rand herself was known to embellish her stories. Filtering the known details, however, it appears that the saga of the flamboyant performer's grand entrance began with Callahan and Rand plotting the strategic entrée in a dark tent outside the fairgrounds on the evening of May 27, 1933. Inside the Streets of Paris concession, Chicago's elite enjoyed the fair's glitzy Parisian-themed opening extravaganza.

It was quite a show. Everyone who mattered was there, laughing and dancing and enjoying lovely food at the Café de la Paix. They had all been invited to
celebrate A Century of Progress, and many of the three thousand or so guests
undoubtedly patted themselves on the back. Huge reserves of energy, enthusiasm,
dedication, and money had gone into putting it all together. But the wonderful
colored lights that lit the Midway—the fair would be dubbed the Rainbow City—
blurred reality's harsh contours and softened the starkness that cloaked Sally Rand
and most other Americans every day of the week. Even the city of Chicago was
bankrupt, but no one would have guessed it, as the cream of Chicago glided through
the party in formal evening clothes or in clever costumes that sometimes aped
their social inferiors—cavemen, Native Americans, peasants, and French maids.
Costumed fair workers drifted among them, portraying artists' models, soldiers,
top-hatted gentlemen, and flower venders.[10]

Meanwhile, in the tent outside, Rand prepared her costume and makeup—a
long white velvet cape, a flowing blond wig, and a floral ankle band. Satisfied,
she approached the exposition's entrance gate, but stunned guards refused her
admission without an invitation. Dejected, she returned to Callahan at the tent.
A clever man, he suggested using the fair's back entrance, accessible only from the
lake. Not unfamiliar with wealthy bootleggers and their lavish cruisers, Callahan
returned shortly with a borrowed yacht. The two conspirators loaded their rented
and very skittish white horse, saddled in white leather. Rand then mounted and
sat side-saddle. She adjusted the wrap that concealed her naked body as Callahan
maneuvered to shore. Rand prepared to stage her entrance.[11]

Beyond the gala's soft, warm ring of light, a virtually nude Lady Godiva disem-
barked unnoticed. She entered the gate and rode boldly through the Streets of Paris
and onto the main stage. Astounded, Chicago's merrymaking high society simply
gaped, and then, seeing her as a novel addition to the planned entertainment, they
burst into applause. The police arrested Rand for obscenity, but the horse remained
to be photographed with the enthusiastic spectators. An exposition attorney facilitated her release, the press reported her prank, and the Streets of Paris hired her
the next day as their headline attraction in the Café de la Paix's floor show. In 1934
the vaudeville comedian Will Rogers wittily credited Rand with the fair's success,
something no one at the extravagant opening affair could have imagined.[12]

Years later Rand gave an interview that evoked Lady Godiva and that night
in May 1933. The ride, she recalled, did indeed secure for her a lucrative niche
in the fair's activities. More than that, it made a social statement. She had felt a
sense of satisfaction at having exposed herself to the elite women who were wearing expensive gowns. Rand claimed that riding naked was like saying, "How dare
you have a dress of thousand-dollar bills when people are hungry?" Wearing those
dresses, she alleged, "was such bad taste."[13]

And so it was a question of taste. Chicago's "high and mighty," as Rand referred
to them, might have said the same about the naked Godiva.[14] The reality was,

though, that Sally Rand's outrageous behavior made a statement about Depression-era Chicago and A Century of Progress. In fact, Rand became the fair's enduring icon for optimism and hope, a true Horatio Alger, rags-to-riches figure. Though risqué displays of female flesh were nothing new—mesmerized spectators had ogled hoochie-coochie girls at burlesque shows and speakeasies for decades—Sally Rand blazed new trails at the 1933 world's fair. It was a fortuitous convergence of disparate circumstances.

Simply put, the fair had to pay for itself, and admission fees could not cover the entire bill. The Midway, though, brought in the cash. Organizers looked to attractions such as the Sky Ride and the food and beer concessions to generate income for the fair. In the beginning they also saw the sensational Sally Rand and her many imitators as other potentially lucrative draws. But the showgirls' public nudity conflicted with the fair's image as educational and crime-free. What about morality, decency, and good taste?

Fair organizers simply looked the other way, at least in the beginning. As they planned and designed the fair, their vision controlled business leaders and exhibit designers, but in their need for revenue, they shunned attempts to control popular culture. That they maintained this laissez-faire approach to the Midway opened the door to a level of sexual exploitation and the spectacle of sexual display for which Sally Rand emerged as the representative.

Amusements on the Midway

For those seeking an escape from the Depression's doldrums, the Midway was pure magic. Concessions included entertainment other than fan dancers and peep shows. Strolling the streets of the Midway, patrons could visit the American Indian Village and the children's Enchanted Island, see how movies were made, ride a roller coaster, experience Battle of Gettysburg panorama paintings displayed in a rotunda cyclorama, watch men wrestle with alligators, and strain to see trained insects in the flea circus. They could gape at barkers spouting obscene language and making lewd gestures while spectators grumbled at show cashiers who had shortchanged them. And then there was the Living Wonders freak show, which displayed physically challenged humans with names and titles to exaggerate their differences. Extremely obese men and women, heavily tattooed men, "Siamese" twins, persons with skin diseases and missing appendages sang, danced, and performed everyday functions in ways that awed spectators. Ripley's Odditorium, wrote a friend of Agnes Nestor, a fair trustee, "certainly was odd!"[15] The friend then noted curiosities that amazed her most—a man who pulled a girl in a cart with his eyelashes and a woman who could swallow her nose.

The Infant Incubator displayed scientific advancements in an atmosphere of medical professionalism, attracting large crowds. Spectators stood in awe as nurses and doctors busied themselves with as many as twenty-five premature babies, including twins and triplets. Regional hospitals sent the babies to the incubator immediately after birth. Each tiny infant's mother delivered her breast milk to the site, where nurses kept it in a modern electric refrigerator until fed to the baby through a catheter. When a baby had attained sufficient weight and health, it "graduated" and left the incubator with its joyful parents.

Fairgoers thronged to the Midway's Midget Village, which boasted the largest midget population ever gathered in one place. The entire village's construction and accoutrements were proportionate to the size of the residents, who operated the businesses and provided musical and theatrical entertainment. Visitors could watch the mayor at work in city hall, shop in the grocery store, or have their hair cut at the only midget barbershop in America. The midgets occasionally married, and visitors could enjoy the ceremony and festivities. Visitors could also dispatch or receive a telegraph, with midget messengers serving as couriers. They cut quite a figure in their tiny regulation uniforms, supplied by Western Union Telegraph.

As with any carnival, souvenir shops attracted Midway visitors whether they had money to spend or not. Though many tourists bought souvenirs to carry home as reminders of their grand diversion, most souvenir venders lost money. That fairgoers had so little to spend accounted for some of the problem. One salesman commented, "We estimated when we went that we would sell three times more than we did."[16] The cost-to-sale price ratio was also a big factor. Since people had so little to spend, venders sold items at giveaway prices and often realized no profit at all. Then there were the clerks' wages, which amounted to a 10 percent commission. The fair too took a cut—5 percent for miscellaneous charges and an additional 10 percent sales commission. To top all this, theft dragged the final tally into the red. All this underscores the fact that alcohol and exotic sexual displays loomed large for managers trying to cover the fair's expenses.

Little Egypt, the sensational belly dancer who in 1893 had helped inspire the transformation of public culture, recreated her famous Streets of Cairo show at A Century of Progress's Oriental Village. By then she was sixty-two. A native of Damascus who lived in Chicago, she told a reporter later that her belly dances had never revealed her midriff, and she was shocked by the nudity she saw on the Midway in 1933. Her comment that she would never face the public as did "the nonchalant young things of 1933" makes a statement about the change in sexual mores that had occurred since Chicago's first world's fair.[17]

Transformation of Popular Culture

Fair management recognized the importance of the Midway. They not only needed its revenues to cover costs, but they also saw it as crucial to providing the carnival atmosphere and exoticism Depression-era fairgoers sought. Charles Gates

Dawes had reminded his brother, Rufus, "What is going to draw your crowds is not museums or scientific charts or similar museum exhibits. . . . People come to see a show, the great surviving memory of the Chicago World's Fair [1893] being the Midway."[18] Lenox Lohr echoed Dawes's reminder. He had visited expositions in Europe and understood that "while the [fair's] theme must have its appeal through those higher concepts of education, science and culture . . . people visit an exposition with a carnival spirit, hoping to be amused and diverted from humdrum routine existence by dreams of fantasy."[19] Charles Dawes, an internationally renowned financial expert, had no doubt that fair amusements would generate the funds necessary to keep the exposition open and prevent bankruptcy.[20]

The commercialization of popular amusements earlier in the century had signaled the rise of a new, expressive urban culture, and this played into the Midway's success.[21] Amusement parks, a real novelty at the time, offered new and daring opportunities for young people to interact, and America's youth thoroughly enjoyed the freedom. Movies, radio, and reading competed with sports and games. A Century of Progress opened during the peak of the Great Depression, and though expendable resources were few-to-none, many fairgoers still sought ways to satisfy their new taste for thrills. Maybe they felt a bit of hope as Roosevelt tried to avert the collapse of the American economic system, and that hope freed them to stroll the fair's Midway. Even if they had very few coins in their pockets, they had plenty of leisure time. For those able to afford a vacation or even a day in the city, the 1933 world's fair offered the era's greatest escape.

The 1893 World's Columbian Exposition had served as one of Chicago's springboards for this transformation of public entertainment. Novelty ruled the day, and the public loved it. Throngs packed the fair's beer gardens, thrilled to the Ferris Wheel, and gaped as the belly dancer Fahreda Mahzar—also known as Little Egypt—gyrated in ways never before witnessed by middle-class Americans. And Little Egypt was by no means the only belly dancer on that earlier Midway. Other "Orientals" performed sexual spectacles wearing native costumes that revealed considerably more skin than visitors ever saw in a mainstream woman's magazine. The Gibson Girl's modest couture may have been the ideal, but some fairgoers—both men and women—definitely relished a taste of the exotic. When Bertha Palmer, president of the Board of Lady Managers, objected to the content of Little Egypt's act, the fair's director general issued an edict to concessionaires to "restrain all future exhibits within the limits of stage propriety as recognized in the country," but the popular performances continued.[22]

The extraordinary popularity of the belly dance at the 1893 world's fair influenced leisure entertainment promoters. They soon added this "cooch" dance to burlesque shows. The dance even entranced some people in small midwestern towns, where it captivated wide-eyed and breathless youngsters such as Sally Rand. According to the historian Robert C. Allen, the "hoochie-coochie" soon became standard fare at carnival sideshows. The dancers appeared as part of the freak-show attractions and in burlesque, providing "an exhibition of direct, wordless, female eroticism and exoticism."[23] In burlesque performance, the cooch was a precursor to the striptease, which would become the standard thirty years later. Burlesque dancers usually removed their brassieres and remained topless while on stage. Many women posed wearing only a G-string. None of the dancers made much of an effort to create an illusion of art.

Since the turn of the twentieth century, public display of women's bodies had been on the increase, from women bicycling in bloomers to "modern" flappers dancing sensual dances and frequenting nightclubs. In some ways the public had been desensitized to risqué behavior. At the same time, it craved even more. And Chicago was no stranger to nightclubs and girlie shows.[24] Concentrated on south State Street in the downtown Loop, just a short distance from the fair, the burlesque theaters featured programs of comic skits, films, strip acts, singing, and dancing.[25] An indication of the demoralized population's desire to escape into girlie fantasies, burlesque flourished during A Century of Progress. As the Depression deepened during the fair's second season, burlesque became increasingly "lewd in character."[26] Both men and women frequented the city's theaters, paying from ten to twenty-five cents at the seamier sites to $1.75 at a classier venue.[27] Women preferred the latter and sometimes comprised nearly one-third of the audience.[28] Chicago's law enforcement agencies looked the other way. The city and the vice industry had long enjoyed a relationship of benign neglect, perhaps conveniently for all concerned. By refusing to police Chicago's popular culture, including burlesque shows, local officials defined what was acceptable as public entertainment. By default, they allowed an increase in the commodification of women's sexuality at the world's fair.

The appeal of burlesque shows and nudity in nightclubs clearly influenced Midway attractions. With Prohibition recently repealed and the expectation that legalized drinking could offer concessionaires a great economic windfall, businessmen initiated sensational forms of evening entertainment at the fair to compete for the dollars of the thirty-nine million paid admissions.[29] Living pictures, nude tableaus, and disrobing acts became model sources for the fair's Midway peep show offerings, which recreated famous paintings or reenacted moments of daily living using nude women performers to lure gazing male patrons. Just as in 1893, some fairgoers raised objections to this startling trend, but most did not. In 1933, fair managers responded to objections to nude dancing, to nudity in the concessions, and to the peep shows much as their counterparts in 1893 had done. They simply issued flaccid edicts that exhibits be kept within the limits of stage propriety.

By the 1930s, young women experienced new levels of freedom, including freer sexual expression.[30] Commercialized sex had become part of the public urban culture during the century's early decades, and Sally Rand simply exploited an existing situation. The shift in attitudes toward drinking, smoking, wearing makeup, and experiencing premarital sex culminated in a heightened emphasis on eroticism.

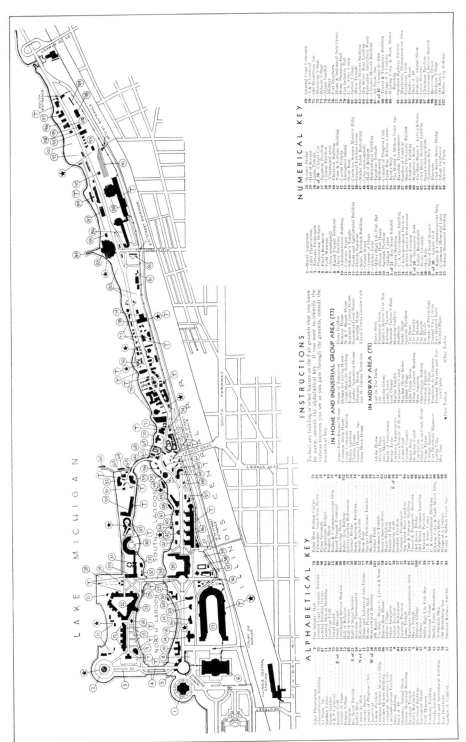

The U-shaped Hall of Science (number 35, just below the South Lagoon, on this map from a weekly schedule of events) served as the centerpiece in the asymetrical design of the 1933 Chicago world's fair. The Midway entertainment zone occupied land at the midpoint from north to south (left to right in this orientation).

Goodyear blimps flew daily over the fair, offering a lakefront view of Chicago's central business district in the distance. Goodyear Tire and Rubber Company, Akron, Ohio.

Sally Rand's sensational fan and bubble dances drew Depression-era crowds eager to experience her unique interpretations of beauty and hope.

Barkers publicized sideshows and peep shows, often drawing criticism for their lewd and indecent gestures and language. Chicago History Museum, ICHi-50681.

From the Sky Ride, visitors could view the Midway amusement zone and the two-hundred-foot-high Havoline thermometer on the other side of the lagoon. Howard A. Bauman, Photographer; Bauman Family Collection, West Bend, Wisconsin.

Recreated Fort Dearborn and the Du Sable cabin (left) offered visitors a glimpse of pioneer life in Chicago one hundred years earlier. Howard A. Bauman, Photographer; Bauman Family Collection, West Bend, Wisconsin.

The concessionaire of Darkest Africa brought African people, deemed exotic at the time, to Chicago for the duration of the fair to demonstrate tribal ceremonies.

OFFICIAL SOUVENIR

DARKEST AFRICA

A CENTURY OF PROGRESS 1933
CHICAGO, ILLINOIS

The squeamish probably avoided the Torture Chamber, Ripley's Believe It or Not Odditorium, the Living Wonders freak show, and alligator wrestling.

The Infant Incubator Company provided professional medical and nursing care to premature babies arrayed in rows.

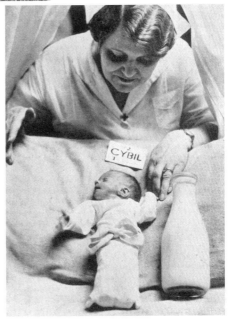

James E. McSweeney, secretary of the Chicago Police Department, deputized the sheriff of the Midget Village. Norine McSweeney Murphy, Park Ridge, Illinois.

Following thirteen years of Prohibition, in 1933 the sale of beer became legal, enabling fairgoers to enjoy a brew in public at the Schlitz or Muller-Pabst cafés.

SCHLITZ GARDEN CAFE — MULLER-PABST CAFE

A CENTURY OF PROGRESS — CHICAGO WORLD'S FAIR 1933   D-3118

This public behavior, which had appealed to young working women since before World War I, became increasingly commoditized in the fair's sideshow concessions, bars, and some restaurants. In those venues young women imitated Sally Rand before Depression-weary tourists grateful for an escape into the sensually exotic.[31] Women needing employment and willing to expose their bodies easily found opportunities in the fair's tawdry theatrical productions, work that helped them attain economic and personal independence.

While exotic dancing in fact trivialized and objectified women, it also offered economic independence and, for some, symbolized their liberation. Fan dancers earned large sums of money compared to that earned by most women of that time, and they exercised levels of control in their work. In addition, they used parody and other subversive means to continue dancing as they wished. Their visibility forced a public discourse. Newspaper accounts provided a range of evaluations of the nude exhibitions, defending it as "good clean fun" or claiming that it appealed "to the lowest instincts . . . vulgar, vile and repulsive."[32]

Besides the convergence of this freedom-loving public culture with escapism, the repeal of Prohibition contributed to the Midway's financial success.[33] This relationship cannot be overstated. For the first time in a dozen years, Chicagoans could consume beer in public legally during the summer of 1933. Hard spirits became legal the next season. During the Prohibition era, organized crime had controlled the city's liquor sales, and so a disturbing culture of crime churned insidiously around most nightclubs and many entertainment venues. Fair organizers, concerned about the city's seamy reputation, sought to clean up its image and counter its negative reputation by maintaining legal operations for liquor sales on the Midway. Consequently, concessionaires such as those who operated the Streets of Paris, where Rand performed in 1933, competed directly with gangsters. Knowing they could legally consume alcohol at the fair, many tourists who might otherwise have traveled to Canada and Mexico to drink now booked a trip to Chicago.[34] Fairgoers and Chicagoans, both male and female, celebrated their freedom to imbibe publicly, and the city saw public intoxication increase markedly. As nights wore on, inebriated revelers flocked to girlie shows, the more revealing the better. Concessionaires and showgirls such as Sally Rand reaped huge profits, and the fair's cut assured financial liquidity. After leaving the fairgrounds, attendees could visit taverns located around the entrances at Eighteenth, Twenty-third, Thirty-first, and Thirty-fifth Streets, negotiate with a female street solicitor, or visit one of the many houses of prostitution located in the Eighteenth Street entrance area.[35]

Sally Rand's Rags-to-Riches Saga

Certain images fix themselves in the public's memory as representative of a significant event. Those images say something about the time and setting to which they relate. As time passes, they assume something of a mythical stature and become icons or symbols of that event. The Ferris Wheel, for instance, will always be associated with the 1893 World's Columbian Exposition, and the Eiffel Tower will forever be linked to Paris's 1889 Exposition Universelle. Both make statements about late nineteenth-century technological achievements. Interestingly, most people no longer remember the 1933 Chicago world's fair's Sky Ride, intended as a symbol for a century of scientific and technological progress. Rather, they immediately associate the fair with Sally Rand, who serendipitously fulfilled organizers' vision of the fair as a metaphor for hope and optimism. She stands out as the enduring icon for A Century of Progress.

After Sally Rand made her daring, unannounced ride as Lady Godiva through the Streets of Paris, she accepted an offer to perform in the Streets of Paris concession for the fantastic sum of ninety dollars a week. In her journey to the floor show stage, however, she had encountered many more obstacles than admission at the main exposition gate and an arrest. In fact, her story is truly one of rags to riches. Harriet Helen Beck of rural Missouri worked her way up from an acrobatic circus performer to a Mack Sennett film stuntwoman, finally landing a role in the director Cecil B. DeMille's stock company. DeMille selected the stage name "Sally" and then, after noticing a Rand McNally world atlas, he chose "Rand" as her last name.[36] In the 1920s, she appeared in a couple dozen silent films including DeMille's *Braveheart, The Road to Yesterday, Bachelor Brides, Gigolo,* and *The Fighting Eagle,* and Howard Hawks's *A Girl in Every Port.* In her most memorable role she played a handmaiden to Mary Magdalene in DeMille's acclaimed *King of Kings.* In 1927, Rand was one of thirteen starlets to be named film's Wampas Baby Star. Stardom was within her grasp.[37]

The 1927 premier of *The Jazz Singer,* credited as Hollywood's first talking motion picture, revolutionized the film industry. At the same time, it ended Rand's promising career. This rising star had a slight lisp—endearing but unsuitable for the silver screen. Devastated, Rand determined nonetheless to achieve star status. She joined a vaudeville act and danced in a musical revue before finding herself stranded and broke when the show closed in Chicago in 1932. There she answered an ad in the *Chicago Tribune* for exotic acts and dancers at the Paramount Club.[38]

Needing a costume for her audition, Rand visited a second-hand clothing store. She bought two very large pink ostrich feather fans and an off-white chemise that could be made into a Grecian robe. The cost: ten dollars. Rushing home, she frantically sewed her costume but had to leave for the club before it was ready. She arrived at the Paramount with only ten minutes before she went on stage. Nervous, she shared her dilemma with a harem girl, who told her that she had once seen someone dance with only fans. Rand nodded in appreciation. Onstage, the pianist played Claude Debussy's "Clair de Lune" and she danced, cleverly manipulating the fans to conceal her naked torso. As the tune reached its finale, she lifted the fans above her head, and the thrilled audience cheered. Within two weeks, she was the club's star attraction. She had worn only net panties that first night. On other occasions she wore a sheer body stocking or nothing at all.[39]

Grateful for the opportunity to win some acclaim in the nightclub circuit in 1932, Rand found that her success did not assure security, particularly in the vice-controlled world of girlie shows and seamy lounges. In Chicago's Prohibition era, mobsters scrutinized liquor sales to protect their investments. Rand claimed to have had confrontations with several gangsters and to have received threats from Vito Genovese when she ignored his invitation to switch to one of his clubs. She later recalled that, as one of Chicago's rising stars, she enjoyed a degree of safety. Her friend Ed Callahan, who had conspired with her in the Lady Godiva caper, was not so fortunate. He met an early demise following the opening of the fair when he quarreled with the Mafia over liquor distribution.[40]

The transformation of popular culture cleared the path for Rand's journey from rags to riches. Juxtaposing precision with grace, concealing with revealing, sexual allure with controlled distance, her disguised nudity and mastery of illusion made Rand's performance the top attraction on the Midway and one of the major revenue draws. The quintessential showgirl, Rand felt herself transformed into "a femme fatale, a coquette, a Cleopatra" as soon as she picked up the ostrich fans.[41] She manipulated the undulating feathers in a slow, controlled, flowing line so that as one fan swept to the side, the other took its place to cover her from her bare shoulders to her knees. She wore high heels and sometimes a thin body suit, or what was then known as "invisible clothing." The body suit—white grease-paint that covered her skin—and special lighting effects heightened the drama. A luminescent vision of purity, the blonde beauty looked like the girl next door living a fantasy in the privacy of her home. Mesmerized patrons strained to catch a glimpse of her breasts or loins. As her dance reached its climax, Rand looked directly into the audience and lifted the plumes above her head. Though men and women undoubtedly experienced Rand's spectacle differently, they all clapped enthusiastically at the finale.[42]

In 1934 Rand choreographed a new dance routine, the bubble dance, to add to her performance program. Creating this program, she drew on her circus and stuntwoman talents to coordinate callisthenic movements while holding a huge ball. With a circumference of over four feet, the lightweight sphere had been constructed especially for her dance by Goodyear engineers. The dance showcased her agility, stamina, and strength. A fantastic innovation, the dance lured viewers such as John Van Gilder from far and wide, all eager to catch a glimpse of the sensational Rand.[43]

An astute businesswoman, workaholic, and perfectionist, Rand performed up to sixteen shows a day. She did her own bookkeeping, and, though represented by the William Morris Agency, she negotiated many of her own contracts. In 1934, her agent, John Hyde, wrote to her that his contact in Detroit, where she performed before she returned to her second season at the world's fair, reported that her show

was "playing like wild-fire, and that you, personally, are the most resourceful artist, businesswoman he has ever met."[44] Letters home to her mother revealed that
she lived a modest life while working long, hard hours, even cooking her own
meals in her dressing room. Much of her income supported her mother and other
relatives, as she frequently mailed cash, goods, and advice home.[45]

Rand credited her idol Isadora Duncan as her inspiration. Both women choreographed their own routines to classical music, both introduced unique dance forms,
and both inspired imitators. Time, popular culture, and the nation's economic
circumstances carried the two into different social circles, however. During the
more prosperous early decades of the twentieth century, Duncan had performed in
revealing tunics that exposed her limbs, a provocative style that pioneered dance
as a modern art form. Her socialite audiences defined Duncan's style as art and
proclaimed it as such.[46] In the era's emerging celebrity culture, Duncan served as an
emblem for women who experimented with new forms of public behavior.[47] Rand,
on the other hand, introduced her fan dance during the Great Depression, and she
drew her following from working-class and middle-class pleasure seekers. Unlike
Duncan, who became an embodiment of sorts for the early twentieth century's
"new woman," Rand symbolized American consumption-based sex and spectacle
as well as a nation stripped of its protective garments. Proud of her profession and
determined that it be respected, she strove to bring it the esteem and dignity that
Duncan had enjoyed.

As the showgirl who achieved rare individual recognition, Rand's own life story
paralleled the storyline in the choreographer Busby Berkeley's film *Gold Diggers
of 1933*. The film used the themes of race, class, and the commoditization of sex
that had been popularized during the century's early decades. Presenting women
as art objects who paraded around the stage in elaborate fashions and performed
spectacularly choreographed leg kicks, productions such as this justified occasional
topless costumes as artistic. Its gold-digger chorus girls portrayed modern, aggressive women, always native-born whites, whom professional misfortune might
push into prostitution.[48] Seeking security and upward mobility, these attractive
characters contrived traps for wealthy men. The characters evolved from idealized
images of ornamental dancers in Florenz Ziegfeld Jr.'s *Ziegfeld Follies*, also known
as the Glorified American Girls.

Rand did not seek a wealthy savior husband. Nor was she interested in the
gold-diggers' other option, prostitution. Instead, when her revue folded, as it did
in 1932, and she found herself sleeping in an alley, she did what she had always
done: she invented a solution. In 1933 it was the fan dance. Rand had the ability to turn adversity into gold, and others jumped on her train. An entrepreneur
in her own right, Rand and her imitators found a consumer base in middle-class
nightclub patrons and tourists. At a time when chorus dance aligned with the
idea of capitalism, they understood how to use their bodies for capital, and Rand
did it spectacularly well.[49] But with increasing fame and success came criticism

from anti-vice crusaders. As a businesswoman protective of her public image and artistic license, she was quite concerned with the "legion of decency" and picture censorship. Resigned to alter her performances to meet local conditions, she wrote that the moral critics could "do a great deal to hurt me this year on the road. . . . We must do the best we can about it."[50] The relentless anti-vice campaign elicited varied responses from government officials and fair officials, none of whom wished to police Rand or the emerging industry.

The Debate about Public Nudity

By the time Sergeant Harry Costello and policewoman Bessie McShane's squad car pulled up at the Chicago Theater on the night of August 4, 1933, Sally Rand had already been arrested three times that day. The crime: indecent exhibition in a public place. Rand completed her fan dance before this, the fourth arrest. Police brought additional charges of disorderly conduct against her brother and Mattie Wheeler, her African American maid, and the production managers.[51] Rand then proceeded to her regular performance at the Streets of Paris after the fourth arrest, accompanied by McShane. "It wouldn't make any difference if you were wrapped up in the back drop," McShane confided. "They'd still arrest you."[52] The arrests, contrived by an undisclosed source to generate newspaper headlines, would draw fairgoers to downtown Loop merchants and, McShane divulged, distract readers from a recent property tax scandal.

In Women's Court the next day, law officers, attorneys, and Judge Erwin J. Hasten debated the nature of Sally Rand's dance, struggling to distinguish it from "lewd, lascivious burlesque."[53] Through it all, Judge Hasten tenderly "beamed down at the defendant, who smiled and nodded to him." The debate: Was Rand's dance art? Was it crude, exploitive, or simply sensationalist? Attorneys for the state questioned detectives and police officers, seeking an understanding. Had they seen Rand dance nude and how did they assess her performance? Parkerson, a veteran policeman, revealed Rand's performance had aroused his passions, and Officer O'Sullivan admitted that his pulse had quickened during the show. Judge Hasten had seen Rand's show himself and acknowledged her as a beautiful dancer. He agreed with one attorney, William V. Daly, that the court should go see the show before making its decision, but he reminded those present that the arrest was for the past act.[54]

When Rand took the stand, she protested. "My dance is art. . . . My public wants me. There is nothing vulgar, lewd, or obscene about my dancing."[55] She calmly and confidently explained that she had conceived of the dance after seeing an artistic depiction of a girl and a swan. Indeed, earlier in her career she had choreographed and performed nature-inspired dances, one being "The Dance of the Butterfly," staged out of doors in Los Angeles in 1925.[56] She told the court that she applied thick white cream on her body to create an ethereal effect, and in lifting her arms during the final four bars, she created the illusion of a graceful statue. If she wore clothes during the dance, she argued, the feathers might catch and disrupt the integrity of her artistic performance. Were her breasts and loins covered throughout the performance? "Yes, with one exception," she demurred. "In the middle of the dance, without ostentation, my gown is removed at the side of the stage. After that I open my fans."[57]

Newspapers immediately broadcast that "the judges incline to the side of art."[58] Judge Hasten fined Rand $25 for indecent exhibition and required a bit of mesh under the coat of greasepaint in upcoming performances.[59] He also instructed her to "veil her charms" in the future.[60] Press photographers took plenty of pictures, and members of the court agreed to pose with Rand, enhancing her notoriety. Though the newspaper's art critic didn't swoon over her performance—he sensed that she was more sincere than remarkable as a dancer—the arrests, the court appearances, and the splash of photos catapulted Rand further into the limelight.[61] She set new box office records. For the next eleven weeks, customers pressed four deep for each of her performances. Admission revenues topped $79,000 during one week that August at the Chicago Theater, and they soared at the fair too.[62] Rand's salary climbed to $1,000 a week for the eleven-week record-setting run, a considerable sum during the Great Depression.[63]

The Streets of Paris took in so much cash that A Century of Progress had to establish a separate banking operation with eight auditors working on its finances to handle its daily receipts. Entrance fees, food, and liquor sales for the Streets of Paris concession reached $100,000 per day, with peep shows taking in as much as $500 per day. The fair received a percentage of the receipts and also charged fees for services. The concession employed over one thousand people and was touted as the most popular site at the fair.[64] Sally Rand was such a large part of that success that the fair management added her show to the official daily program of events in 1934. She moved her production from the Streets of Paris to the Italian Village and later to the Oriental Village, where she was able to secure more lucrative compensation for her artistic skills. She expanded her show and following by adding new numbers and a chorus of young women clad only in breech cloths and grease paint.

A Chorus of Young Women and Other Seedy Entertainment

In addition to showcasing Rand as a star, the fair provided an opportunity for other dancers to develop a local level of fame. For many of the dancers and performers, nudity offered a path to success, and during the Great Depression in Chicago, they had few options. Those who achieved celebrity status knew that publicity meant a larger box office, and that meant a larger salary, more control, and a chance to reach stardom. Faith Bacon, who claimed to be the rightful originator of the fan dance, described her dance at the fair's Hollywood stage show for a local reporter, explaining that any kind of clothing was distracting as it made the audience more conscious of what was covered. Long legs, long hair, a small waist, full breasts, and two fans were required to create this ethereal art. Bacon emphasized "above all things, try to get yourself arrested as much as possible. Bite the policeman, or throw a jug at the judge. Be sure you spell your name right to the reporters."[65]

Many dancers and models never achieved special recognition, especially those who worked in the peep shows. Their salaries were lower than the salaries of floor-show star entertainers, with the average peep show performer earning about twenty dollars a week.[66] While the headliners drew in the large crowds, the sideshows provided curiosity seekers with additional tales to take home. Barkers in front of the sideshows promoted and frequently exaggerated the value of the sights to be seen inside. Often, lured by the barkers, a small group of patrons entered a small, dark space to experience a couple of minutes of entertainment or hoax for their ten to twenty-five cents. Crowds responded vocally, expressing their appreciation or disappointment, as they were amused, angry, or embarrassed.

The Streets of Paris, where Sally Rand headlined the floor show during the first season, offered some of the seediest entertainments during the opening months of the world's fair, and it received the criticism or credit for instigating widespread nudity in concessions.[67] For the quarter admission to its show "Life Class," patrons received a crayon and a piece of paper on which they could sketch as if they were in a French art studio. A young woman model posed in a chair on a platform, wearing a scant pubic covering and a piece of chiffon around her neck. In "Visions of Art," colored lights flashed on three topless women, who danced to music and assumed different erotic poses. Each wore a tiny, transparent cheesecloth barely covering at the pelvis. For fifteen cents, patrons could throw three baseballs at a plaque in "La Belle au Bois Dormant." When they scored, a scantily dressed young lady, who had been in a bed covered with a sheet, rolled out of the tipped bed. More than one of the fairgoers must have been surprised when, after entering "The Nudist Colony" and peeping through holes, they found their own faces reflected in mirrors with a painting of a nude man below each mirror. The Streets of Paris did not represent Paris or France, even though its publicity claimed to recreate a true French atmosphere. When the concession flew the French flag, the French ambassador protested until it was removed.[68]

Fair officials would not enforce nudity restrictions, but they drew the line at prostitution. Shortly after opening, the fair authority closed the Dance Ship concession, a taxi dance hall where a man could hire a dancing partner for ten cents per dance. For all practical purposes, it was a house of prostitution. The year before, taxi dance halls in Chicago had been closed by Mayor Bill Thompson, but several still operated outside the city limits. Locals as well as tourists patronized these sites. Critics complained that young women who worked in these halls told "the men to stand still while they wiggle and writhe their bodies up and down the bodies of the men in the most suggestive and objectionable manner." Then a "date" could be arranged. Frequently the date took place in an annexed room where the couple engaged in sex for a fee.[69] On the fairgrounds, however, solicitation for prostitution was prohibited. The Public Protection Division of the fair acted on reports of violation with immediate removal of the offenders as substantiated in investigative reports made by agents of Chicago's Juvenile Protective Association.[70]

The Council of Social Agencies of Chicago monitored all entertainment at the fair. Jessie F. Binford, the executive director of the Juvenile Protective Association of Chicago, chaired its advisory committee. The council sent observers to write reports on entertainment concessions such as the taxi dances so that the committee could advise the fair officials of conditions that it deemed exploitive or dangerous for young people. Binford's first report criticized many of the sideshows and taxi dances, where men purchased tickets to dance with young women who performed lewd acts during the dance. She acknowledged that it was difficult to change conditions in the city as a whole. She felt, though, that "the Century of Progress has absolute control and a very great responsibility" and that the fair would not want to continue to have "places of amusement that are vulgar, obscene, indecent and very offensive to the taste" of the patrons.[71] The fair responded by ordering additional clothing on some models in order to meet expected standards of decency, and fair staff received instructions to enforce the regulations.[72]

Dance Ship management knew how to split legal hairs, which made it difficult to close it down. The hall's management argued that a patron did not pay preselected dancing partners with prepurchased tickets as was done in taxi dancing; rather, the patron could invite any hostess to dance as the whim suited him. Such hair-splitting forced fair organizers to find other infractions as an excuse for the shutdown. They explained that the concession violated fair regulations regarding the sale of draft beer rather than bottled beer, the use of its own cashiers rather than cashiers employed by the fair, and the playing of copyrighted music without consent. Max Silverberg, the concession operator, was "reported to have been always associated with the 'fast set,' gamblers, etc., and has been classed as a minor 'racketeer' and his activities to some extent alleged bordering on illegitimate lines."[73] Supposedly, he occasionally resided in an apartment hotel housing gangsters and prostitutes.

Martha McGrew, assistant to the fair's general manager, Lenox Lohr, forced the elimination of taxi dancing, however defined, from the fair. She wielded considerable power with fair officials, and her opinions and suggestions frequently influenced their decisions. While not in a position of authority, she reportedly was the most feared as well as the most courted person in the fair enterprise.[74] McGrew also enacted a 1:30 A.M. curfew at the fair to reduce the problems of drunken, unescorted women who might "take a notion to fall in the lagoon."[75] To comply with the fair management crackdown, the Dance Ship changed its name to the Pirate Ship and altered its programming by bringing in Texas Guinan and her nightclub revue with forty showgirls to present "A Century of Whoopie" in competition with the Streets of Paris and Sally Rand.

The actions taken by the fair officials, however, failed to satisfy some fairgoers. Mary Belle Spencer, a lawyer and the widowed mother of two children, filed a bill for injunction to prevent the Streets of Paris from exhibiting or displaying nude women in concessions as well as picturing them on signs. She argued that nudity "represented a cess-pool of iniquity, a condition of depravity and total disregard of purity and display of the most disgraceful lewdness and abandon ever publicly shown in any institution of the character such as this Century of Progress purports to represent."[76] She based her argument on both State of Illinois and Chicago municipal codes.[77] Spencer claimed to represent property owners, who would suffer when visitors refused to consider Chicago as a future place for home or business. She provided an inventory of those offended, pointing to international visitors who faced this "licentious and libidinous assortment of carnal shame," to the shamed citizens of Illinois, and, finally, to mothers and their "children whose outlook on life might be changed and corrupted by their viewing the exhibitions of immoral character . . . and who ordinarily would not suspect or believe that . . . such carnal sights would be permitted."[78]

Although Sally Rand and Dorothy Kibbee, one of the art class models, had been subpoenaed to the Spencer case in July 1933, Superior Court Judge Joseph B. David was interested in neither hearing their testimony nor witnessing any performances. As he assessed the situation, "They are just a lot of boobs to come to see a woman wiggle with a fan or without fig leaves. But we have the boobs and we have a right to cater to them."[79] Jay J. McCarthy, an attorney representing Spencer, failed to convince the judge that nudity corrupted public morals. After listening to McCarthy's long dissertation on the law, an irritated Judge David refused to discuss lewdness and stated that "the human body is a beautiful thing. . . . Some people would want to put pants on a horse. . . . If a woman wiggles about with a fan, it is not the business of this court. . . . I would be the last person to cast a blotch upon A Century of Progress." He concluded that improprieties should be handled by the South Park police or the county sheriff.[80] Spencer admitted later that she brought action against A Century of Progress not only for altruistic reasons; she also wanted to attract clients to her law practice.[81]

Even though Judge David refused to forbid total nudity at the fair, publicity forced fair officials to take some action. Thomas H. Slusser, a fair attorney, advised that a memorandum be sent to directors of operations, concessions, and promotions stating that if the Illinois Revised Statutes criminal code on obscene shows was violated, then offending persons could be arrested and prosecuted. He added that "what is or is not an obscene show is obviously a question of fact in each case" and that management should exercise care that no exhibition violates the code.[82] Rufus C. Dawes, the fair's president, informed concessionaires that they had to modify nudity in their shows. J. Franklin Bell of operations and maintenance ordered women in shows to wear a minimum of loin and breast coverings and informed concessionaires that "police supervisors" would monitor for nudity and obscenity.[83]

The conflict between banning the girlie shows and being able to pay the fair's bills troubled fair organizers. Lohr frequently toured the fairgrounds with his wife, professional women, society women, wives of visiting dignitaries, and distinguished female visitors. Their remarks, plus those of his assistant McGrew, influenced his thoughts, but his actions fell far short of what some felt necessary.[84] While the debates of the day questioned whether nudity was art or indecent exposure, all the key players used it as a means to successful economic ends. Jessie E. Binford concluded that one thing was clear: "the way to make money is to show a naked woman. The rest is a struggle over the point of permissible nudity."[85]

The fair organizers' three-point coverage decree—cover both breasts and the pelvic area—did not include any means of effective enforcement. On the evening of July 31, 1933, Mayor Edward J. Kelly and State's Attorney Thomas J. Courtney toured some of the objectionable concessions. The mayor found Hot Cha San's graceful dance at the Oriental Village acceptable because, although she was totally nude, her gilt-painted skin gave her a statue-like appearance. Yet he found the other shows at the Oriental Village, Streets of Paris, Cuban Rhumba, and Old Mexico to be cheap, tawdry, and downright suggestive. He summoned Lenox Lohr and George T. Donoghue, superintendent of the park system, to his office and ordered the shows cleaned up or closed.[86]

Lohr was definitely in a quandary, and he welcomed the mayor's decision. He had at one point publicly stated that he personally found nothing lewd, immoral, or shocking in the fair entertainment performances, that 99 percent of the visitors were satisfied, but that it was difficult to determine the boundary between proper and improper.[87] To make matters worse, though Judge David had warned concessionaires six times to obey the law, his failure to issue an injunction against the Sally Rand show in the Streets of Paris had prevented the fair officials from taking decisive action.

The way in which dancers complied with the mayor's decree became a show unto itself. Plainclothes park police kept their eyes on the situation. With the exception of Hot Cha San, who continued to wear a coat of gilt, dancers wore brassieres and panties for the next few nights. Sally Rand protested, but she reluctantly complied by wearing a little piece of gauze. Rosalie, the fan dancer in Old Mexico, added only adhesive tape. Other women demonstrated their compliance by hanging panties and a brassiere on one of the signs or by wearing red flannel underwear. Fulfilling Judge David's vision that "some people would want to put pants on a horse," Lady Godiva and her horse both wore lace panties on stage. Several dancers began to wear invisible clothing, and they credited the cause of its design to the mayor.[88]

Dancers and concessionaires legally met the three-point coverage expectation, but the audience perceived total nudity. Fairgoers, police, and evaluators from the Juvenile Protective Association could often not be sure if the dancers were actually nude or not. Special lighting effects masked the "invisible" body wear. In an effort to exercise control over invisible clothes, Hazel Ward, a policewoman hired by the Streets of Paris, forced Sally Rand to dance in a full-length gown.[89] Through it all, the fair police only closed one show, the Theater Comique, a production that featured men impersonating women. The social mores of the 1930s, which increasingly promoted overt heterosexuality, found some acceptance in the display of the female body, but cross-dressing was an unacceptable transgression.

In the summer of the 1934, nudity returned to the fair concessions because fair officials again refused to enforce obscenity regulations. Topless dancers, nude dancers covered with grease, or dancers covered only with flower petals, tape, or transparent gauze could be found in concession entertainment, peep shows, and dinner floor shows. The "Life Class" added a nude male and the "Love Machine" puppet show animated sexual intercourse. Barkers became more suggestive in their sexual remarks, although they had eliminated profane language. Shows became more numerous, and competition forced the sensationalism beyond the permissible limits of the previous year.[90] Wanting to cash in on the bonanza, several villages, which had previously been educational in theme, introduced peep shows or nearly nude floor shows.[91]

On July 7, 1934, Judge John P. McGoorty of the Superior Court denied a writ of injunction for closure of an indecent display by Cati Mount, operator of the Olympia show. The show featured a nude model replicating the pose of the reclining courtesan in Edouard Manet's famous *Olympia* while the barker, Peggy Hawn, spewed suggestive one-liner jokes.[92] Although the judge identified similar peep shows as "utterly indecent, pagan, and immoral" and determined that it was "a disgrace that A Century of Progress should derive revenue from displays intended to rouse the lower, evil passions," he again shifted the responsibility away from the courts and back to the fair officials and police.[93] Police officers had requested that Mount cover her breasts with velvet petals, but the judge restrained that action. Fair officials, preferring that someone else assume responsibility for monitoring and enforcing official decisions, responded by claiming they could not have a censor with each show.[94] Why would no one accept responsibility? While evidence is sparse, one thing is clear: Chicago and its law enforcers had enjoyed a longtime relationship of neglect with vice and burlesque, and so edicts calling for a change in the status quo often fell on deaf ears.

Fair officials, concerned with satisfying the concessionaires and the public, shifted their position in the debate over nudity according to the amount of negative publicity generated. They needed to ensure the exhibition's popularity as well as its financial success. Concessionaires complained that they were forced to sensationalize their displays in order to raise enough revenue to meet the fair's contract requirements. In the second year, the fair officials loosened some of the financial constraints for concessionaires in the contracts but failed to include any provisions for banning nudity and enforcing punishments. When Lohr wrote his book about the international exposition, providing a blueprint for managing a world's fair, he dismissed the problems on the Midway by noting that "fan dancers and oriental dancers presented a serious dilemma."[95] He reported that they violated the law, sought notoriety, and were disappointed if not arrested and taken to court. He did not mention Sally Rand by name nor did he acknowledge the financial rewards from dancers' performances that accrued to the concessionaires, and he didn't note how the fair operation contributed to the situation when it chose not to crack down on indecency incidents. His assistant McGrew refused to cooperate with journalists who credited Rand as crucial to the fair's turnout and financial success. Lohr and McGrew preferred to promote the fair as a successful exposition that promoted science and education.[96]

The actions and inactions of the fair officials were surpassed only by those of law enforcement and the courts in their inability to behave decisively regarding public nudity. The judges ignored the state and municipal laws that clearly designated many of the displays at the fair as illegal. Instead they gave the authority back to the fair officials and the police, whom they knew would not initiate drastic changes. The police were unable to accomplish anything beyond increasing publicity for the fair concessions and collecting fines from the offenders. Fair authorities and state officials allowed an increase in the sensationalizing of women as objects of sexual fantasy to take place at the fair, especially in the peep shows that appealed to men and offered little artistic merit. Fair literature had boasted that "the Midway of 1933 will be just as startling and fascinating a place as was the original of 1893."[97] They did not exaggerate, and, in fact, provided an environment that allowed for a more broadly defined concept of what was acceptable as public entertainment than attendees in 1893 could have ever imagined.

The debate over Sally Rand, the fair's risqué Midway shows, and public nudity influenced later Hollywood production codes. In December 1933, the winter after Rand made the fan dance a sensation, Will H. Hays issued a set of twelve bans for film publicity. Number four illustrated the power of Rand's influence: "Thou shalt not photograph the so-called fan dance type of photograph in which delicate parts of the anatomy are covered by fans, feathers, lace, or other types of scanty or peek-a-boo material."[98] The next year, when Rand danced her fan dance in the film *Bolero*, the Production Code Administration informed Paramount that they needed to "eliminate views of dancer wiggling her posterior at audience."[99]

"A Century of Progress" as a world's fair theme presented human progress from scientific and technological perspectives. For working-class women to advance beyond what had been accomplished in the previous century, some had to take more drastic measures than others. Among them were those women who danced at the fair, including Sally Rand. They sought to earn a good living in hard times and to increase their visibility and independence. Although Rand and a few others achieved fame, most dancers and models were working women seeking economic stability with little hope of stardom. Interestingly, the sexual revolution of the early twentieth century did not trickle down from middle class to working class. Rather, it was a change initiated by working-class women charting their own sexual terrain for pleasure as well as financial rewards.[100] Singled out by the media as the fan dancer extraordinaire, Sally Rand became the popular heroine of sexual service work as she embodied the role of dancers and models at A Century of Progress.

Sally Rand definitely broke ground in her field. Her experience in circus performance, Hollywood film acting, stage theater work, and burlesque theatrics culminated in her ability to produce a dance that created a fantasy, both sexual and artistic. She brought credibility to burlesque dancing by taking it into the public arena and presenting it with pride and a level of perfection that made it an art. An ideal role model for the aspiring dancers around her, she put all of her energy into her career, debunking the stereotypical image of the nude dancer as an immoral woman and demonstrating the depth, diversity, and potential "class" of sex service workers. The standards that she set for fan dancing established it as a nude art form. Her physical attractiveness and wit, combined with a keen sense of timing, made her a favorite of the press. Rand defied those who would define public morality by banning nude dancing, and in so doing she represented those who enjoyed a bit of vice and sex in films, tabloids, magazines, and on stage. By publicly displaying her body she demonstrated a sense of privileged mobility with a sense of danger but within a safe and self-controlled environment. Her charismatic sexuality allowed her to expand the showgirls' confined space and audience from the speakeasy nightclubs of the roaring twenties to the center stage of a world's fair.

Initial discussions of mounting a Chicago fair occurred prior to Black Tuesday, the cataclysmic fall of the stock market in October 1929, during those years when confidence and gaiety still ruled the day. But as the campaign for a fair intensified and plans took shape, the economy deteriorated dramatically, forcing organizers to reconceptualize the fair's social and economic significance. It became something that neither early advocates nor opponents could have imagined. Sally Rand stepped into that new set of circumstances to inspire reactions no one could have engineered.

2

Chicago Boosters
Set the Stage

The opportunity is here, by adopting high ambition, to summon a
great spirit and unite the efforts of a great community to achieve it.
—Rufus C. Dawes, Association of Commerce Speech

Mayor "Big Bill" Thompson entered the city council chamber at Chicago's city hall on December 13, 1927, to find civic leaders absorbed in a charged discussion. Should they or should they not hold a second world's fair? Who would finance it? What location would guarantee its success? Given the state of municipal affairs, could they really pull it off in a nonpolitical, professional, and legitimate manner?

Soon after Thompson took his seat, an expectant and calculating Charles Simeon Peterson, the city treasurer, gave the floor to the banker and business mogul Rufus C. Dawes.[1] That Peterson had called on Dawes at the conference just after Thompson's arrival was not a fluke. Peterson had enlisted the support of Chicago-area business leaders, including Gen. Charles Gates Dawes, the vice president of the United States. General Dawes had insisted that Peterson meet with his brother and business partner, Rufus.[2]

Rufus Dawes knew that skepticism about a fair abounded, but it coexisted with a commitment to show the world that Chicago was much more than a den of vice. In an address calculated to stir the emotions and civic pride of attendees, many of whom he knew through memberships in private clubs and business associations, Dawes emphasized that a second world's fair must be more glorious than Chicago's 1893 World's Columbian Exposition. Most important, this fair must make a bold statement about twentieth-century Chicago—self-assured, innovative, and at the forefront of technological and industrial progress. And it must not fail. But could it succeed? Make money? Dawes argued that to ensure success, Chicago's citizens—business people, bankers, artists, intellectuals, and persons of all classes—must cooperate.

Numerous others at the meeting shared Dawes's enthusiasm and resolved to hold "a second exposition as wonderful and exhaustive and as representative of the progress of the world in 1933 as was the Columbian Exposition in 1893."[3] When Mayor Thompson again took the floor, he dedicated himself and his administration "to carry out the ideals so well expressed by Mr. Dawes" and gave the nod to establishing an organization committee with full power to proceed with plans for what would be Chicago's 1933 world's fair.[4] The following week Rufus Dawes became president of the Chicago Second World's Fair Centennial Celebration, with Charles Peterson as his vice president.

Debating the idea of a fair in late 1927, Chicago's politicians, prosperous business people, and social elite could not foresee that the fair's opening would fall in the peak year of the Great Depression. The shrewd planning by Peterson and Dawes for the December 13, 1927, meeting at city hall, which won the mayor's support, foreshadowed later planning policies that enabled the international exposition to survive and even flourish amidst economic crisis.

Chicago's most successful engineers and business entrepreneurs—most of whom, like Dawes, had served in World War I—collaborated to conceive and then create an incredible exposition that became a testament to their own determination, personal ethics, and city boosterism. After 1929, they hoped the fair project would restore the respect and credibility that corporate leadership had lost following Black Tuesday, but they could not anticipate the fair's critical role in buttressing Chicago's economy during 1933 and 1934. Nor could they foresee during the fair's early planning that the Great Depression would prompt them to put a unique spin on their use of "progress" as an organizing mantra: earlier fairs had exhibited technological advances, but Chicago's 1933 fair used the very idea of progress to buoy national optimism during the Depression's darkest years.

A Fair-minded City

Since its very earliest days, Chicago has been a "fair-minded" place, a site at which traders displayed and exchanged their goods. The Ottawa, Ojibwa, and Pottawatomie bartered first with each other and later with Haitian, French, Scottish, and English traders at the mouth of the Chicago River. The settlement's role as a lakefront economic and meeting center expanded as its population grew. By the late nineteenth century, the bustling urban center had hosted numerous fairs and expositions, from the 1847 River and Harbor Convention to the 1893 World's Columbian Exposition. The city had fulfilled its youthful potential as a commercial hub and had promoted itself through its fairs and expositions.

Chicagoans celebrated the four-hundredth anniversary of Columbus's discovery of America with the Columbian Exposition, the most impressive of all world's fairs to that date. The exposition expanded the existing fair model, introduced by Great Britain at its 1851 Crystal Palace Exposition, which displayed examples of technological progress in competitive exhibits. The 1893 fair did so by building a utopian urban landscape.[5] Responding to the social consequences of Chicago's rapid growth—poverty, political corruption, radical labor agitation, and crime— as well as to elite society's idealized moral standards, the Columbian Exposition suggested a secure social order while promoting the idea of progress.

Dr. T. W. Zaremba, a coordinator of the Interstate Industrial Exposition, organized the Chicago Columbian Centenary World's Fair and Exposition Company in 1885. In the same year, Chicago's Commercial, Union League, and Iroquois clubs, all private organizations where the city's business elite socialized and networked, established a joint committee to discuss a world's fair. When, in 1888, Congress passed a bill providing for a permanent exposition to honor Columbus's discovery, Philadelphia, St. Louis, Washington, D.C., and New York each challenged Chicago for the honor of being the host city.[6] A bitter battle ensued between the East and the West. Chicago business leaders and Mayor DeWitt Cregier organized, aggressively campaigned, and made a financial commitment that assured their city the exposition site. Conflicts that developed between the national committee and Chicago's local organizers would provide problem-solving strategies for fair organizers thirty-five years later.

Many business entrepreneurs had envisioned a permanent trade fair in the United States, similar to the European industrial fairs, and they saw Chicago as its center. The Chicago Plan Commission, however, let dust collect on the idea. Then during the summers of 1921 and 1922, private investors, encouraged by Mayor Thompson, staged the International Pageants of Progress at Municipal Pier, later renamed Navy Pier. Industrial exhibits, special events, air and water demonstrations, and fireworks drew large crowds the first year. Regrettably, numerous unforeseen circumstances undercut the second summer's success—bad weather, a transportation strike, a Prohibition raid, and accusations of corruption. Significantly, the Pageants of Progress exposition convinced many city boosters that private administration with limited political input would propel the 1933 fair along the most successful—and profitable—trajectory.[7]

As visions for the 1933 exposition became more focused, organizers enthusiastically touted the fair's benefits. They forecast improved community relations, urban revitalization and beautification, enhanced civic pride, and a boom in tourism. They also predicted an improved city reputation and economic development for municipal government. Likewise, chambers of commerce and business associations as well as service and social organizations would benefit. Fairs appeared open and accessible, free of urban ills, slums, and billboards. They sparked improved municipal services, including parks, transportation, sanitation, fire protection, and electrical services. Clearly, organizers anticipated virtually unlimited benefits and a chance to showcase Chicago's cultural and economic wonders to the world.[8] They determined to make their utopian vision a reality.

A Corrupt and Prosperous Chicago in the Roaring Twenties

Urban America experienced great prosperity during the 1920s. Corporate consolidation and leviathan-like bureaucratic structures spurred higher productivity. At the same time, people struggled to cope with business, technological, and social change. Also during this decade, advertisers promoted a new vision of consumption, and electrical appliances and the automobile altered the American lifestyle. Prosperity impelled culture and science in new directions while political scandals and social tensions abounded. As this new, sometimes confusing society took form, conflicts surfaced and then intensified over immigration, race, urbanization, religious fundamentalism, and Prohibition.

Both the image and the reality of Chicago in the 1920s reflected the contrasts and conflicts, the highs and the lows, of the national urban experience. The city's reputation as a center for rampant crime, gang warfare, and corruption regularly made headlines nationwide. Yet, the city radiated energy, prosperity, and even magic by attracting enterprising and commercial talent.

The Plan of Chicago, published in 1909 by Daniel H. Burnham and Edward H. Bennett, gave form to the city's great potential.[9] Early in the century, Burnham, the principal designer for the 1893 exposition and its utopian vision of beauty and order, secured the sponsorship of Chicago business and political leaders through the Merchants Club—later the Commercial Club—for a city planning project. Burnham worked with Bennett to produce a plan that preserved the lakefront for public recreation, and the plan proposed highways, railways, parks, and streets to enhance the city as a cultural center. The city used the plan as a guide for official policy, which nurtured a dynamic in the business community that set the stage for a second Chicago world's fair.[10]

While the 1909 plan addressed traffic congestion and other problems associated with an urban workplace in continual flux, it could not remedy problems such as labor unrest and racial violence associated with friction among some population groups. Labor-related conflicts stained Chicago's first decades in the twentieth century as strikes, lockouts, and pickets demonstrated the dissatisfaction of teachers, laborers, and public employees. Brutal race riots erupted in 1919, resulting in thirty-eight deaths and hundreds of wounded. Strife accelerated when African Americans migrated in large numbers from the South after 1924.[11] Fueled by the hostility of Chicago's Ku Klux Klan, angry outbursts occurred in the workplace and unions.

Nothing damaged the reputation of Chicago during the twenties and thirties as much as violent crime, and the city became known as the crime capital of the world. Chicago's organized crime flourished during Prohibition, generating huge profits from the illicit trade of alcohol. All the excitement captured the public imagination, spurred by the press and films.[12] Readers held their collective breath as newspapers and the Chicago Crime Commission detailed beer wars, gangland murders, bombings, juvenile delinquency, prostitution, and racketeering.[13] *The Illinois Crime Survey* reported that there had been 760 murders in 1926–27 alone, most related to bootlegging and gambling. Yet there were no convictions during this time for gang murders, which suggests duplicity among law enforcers and politicians. The survey attempted to salvage Chicago's sordid reputation *and* its tourism industry by rationalizing that the gangsters directed most violent crime toward other gangsters. Consequently, it argued, visitors and citizens were safe in Chicago. On the other hand, it acknowledged that the inefficiency of the law, courts, police, juries, and legal system, combined with the selfishness of the ordinary citizen and the low expectations of civic government since the world's fair in 1893, also allowed violent crime to proliferate.

Skeptics argued that Chicago's reputation as a hotbed for organized crime would undermine a fair's success. Prompted by the St. Valentine's Day Massacre, on February 14, 1929, and the fears it generated nationwide, Rufus Dawes remarked that Chicago did not conceal its corruption or crime. Rather, he pointed out, the press advertised the city's vices and often exaggerated them. "The character of Chicago," he said, "has always been better than its reputation."[14] He offered solutions, suggesting that Chicago's reputation could be improved by broadcasting the city's business and technological successes along with its cultural richness. Chicagoans such as Jane Addams believed that publicizing urban ills would lead to solutions to cure them. Would a world's fair strengthen Chicago's character, redeem its reputation, and show the world the great attributes of this modern, urban center?[15] Unequivocally, yes, was Dawes's answer.

Lt. Col. Robert Isham Randolph, president of Chicago's Association of Commerce, organized a secret committee of millionaire businessmen to clean up crime and the city's reputation along with it. On the first anniversary of the St. Valentine's Day murders, he announced that Chicago would be crimefree by 1933 so that everyone could feel safe at the fair. Known as the "secret six" in the press, the committee raised a million dollars, much of it from the utilities magnate Samuel Insull, to finance its own strike force and especially to target Al Capone and his operations. It cooperated with federal treasury officials by exchanging information and providing funds, which eventually resulted in Capone's arrest for tax evasion.[16]

Chicago's muckraking press bared the city's mismanagement and inefficiency with exposés of Mayor Thompson and the corruption of his early administrations. The Republican mayor was a city booster, builder, and self-promoter, and he clashed with many local business leaders, including the Sears and Roebuck magnate and philanthropist Julius Rosenwald and the McCormicks of the *Chicago Tribune* newspaper. Thompson served two terms (1915–23), both riddled with corruption, and then decided not to run for reelection. A defeat, he recognized, would destroy his chances for a Senate run. The Democrats nominated Judge William E. Dever, a former alderman, to run a reform campaign in 1923.

The Dever campaign pledged "a cleaner, better, safer, and greater Chicago" with improved education, a municipally owned transit system, and more parks and playgrounds.[17] He appealed to men in civic and industrial life as well as to women voters, both Republican and Democrat.[18] Newspapers listed independent and Republican supporters as members of the Independent Dever Club. The names of many who later served on the centennial committee appeared on the list. One of them, Myron E. Adams, would later propose the exposition idea to the new mayor. The Independent Dever Club campaign brochure stated that "during the past few years our City Hall has become a center of political corruption, so open and scandalous that it has never been equaled in Chicago or any other American city. The mixture of graft and spoils and waste that is called Thompsonism has disgraced Chicago's name."[19]

Five months into office, Dever began his campaign against illegal liquor sales. He personally believed that Prohibition caused crime, but he supported the laws regardless of his own opinion.[20] He insisted that Chicago was not the "crime capital of the world" and that the slogan was an exaggeration. Since most killings occurred outside the Chicago city limits where the Chicago police had no jurisdiction, he claimed, those acts of violence should not be attributed to Chicago. Curiously, while Dever took credit for cleaning up the city, he failed to note that organized crime had simply moved its headquarters beyond the city limits to elude police raids. The shift resulted in an escalation of violence among rival gangs, and both local and national headlines continued to shout, "Nothing is safe in Chicago" and "Chicago Life is Survival of the Fittest."[21]

Dever's efforts to create good government failed to please labor, remove politics from the school board, or eliminate drinking and organized crime. These failures made it possible for Thompson to stage a comeback after Dever's single term. *The Illinois Crime Survey* summarized Dever's failures in its conclusion by noting that crusades arouse public sentiment but rarely address actual problems.[22] Success was illusory; voters ultimately rejected Dever's municipal transit ownership plan and refused to reelect him.

Did Dever's single term, a hiatus between what would be Thompson's terms (1915–23, 1927–31), offer fair organizers anything significant? Yes. It gave prominent business people hope that their dreams for a fair could be realized. It also gave them a window of time during which they could showcase Chicago's many positive aspects. During those few years, they grabbed the chance to sell the concept of a world's fair run in a nonpolitical and professional manner.[23]

Origins of the Idea

The idea of a second major fair enjoyed wide appeal during the century's early decades, cropping up numerous times between 1919 and 1926. For example, one businessman, William E. Clow, suggested it annually to Chicago's Commercial Club, which took no action.[24] David A. Steel, associate editor of *Railway Age,* proposed a celebration of the centennial of American railroads in the form of an exposition in Chicago, and on November 12, 1924, the city council endorsed a resolution to hold a railroad fair in 1930. The plan linked the exposition to Chicago's hundredth anniversary. As it happened, Baltimore threw a successful railroad centennial fair in 1927, and that exposition actually aided Chicago's organizers as they planned the 1933 fair.[25]

The person credited with the idea for the 1933 fair was a city planner and U.S. Army chaplain, Capt. Myron E. Adams. A Chicago booster and visionary, Adams had submitted plans in 1918 for another use of the lakefront south of the central business district. His plan, a "Boulevard of Victory" honoring the United States and its world war allies, earned headlines in Chicago newspapers and prompted consideration by the Chicago Plan Commission and South Park Board. Other post-war activities, such as those concomitant with his position as executive manager of the Fort Sheridan Association, made Adams very familiar to prominent Chicago business people, including Samuel Insull and Col. Albert A. Sprague. Both men later played key roles as fair organizers. Adams not only conceived the idea of a fair situated along the lakefront but he convinced Sprague, Chicago's commissioner of public works, to back him. After discussion with Sprague and other city notables, he submitted a plan for the celebration of Chicago's centennial to Mayor Dever on August 17, 1923.[26]

Intentionally vague, the Adams plan left room for changes and expansion. However, by suggesting an exhibition promoting progress that would bring world attention to Chicago's lakefront and civic spirit, Adams established a foundation of ideas from which the fair vision was eventually realized. For instance, he suggested the hundredth anniversary of Chicago's incorporation, which would be 1937, as an ideal occasion to commemorate the city's diversity while involving as many as possible in the celebration. He envisioned permanent, beneficial improvements to the city that would implement Burnham's 1909 plan. He suggested holding the fair on the lakefront, and echoing Burnham's plan, he sought improved transportation within the downtown area. Further, he visualized temporary as well as permanent buildings, such as temples of agriculture and transportation. Though he did not specifically suggest a second world's fair, Adams did recommend that the "Chicago Centennial should be in keeping with the progress of the city and of the world since the famous [1893] World's Fair Exhibition."[27] To emphasize this, he recommended a replica of the original village cast against the modern city's skyline. This juxtaposition, he urged, presented a visually stunning and historically significant message. Without doubt, such an exposition would spur "the imagination and the energy and good will of patriotic citizens."[28]

Mayor Dever approved Adams's plan immediately, and he considered announcing it in his inaugural message to the city council. Then after having given it more thought, he decided on a more cautious approach: before publicizing the idea, it should first be approved and supported by community leaders who might assume responsibility for executing the plan. Mayor Dever suggested that Adams consult leading citizens and members of civic organizations to determine their attitudes and potential support.

Before submitting the proposal for a centennial celebration to the city council, Dever outlined the plan to Corporate Counsel Francis X. Busch, Commissioner of Public Works, Col. Albert A. Sprague, and others whose support he deemed crucial. He forwarded to them letters of support from Charles H. Wacker of the Chicago Plan Commission and Dr. Otto Schmidt of the Chicago Historical Society. He wanted permanent results on a vast scale of increasing benefit. With the backing of prominent Chicago citizens, Dever submitted the communications on December 9, 1925, to the Committee on City Planning, Parks, and Athletics, and on March 3, 1926, that committee forwarded the proposal to the city council. Five days later the city council endorsed the plan, passing a resolution empowering the mayor to appoint a committee of one hundred fifty representative citizens to create and organize "an exposition or celebration to commemorate Chicago's Centennial Anniversary."[29] On March 31, the city council approved the mayor's appointed committee, to be called the General Committee. The next day, the mayor sent letters appointing members to the committee who would "take an active interest in its deliberations and work" and announced the first meeting at city hall.[30]

Following city council approval, the newly formed General Committee met on April 8, 1926, in the council chambers. About one hundred members elected Mayor Dever as the temporary chair and Myron E. Adams as the temporary secretary. The committee authorized the mayor to appoint a Ways and Means Committee, which would submit a list of permanent officers and an organization proposal.[31] It also discussed the two suggested dates, 1933 and 1937. Nineteen thirty-three marked the centennial of Chicago's incorporation as a village; 1937 marked the centennial of its incorporation as a city. Dr. Schmidt of the Chicago Historical Society favored 1933 as the centennial of Chicago's first appearance as a corporate organization. That year would see the Great Depression at its worst.

From the very beginning, Mayor Dever sought to separate the fair from municipal governments. To this end, he stated that he should not be chair and that meetings should take place at another location. This separation would free the committee to proceed without pressure from city hall.[32] Dever presided at the next meeting. The committee selected Edward Nash Hurley as the chair of the Organizing Committee of a World's Centennial Exposition. The committee met from

June 11, 1926, until July 8, 1927, at which time it submitted a report to Dever's replacement, "Big Bill" Thompson.

The press had initially scoffed at the idea that Dever could pull off the proposed fair. The day after Adams had presented his idea to Dever, the *Chicago Tribune* ran an editorial cartoon depicting Chicago as unable to solve its transit problems and powerless to muster the "I Will" spirit that had built the 1893 fair in just three years.[33] Undaunted by skeptics, Dever proceeded to establish a fair organization that was not directed by municipal politics.

Throughout the next two years the image of the City of Chicago and of its mayor made national news. While on one page newspapers heralded Dever as a dynamic reformer engaged in beer wars to enforce Prohibition laws, on another page they sensationalized violent gang wars and their associated crimes. Nonetheless, Dever remained steadfast in his belief that a centennial exposition would help restore confidence to Chicago's restless voters and divert some headlines away from Al Capone. At the end of his term another editorial cartoon—this one in the *Journal*—depicted the allegorical figure "I Will" congratulating Dever on his accomplishments, including the creation of the commission for the 1933 world's fair.[34]

The Failed Hurley Plan

As an engineer, industrialist, and economist, Edward Nash Hurley brought considerable expertise to the table.[35] He knew business and community leaders nationwide, and, most important, he understood the strengths and needs of Chicago; but his plans, overly ambitious and democratic, failed. Once reelected in 1927, Mayor Thompson refused to underwrite Hurley's plans in any way. In the meantime, Hurley proceeded. After attending the initial meeting of the General Committee on April 8, 1926, Hurley wrote a letter to Mayor Dever expressing his belief that the fair should be international in scope "so that the attention of the world may again be attracted to our great city and state which are commercially and geographically in the heart of America. . . . It is most vital to our own prosperity and to the prosperity of our country."[36] The world war had heightened Americans' interest in international events, he stressed, and an international exposition would appeal to the general population. He and other Chicago business leaders saw a fair as a means of bringing attention to products produced in Chicago and across the Midwest in an increasingly competitive global marketplace.

As chair of the Committee on Organization, Hurley aggressively sought input for the proposed celebration. He sent approximately two thousand letters to members of the General Committee as well as to business and community leaders, inviting them to respond in writing with suggestions for a plan to celebrate Chicago's hundredth anniversary. Knowing that an exposition name would have an impact on the fair's legacy, he asked for suggestions for an official name and noted that the 1893 fair had both a corporate name—"The Columbian Exposition"—and a featured name—"The World's Fair." Of the committee members who received letters, one hundred thirty replied favorably. Only three opposed the idea.[37] In addition, local newspapers conducted contests and collected names for the fair from approximately four thousand readers.[38] After reviewing the suggestions, the Committee on Organization selected "The New World's Fair 1933." The exposition's name would go through several changes until, as the vision crystallized, fair leaders finally selected "A Century of Progress" in 1929.

While collecting ideas during 1926, Hurley, Dever, and members of the committee traveled to Philadelphia for Chicago Day at the Sesqui-centennial International Exposition. Their first-hand observation of a world's fair allowed them to gather invaluable information relating to the benefits and difficulties of staging a major exposition. They returned to Chicago determined to avoid the mistakes in politics and management and the financial pitfalls that the Philadelphia fair had experienced.

In addition to discussing the fair's name and scope, the committee addressed location, financing, organization, and types of buildings to be constructed. Committee members met regularly and also created subcommittees for grounds, information, and labor. Permanent contributions to the city elicited particular enthusiasm, as did the inclusion in the planning of approximately one hundred fifty civic and commercial organizations. During his chairmanship, Hurley spent over four thousand dollars of his own money to forward the committee's work, municipal funds not having been appropriated for the purpose.[39]

As Adams had suggested, the committee decided to stage the exposition on the lakefront from Twelfth Street south to Fifty-seventh Street, anchored at the north by the stadium and museums and at the south by the Rosenwald Industrial Museum.[40] The Chicago Plan Commission had projected the site for development as part of an expanded Burnham plan, and the proposed permanent buildings of the exposition were to become part of that development. In addition, the committee saw numerous advantages to the site, including neighboring public institutions, access to freight and passenger railroads, and, of course, the lakefront harbor.

The Committee on Organization did not follow the traditional form of a world's fair, which included temporary structures and competitive industrial exhibits. Rather, the committee promoted permanency and service to humanity. All the proposed twenty-five units would implement contemporary business efficiency, but, interestingly, the committee never addressed financial feasibility in any detail. The most ambitious plan proposed was the public health unit, the International Temple of Medicine on the Chicago lakefront.

Hurley and his Committee on Organization found Mayor Thompson's general lack of support exasperating, so on July 8, 1927, they tendered their resignations. It was only natural that they would be concerned over whether Thompson would support a fair or its vision of a fair. When Hurley initially approached Thompson for input the previous year, Thompson offered "to do everything in [his] power to help."[41] Since then Thompson had lost his bid for the Senate and planned a return to the mayor's office, and at that point his true feelings surfaced. He publicly voiced his reluctance to support the project.[42] For one thing, Thompson and some business people in Chicago vehemently opposed plans for a permanent hospital and medical center on the lakefront as part of a centennial celebration. They felt that these "utopian visions" did not reflect the interests of the city's social and business elite, who would help finance and promote the fair. They also cited unsuccessful fairs since 1893, changes in travel habits, and the lack of adequate transportation as areas of concern. It soon became clear that Thompson wanted a program of public and lakefront improvements, including an immense exhibition hall that would attract conventions and other kinds of expositions to Chicago. Thompson and his advisory committee, under the leadership of George F. Getz, cancelled the 1933 exposition on August 1, 1927.[43]

The Peterson Reorganization

Fair supporters refused to surrender their dreams, and they convinced Mayor Thompson to reopen the discussion. Charles Simeon Peterson, a Republican who was not only Thompson's city treasurer but a member of the board of county commissioners, played a key role in the turnaround. Thompson promptly appointed Peterson temporary chair of the Chicago Second World's Fair 1933. Peterson enlisted the enthusiastic approval of the vice president of the United States, Gen. Charles Gates Dawes.

In a significant divergence from the Hurley plan, Peterson suggested including women on fair committees. Peterson recalled that a separate women's committee had successfully planned exhibits for the Columbian Exposition. He persuasively reasoned, "We see women in positions of trust in the business world, proving their capacity for leadership as well as for detail, and so some of the members of the committee feel that it is advisable that the women who have shown themselves in the varied activities women of Chicago are now interested in, should be given a place on many committees that will be created to carry the fair through to success."[44]

Peterson soon appointed the political activist Anna Ickes, who had served on Dever's Ways and Means Committee, and Ruth Hanna McCormick, a suffragist and elected legislator, to spearhead a campaign to involve leaders representing women's activities. Congresswoman McCormick then named twenty-one women to serve on a permanent committee. In addition, twelve women represented national ethnic groups and twenty-two women served with their local organizations, including settlement houses, labor organizations, service clubs, and professional groups.

If Peterson's original appointees had remained onboard, women's place at the fair might have been quite different. However, changes among those women who ultimately served as organizers altered women's representation. McCormick, unfortunately, lost her bid for the U.S. Senate in 1930, and she then moved to the Southwest. In another loss, Anna Ickes moved to Washington, D.C., with her husband, Harold Ickes, Roosevelt's choice for secretary of the interior. Later, society women who were not activists replaced McCormick and Ickes, and this minimized women's leadership role at the fair.

With a nod from Thompson, plans for the fair moved forward under Peterson's guidance. On November 27, 1927, Peterson invited eleven prominent Chicago business leaders to meet at the Chicago Athletic Club. Attendees recommended a public meeting in the near future. Peterson then created a body called the Temporary Committee, consisting of sixty members, including many of the active members of the Ways and Means Committee and the Committee on Organization.[45] He also sent letters inviting other Chicagoans to become members of a permanent committee, and he set the first meeting date for Tuesday, December 13, 1927. The meeting would be held in the chambers of the Chicago City Council, and its agenda centered on determining a fair's feasibility.

The December 13 meeting closed the initial phase of Peterson's work. Peterson opened the discussion with a review of his recent fact-finding trip to Europe. With Thompson's support, he had wanted to determine whether Europeans would participate in the fair. Would they send exhibits? Would tourists from abroad make the effort to visit? Upon his return, he felt confident that Chicago, America's great central market, could expect better European representation then previous fairs. After this report, Peterson sought further input from those present at the meeting. Would local citizens support the fair concept? Of the approximately two hundred attending the meeting, only four expressed disfavor. Peterson then projected preliminary finances based on admissions, concessions, floor space sales, and fundraising. According to the South Park Board, he reported, the park along the lakefront would be available for exposition use. Finally, he assured the participants that if "sound public sentiment is indicated to his Honor in favor of holding a second World's Fair in this city, . . . the mayor in his usual energetic and supremely aggressive way and spirit will cooperate."[46]

Further discussion confirmed the fair interested most business professionals, that transportation by road and rail would be improved and increased traffic welcomed, that local improvements would be completed in time, and that the city council was supportive. Other speakers reviewed numerous topics, including the development of the city, Chicago's "I Will" spirit, the need for a plan to control crime, lessons learned from the 1893 fair, and the reasons other fairs had failed.

George Woodruff of the National Bank of the Republic, who later served as treasurer of the Chicago world's fair, noted that fairs of the previous two decades had used the 1893 fair as a model. He envisioned the 1933 fair as breaking with that model and setting the course for future fairs. The 1933 fair, he predicted, would not only address the immediate moment in history; it would point toward the future. But, he warned, Philadelphia's 1926 Sesqui-centennial International Exposition and other recent fairs had failed financially. The 1933 fair must not be added to this list. Without question, this fair's administration must run on a strict, business basis with strong leaders in charge.

Rufus Dawes directed his remarks primarily to Mayor Thompson. He related his experiences as an active member of Hurley's Committee on Organization and the head of the subcommittee on information. Under Hurley, Dawes had learned just what the business community would and would not support, and these lessons had helped forge his new vision for a fair—a vision, he argued, that would motivate a greater variety of business leaders to participate. He had strongly urged Hurley, for instance, to be cautious in his remarks about permanency, realizing that it would be better to emphasize the permanency of better conditions rather than of buildings and physical properties. Further, he had foreseen the need to work with Congress and national leaders, who would not support a local improvement program. This fact made his connections in Washington, reinforced through his brother, all the more vital to the fair's success. The civic leaders at the meeting readily agreed to establish a fair committee, and they nominated Dawes for the president's position. In addition to the organization committee, Mayor Thompson appointed a general committee of several hundred men and women, an important move that ensured the fair would remain in private hands. Immediately following passage of the resolution to establish the committee, Peterson, who chaired the committee, and nine other prominent businessmen began developing plans.[47]

Rufus Dawes told the committee that "after due deliberation and consultation with his brother, Vice President Charles G. Dawes, Illinois Senator Charles S. Deneen, and other close friends, he had decided to accept" the nomination as fair president.[48] He had spent the past several days reviewing the most pressing issues. He was primarily concerned that the South Park Board provide definite assurance of site availability; that a committee of bankers develop a financial plan; and that Governor Len Small pave the way for a special session of the Illinois legislature to enable legislation if necessary.[49] Dawes also requested Peterson as one of the vice presidents and Daniel H. Burnham as secretary of the organization committee.[50]

The city's one hundredth anniversary offered a pivotal moment to advocate for action. The ideas and proposals of the fair's early boosters—Adams, Dever, Thompson, Hurley, and Peterson—set the stage for concrete planning because they allowed organizers to determine what was possible and what was not. By seeking input from key business and political leaders, planners of each successive phase of the process refined the concept of a centennial celebration until finally the working idea of a world's fair evolved into a realistic possibility. What was required at this juncture, however, was to transform the idea to hold a world's fair into a vision that would ensure success. As president, Rufus Dawes needed to use his business acumen and the vast networks from his family, the business world, and private clubs to create both the vision for a world's fair organization and the realization of a financially successful exposition.

The Dawes Brothers

Rufus Dawes naturally consulted his brother Charles before accepting responsibility for such an enormous civic project as the 1933 fair. The brothers had collaborated as business associates for thirty years. While Charles had handled financial matters, Rufus had handled the nuts-and-bolts matters, particularly as organizer and manager of their utilities ventures. He served as president of Union Gas and Electric Company, Metropolitan Gas and Electric Company, Central Indiana Gas Company, New York and Richmond Company, and Seattle Lighting Company. As evidence of the success of the family corporation, Dawes Brothers Inc., in the two years immediately before Black Tuesday, it sold control of fifteen utilities companies, each worth between one million and fifty million dollars. According to Charles, Rufus definitely stuck to the budget.[51] While Charles smoked his pipe upside down as a promotional trademark, Rufus dressed meticulously, emphasizing their differences in style.[52]

The brothers had worked together for the federal government. When Charles was federal budget director, he employed his brother Rufus as an adviser, paying him one dollar a year. After World War I, Charles served as chair of the Committee of Experts, which wrote the Dawes Plan to stabilize Germany economically, and Rufus served as an adviser to the committee. The brothers' working partnership in planning and staging the fair reflected a long-established division of responsibility. A huge benefit to fair management, they complemented each other and created a natural check and balance system.[53] A statement in a fair brochure perhaps best summarized the difference in the brothers' styles: "The Dawes plan is bold, like Charley, and conservative, like Rufus."[54] *Time* magazine reported that Rufus never crossed or argued with his older brother. Rather he simply let him explode and then went ahead and did what needed to be done.[55]

Brothers, partners, personal friends, and neighbors: Rufus and Charles Dawes were bound by common interests. Both lived on Lake Michigan in Evanston, a suburb north of Chicago. Both enjoyed archaeology and genealogy and shared an intense pride in family and community. They trusted and supported one another, shared ideas, and sought each other's opinions. Charles occasionally felt resentment at Rufus's suggestions on methods of raising money, while Rufus felt Charles's suggestions placed limitations on construction. But the brothers wrote openly to each other about their feelings and frequently reiterated intentions to continue sharing information and advice.[56] Their letters to each other always closed with "your affectionate brother."

Born during the first few years following the Civil War, Charles (b. 1866),

Rufus (b. 1868), and their brothers Henry and Beman grew up in Marietta, Ohio, in a well-heeled family familiar with business, public service, and politics. Their great-great-grandfather William Dawes raced from Boston to Concord while Paul Revere took the route from Charleston to Lexington, both shouting word of the British approach. Another great-great-grandfather, Manasseh Cutler, served in Congress and, believing in the promise of the West, helped draft the Northwest Ordinance of 1787. Their father, Rufus R. Dawes, who had been a Union general in the Civil War, served in the House of Representatives. In 1889, Rufus took charge of the family lumber business when their father's health failed. Four years later, both brothers, in their mid-twenties, visited the World's Columbian Exposition, where they observed the fabulous Ferris Wheel on the Midway Plaisance. Charles Dawes's father-in-law had helped finance this remarkable attraction. Charles and Rufus admired their own father and followed his advice, "The only success in life is the development of character."[57]

Though always active in Republican politics, Charles Dawes independently sought an elected position only once, that being an unsuccessful run for the U.S. Senate in 1900.[58] The long list of his business accomplishments and political appointments, however, underscores his brilliance as a politician and financier. He consistently used his organizational and financial skills, plus his wide network of contacts, in a variety of paid and unpaid positions. A lawyer with astonishing financial expertise, he followed a career path that led to the presidency of the Central Trust Company of Illinois, often referred to as the "Dawes bank." In addition, he worked on Republican campaigns and fought for currency reform, better antitrust legislation, and clean party policies. He organized the "Minute Men of the Constitution" in Illinois to fight political fraud as well as crime and corruption in labor organizations.[59] After refusing several federal cabinet positions, he accepted the roles of comptroller of the currency under William McKinley and budget director under Warren G. Harding.

Through his business contacts, Dawes received a commission as a major in the Army Corps of Engineers. Soon thereafter, however, Gen. John J. Pershing, a friend from his early years of law practice, promoted him to head of the newly created General Purchasing Board of the American Expeditionary Forces. Dawes developed an organizational plan and successfully oversaw the coordination of purchase and supplies between the French, British, and American military. His business organizational skills as a wartime general and as an executive in various positions in Washington, D.C., led President Calvin Coolidge to appoint him as chair of the Committee of Experts to solve reparations problems in Europe, for which he received the Nobel Peace Prize. He later served as vice president under Coolidge. President Herbert Hoover appointed him ambassador to Great Britain, hoping to prevent an armament race and to improve relations, and then later named him president of the Reconstruction Finance Corporation.

Between their childhood in Marietta, Ohio, and their adult years in Chicago, the Dawes brothers witnessed a fundamental societal shift from small-town values to the glorification of business models, including the bureaucratically based division of labor, continuity and regularity, functionality and rationality. As extremely successful businessmen, the Dawes brothers undoubtedly helped develop these models further. The 1933 exposition's tremendous success can be directly linked to the Dawes brothers' management and organizational techniques. The two men applied these techniques to fair financing, organization, themes, and promotion. After the stock market collapse in October 1929, organizational planning and policies established by the Dawes brothers and their general manager, Maj. Lenox R. Lohr, provided not only the means for a successful fair but also a model enterprise touting optimism and hope for the country.

Financing the Fair

Even before Black Tuesday, financial problems dogged Chicagoans, and fair officials were not exempt. The bankrupt city itself found it difficult to pay its own employees. Negative attitudes toward the fair expressed by some civic leaders—William Wrigley Jr. and William R. Abbott among them—exacerbated financial concerns for fair organizers, who knew they must rely on private support to make the fair a reality. The skeptics, all prominent in business, went on record in February 1929 as refusing to endorse the world's fair project. Further, they predicted that the fair would "be the biggest fiasco ever occurring in Chicago."[60] Troubled and disappointed, Charles Dawes promptly assumed full responsibility for financing the fair under a plan suggested by the fair's treasurer, George Woodruff.

Fair organizers determined that twenty million dollars in private and corporate funds, not taxpayer money, would finance the fair. Charles Dawes agreed to raise the bulk of those funds from his business and social circles. A meeting with Julius Rosenwald suggests the influence Dawes wielded with his friends: when Dawes called on Rosenwald asking that he support the fair, Rosenwald simply signed a check and instructed Dawes to fill in the amount. What amount did Dawes write? One million dollars.[61]

Fair management intended to work within its income, dealing on a cash basis and building only as money became available. Unquestionably, fundraising and fiscal management during Depression years presented formidable challenges and demanded creativity. Strong marketing campaigns targeted support from wealthy citizens, corporations, and the public in general. For example, Maj. Stuyvesant Peabody, who chaired the Enrollment Committee, directed the fundraising volunteers known as the Chicago World's Fair Legion to ask every adult in metropolitan Chicago to support the exposition with a subscription of five dollars.[62] In exchange, each subscriber would receive a certificate of membership and ten complimentary admissions. In addition, printed brochures broadcast enticing fair details, and lively speakers campaigned throughout the city and suburbs, all hoping to stir enthusiasm and capture the public's support.

Organizers also sold bonds, and the first sale raised ten million dollars. Dawes and the Finance Committee projected that a lien on the first forty cents of each dollar of admission fees would cover the bonds at maturity. The guarantees by responsible individuals and firms provided a double guarantee. Clearly, Dawes would not allow default on the fair's financial commitments. In the agreement under which he accepted chairmanship of the Finance Committee, a clause stipulated that he and his committee control all disbursements from the bond fund and, to ensure steady progress, have the right to circumvent other committees' decisions in extreme situations. Controlling the early stages of development promoted progress with a minimum of friction, which made it easier for Dawes to approach his contacts for additional funds. After Black Tuesday, Dawes still managed to raise the required funds by appealing to people and corporations whose wealth had survived the 1929 crash.

The controls Charles Dawes placed on the use of funds prevented wasteful expenditures. Fundraising results, for instance, would determine the amount spent on publicity, agreements and contracts, and building construction. To maintain investors' interest and involvement, Dawes used publicity to create a sense of continuity and momentum.[63] After reading the minutes of a trustees' meeting at which it was suggested that two million dollars be spent on publicity, he replied that the real publicity campaign should not begin until 1932, arguing, "One gang murder on the front page destroys all preceding propaganda of the self-praising kind. The best propaganda for Chicago is the Century of Progress."[64]

Organizers prioritized opening the fair on time. If adequate funds to erect all the fair buildings and exhibits could not be raised in time, the fair would open in May anyway. If only the transportation exhibit with its four divisions plus the radio and electricity exhibits had been constructed, so be it. These exhibits alone could be expanded to stage a world's fair.[65] The fair's size, though important, was not as crucial as the presentation of an exciting new concept. Organizers valued quality over quantity.

Winning Government Support

Charles Dawes brought more to the table than his skills as a financier, and this proved critical because, in the end, the cooperation of government and private sectors ensured the fair's success. Dawes had powerful contacts in all the right places, and he called upon them when needed. As a result, the congressional approval necessary for a truly international fair came easily. Further, Dawes's network in the business world made raising funds a rather simple matter for him. Both realms of influence—political and business—came into play when the joint congressional resolution that authorized the president to invite other nations to participate in the Chicago world's fair added the stipulation that at least five million dollars must be raised and be available to the fair organizers.[66]

Congress did not automatically support proposals for world's fairs. In fact, financial shortfalls at the fairs in Buffalo (1901) and Philadelphia (1926) predisposed congressional leaders to veto new applications. But Dawes, a savvy politician and shrewd businessman, understood what he needed in a resolution to secure federal congressional recognition for the Chicago world's fair, and he lobbied other congressional members for support while fine-tuning his ideas. Charles promoted his brother's visionary plans for Chicago's fair while demonstrating that the fair would not need federal appropriations to reach his brother's goals. He knew that if the fair's financial program was already underway when he applied for government representation, his proposal would meet less resistance. For his part, Rufus feared that the Congress would not pass the resolution and that negative ramifications of the failure would reverberate through the fair's financial plan.[67]

Charles Dawes also traveled to Illinois to lobby politicians there for support. Before returning to Washington, D.C., he learned that a favorable report on the resolution had reached the U.S. House of Representatives. Later that month, the House passed an amended resolution, stipulating that the government was not obligated to pay any expense of the fair. The resolution then passed to the Senate's Finance Committee and secured another favorable report. The Senate promptly passed the joint resolution.

The favorable vote skidded under the wire just before Coolidge left office and so can be pointed to as one of Charles Dawes's final triumphs as vice president. President Coolidge signed into law the resolution to support the fair on February 5, 1929, one month before turning the White House over to Herbert Hoover. Charles Dawes had spent nearly sixty days piloting the resolution through Congress. Later that year, when Rufus Dawes, his wife, and Maj. Lenox Lohr lunched at the White House, President Hoover officially issued the proclamation inviting foreign nations to participate in the Chicago world's fair of 1933.

Without doubt, Charles Dawes was accustomed to achieving his goals. He spent his entire life meeting specific objectives by means of well-defined authority and responsibilities. He cherished his right to accomplish things swiftly and on his terms. He believed truth was the right way and only way.[68] Significantly for fair management and design, he also believed that an engineering officer had the necessary skills to tackle major projects and complete tasks successfully under any circumstances.

The Business, Military, Engineering Organizational Plan

Trends in business management clearly influenced the way committees managed the 1933 fair. During this era of expanding bureaucracies, corporations implemented new business methods based on an efficiency model. Business leaders such as Charles Dawes reorganized management layers to provide better control over production and distribution. As businesses added more executive positions to the layers, engineers frequently moved into leadership positions, and some advanced to chief executive roles.[69] Consistent with business and political practices of the time, males dominated these fields. As fair organizers, the Dawes brothers, both progressive businessmen and adherents to the new management models, ensured that Chicago's second world's fair would follow this trajectory. While including women in their plans to a limited extent, for the most part they invited women to fill roles that fell within women's traditional sphere.

In the early twentieth century, Frederick W. Taylor, an engineer, developed an efficiency model built on the methods of his field. The model has become known as Taylorism. Taylorism increased the number of specialized middle managers, thereby transforming industrial organization through scientific, labor-saving strategies. Some business managers published journals, which included examples of organizational charts and success stories. One such journal was the *Military Engineer*, a publication of the Society of American Military Engineers. Its editor, Maj. Lenox R. Lohr, followed this tradition. Further, Lohr also personified the qualities most revered as part of the new management model: versatility, sound business sense, and astute leadership abilities. In 1928 Lohr attracted the attention of the society's national president, Charles Dawes.

Born in 1891 in Washington, D.C., Lohr developed leadership and manual training skills in high school before earning a degree in mechanical engineering at Cornell. He had served in the Army Corps of Engineers in Europe during World War I, advancing in rank to major. Following the war and two years of teaching at West Point, he reorganized the Society of American Military Engineers magazine operations with his assistant, Martha Steele McGrew, rescuing it from an almost certain demise. Lohr's editorials expressed his vision of the engineer as a public servant with a teaching mission. By effective organization, he said, engineers could coordinate forces to attain their objectives both economically and effectively.[70] When he wrote that "history teaches not so much from success as from failures, for when failures are eliminated success comes automatically," he outlined what would be his management style and policy for Chicago's world's fair.[71] He determined that, with careful organization and planning, the fair would be both economically sound and educationally effective.

Recognizing all that Lohr could contribute, Dawes soon invited him to come onboard as the fair's general manager. Dawes outlined details of the fair, depicting it as a grand civil engineering project. Dawes remarked to Lohr, "An engineer is supposed to be able to do anything."[72] Lohr accepted, and then he resigned from the army.

A few weeks later Lohr delivered a four-page memo to the fair president, Rufus Dawes, that outlined his policies and a preliminary organizational plan.[73] He followed a decentralized plan with all departments united through the general manager's office. The plan held each department director responsible and accountable for the efficiency and accuracy of his own assignment and personnel. No department would have full authority, but each would operate freely under the advice and counsel of the officers above in the hierarchy. Communication among departments, directors, and officers assured compatibility. A system of rules and procedure would clarify the information flow among levels. In addition, Lohr insisted that all fair workers be paid employees, not volunteers, in order to assure control and loyalty.

Lohr understood the benefits of organization charts. His handbook from the army engineering service as well as several articles he had edited for the *Military Engineer* graphically illustrated the relationship of one official or department to the others within a specified organization.[74] At Lohr's urging that they establish a logical system of accountability and efficiency, fair organizers consulted a business organizational specialist firm, the Business Research Corporation of Chicago. This firm studied the organization of four earlier world's fairs—Chicago's 1893 World's Columbian Exposition, St. Louis's 1904 Louisiana Purchase Exposition, San Francisco's 1915 Panama-Pacific Exposition, and Philadelphia's 1926 Sesqui-centennial International Exposition. It created a proposed organizational chart for the 1933 fair, based on a comparison of the fair's policy draft on committee functions with the committee organization of these four previous expositions (figure 1).[75]

As the fair organization evolved, some departments merged and others completed assignments or expanded to encompass new operations. Eventually, the ten originally proposed major departments were reduced to seven.[76] As general manager, Lohr remained at the center of the organizational plan, in charge of overseeing the entire project. He was responsible only to the board of trustees through the president, Rufus Dawes. Sensitive to the different leadership styles of the Dawes brothers, Lohr had accepted his position with the understanding that his loyalty would be to Rufus Dawes, not Charles Dawes. In turn, Rufus Dawes would not subvert staff loyalty to Lohr.[77] Immediately below Lohr, the secretary and comptroller departments handled and routed procedural operations. The president, vice president, and treasurer operated between the board of trustees and Lohr. The president, vice president, treasurer, general manager, and nine others formed the Executive Committee, which made decisions between board meetings.[78] The fair

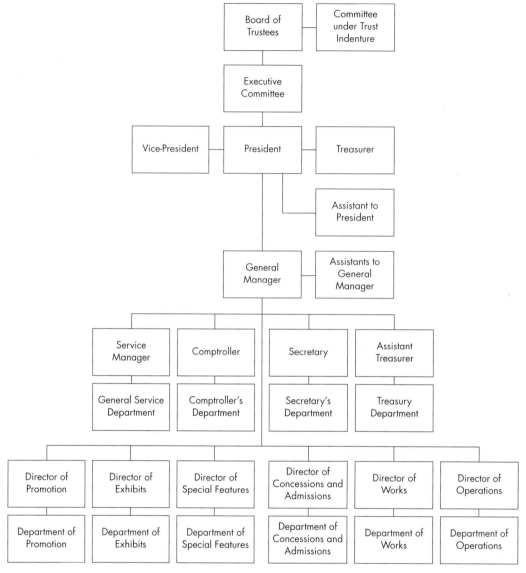

Figure 1. Proposed Organizational Chart of A Century of Progress International Exposition, 1930.

officials in the bottom layer led the five departments that produced products and functions: promotion, exhibits, concessions, works, and general service, which pertained to operations and maintenance (figure 2).

Virtually all top fair officials belonged to a "Good Old Boy Club" of sorts. There were no real strangers among them, and they used their social relationships to promote the fair's goals. These officials, primarily white men in their forties to mid-sixties, operated within the upper echelon of their fields, whether law, banking, science, or business. The majority had served in World War I. Though

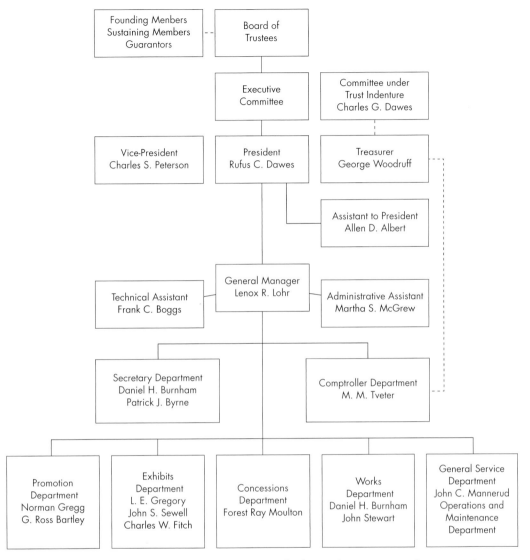

Figure 2. Implemented Organizational Chart of A Century of Progress International Exposition, 1933–34.

of various religions and political affiliations, they belonged to many of the same private social and civic organizations, including the Chicago Club, Commercial Club, Union League Club, City Club, University Club, Chicago Athletic Club, and Tavern Club. Through their relationships in men's clubs, they fought for better government, supported cultural institutions, and worked to beautify the city.[79]

Using the new business efficiency model, fair organizers developed a top-down plan but with advisory group input. Advisory groups included, for instance, an Architecture Commission, which counseled the Works Department on construction design; the National Research Council, which advised on the theme and scope of science for the exhibits; and neighborhood ethnic committees, which participated at various levels in promotion, exhibits, and concessions. One extremely influential advisory committee included some four hundred wealthy and entrepreneurial founding members, sustaining members, and guarantors. Their financial contributions not only earned them special recognition and privileges at the fairgrounds but also allowed them to nominate members for the board of trustees. Over one-quarter of the trustees were drawn from this pool of advisers.

Just as important as establishing an organizational framework was the selection and appointment of officers, directors, and staff. Lohr not only brought his knowledge of military engineering to the project, he also brought some of his staff and colleagues. In fact, several branches of the military provided leaders for fair operations. From the *Military Engineer*, Lohr's assistant, Martha McGrew, joined as his administrative assistant; Lt. Col. J. Franklin Bell, a contributing author, solicited and managed the fair's industrial exhibits; and Lt. Col. Robert I. Randolph, an active member of Chicago's chapter of the Society of American Military Engineers and the crime-fighting president of the Association of Commerce, headed the Operations and Maintenance Department.[80] In addition, many other engineers and former military men joined the fair organization in leadership roles. Col. Frank C. Boggs, Lohr's technical assistant, had served on General Dawes's staff as a supply officer of the engineers' service during the war; Col. John Stephen Sewell, an engineer who contributed articles to Lohr's magazine and a personal friend of Charles Dawes, was one of the directors of the Exhibits Department; Adm. L. E. Gregory, former naval chief of the Bureau of Yards and Docks, had preceded Sewell; and Col. Charles Walton Fitch, Lohr's childhood friend, followed Sewell in exhibits.

Dawes and Lohr selected other directors and experts from the corporate and academic fields. The architect Daniel H. Burnham Jr. held several positions, including director of the Works Department, secretary, and vice president. Forest Ray Moulton, an astronomy professor, directed concessions; John C. Mannerud had managed the Carson, Pirie, Scott department store before heading the General Service Department; and Col. John Stewart also had administered a private firm before taking over the Works Department. When G. Ross Bartley took over the Promotion Department, he brought knowledge of protocol from his work as a Washington correspondent.

All the chosen leaders had demonstrated characteristics and values essential to military engineers and corporate executives: courage, sound judgment, knowledge, initiative, industry, and loyalty.[81] These men together forged a managerial hierarchy of dedicated executives committed to the Dawes brothers and Lohr, to professional expertise, and to staging a spectacular technological triumph in less than five years. Lohr related this achievement to the fair's business, military, engineering organizational plan. "Ours is not unlike a war construction problem," he wrote to Martha McGrew, "where it is found that structures could be made to stand with only a fraction of material formerly used, and without sacrificing real safety."[82] He had identified the fair as a civil-engineering enterprise.

The first building erected on the South Park land that would become the fairgrounds was the Administration Building. Located just inside what would be the Eleventh Street entrance, this symbol of power and authority operated as a laboratory for new material and construction.[83] Edward H. Bennett, Hubert Burnham, and John A. Holabird, members of the initial fair architectural commission, designed the building as both the first structure on the fairgrounds and a demonstration of the use of modern, experimental materials for architecture. The E-shaped structure served as a symbol of welcome, displayed the themes of science and industry with towering allegorical figures on the front facade, and provided space for offices, workshops, and receptions. There were laboratories in the basement for experiments in lighting, color, and display techniques. This multifunctional gateway to the fair, with a terraced view of the lagoon and Lake Michigan, offered visitors an impressive introduction. It also served as Lohr's headquarters, from which he directed the fair as an engineering project, sometimes spending twenty-four hours a day there, just as a military engineer would when serving in the field.

Over the course of several years, the Dawes brothers and Lohr developed an organization and produced a vision for a fair that set a new course for fairs of the twentieth century. They implemented modern business methods in the organizational structures and processes and yet retained a sense of the entrepreneurial family enterprise. They united diverse members of the population and built a team of enthusiastic and devoted workers on all levels. They received municipal, state, and federal authorization that elevated the exposition to an international level. They raised adequate funds to begin construction. Together they had transformed the idea of a centennial exposition into the reality of a Chicago world's fair. After Charles Dawes met with civic leaders to ensure that the fair was financially feasible, he released a statement to the press in which he justifiably concluded that no one in his right mind could predict that the city of Chicago would "change its motto from 'I will' to 'I surrender.'"[84]

The Dawes brothers, Lenox Lohr, and their team of motivated leaders were ready to reshape Chicago's lakefront and reputation. Together this group would design a radical plan for the 1933 international exposition, beginning with its visionary theme and incorporating futuristic architecture and dynamic exhibits. As the nation slipped into the Great Depression, their vision crystallized into one that economically and emotionally bolstered Chicago's economically exhausted population by creating a magical, colorful escape grounded in modern technology.

3

A New Vision
for a World's Fair

The Fair stands as a symbol of the architecture of the future . . .
strengthened only by the background of scientific engineering
and inventive genius.

—Harvey Wiley Corbett, *Architectural Forum*

Charles Gates Dawes arrived in Chicago on May 24, 1929. He soon announced his intention to raise ten million dollars for the fair from Chicago sources before he left to serve as ambassador to England. He phoned civic leaders whom he regarded as essential to the effort, all powerful leaders in their own fields who also served on boards of key organizations.[1] Most belonged to the same private clubs as Dawes and also had connections to the banking business. Dawes planned a meeting in his office with his brother Rufus; the fair treasurer, George Woodruff; and several other influential guests—newspaper editors and publishers Col. Robert R. McCormick and Walter A. Strong; merchants James Simpson and Silas H. Strawn; and Melvin A. Traylor and John W. O'Leary, who represented banking and industry.[2]

To secure their commitment to the exposition, Dawes appealed to their sense of duty to Chicago and to their ties as personal friends. His reasoning and optimism united the group and dispelled their doubts about the practicality of the fair. He probably used the techniques described in his World War I memoirs. When he needed speedy results for Gen. John J. Pershing, he recalled that "by smoking cigars, by great emphasis, by occasional profanity no matter how dignified the gathering or impressive the surroundings, I generally got everyone earnestly in discussion of the very crux of the question in the first half-hour."[3] By the end of his meeting with McCormick, Strawn, and the others, all supported the fair, but they requested several changes. First, the name would change from the Chicago

World's Fair Centennial Celebration to A Century of Progress.[4] Second, the scope of the fair should be expanded to include more active participation by local industries, and sports activities would take place throughout all areas of the city.

Changing the fair's name was originally just a conciliatory maneuver to obtain the cooperation of prominent skeptics. Fair organizers, however, soon recognized the genius in it. They quickly adjusted their focus, turning the idea of progress into their celebrated fair theme. This was a strategically brilliant maneuver, for Black Tuesday's emotionally devastating fallout begged for some kind of optimism. The very notion of progress promised buoyancy, hope, and resilience for Chicago and its future. Further, the word gave fair participants, whether corporate exhibitors or barkers on the Midway, a marvelous advertising tool. The thought of translating an abstract concept into concrete forms—architecture, art, and exhibits—thrilled and challenged fair officials while offering them the opportunity to reinvent the world's fair. It also gave them a way to create a legacy for the World War I generation, and it gave business leaders a public forum through which to regain the public's trust and respect after the stock market crash. First, though, fair management must define what progress meant to its generation and determine how best to showcase it on the fairgrounds.

The Idea of Progress at World's Fairs

In 1922 the renowned Cambridge professor John B. Bury defined "progress" as a theory involving a synthesis of all things past and a sense of optimism for the future. In other words, the theory saw humans as slowly but persistently advancing toward general happiness. Bury tied the idea of progress inextricably to respect for industry and labor and insisted that progress is linked to the material world, distinctly separate from religion and spirituality. He saw that this continuity and optimism about change in the material world defined the dominant culture and consequently shaped gender roles and realities. Clearly, men were the actors who both promoted and initiated the change that they identified as progress, and they benefited far more than women in this scheme because of their access to education, power, and capital. Bury tied the belief in progress to material progress, especially for the "average man" who had visited the first world's fair in 1851 and had witnessed industry's scientific and technological advancements. Society often measured its notions of slow and steady change in very personal ways—asking, for instance, how has technology improved my job, my income, and the ease with which I travel or harvest my crops? How has the law changed to give me more freedom, more power?[5]

In turn, white Americans identified themselves as the focal point of progress. They saw progress, like Manifest Destiny, as a God-given right and, in fact, a way of life. The ideal shaped the way they created their world and all their pursuits, including those of science and technology. By extension, then, Americans saw science and technology as paths toward personal and societal perfection.[6] World's fairs provided a venue for this utopian vision and the Great Depression provided a need for optimism.

In 1930 a major publisher invited the prominent historian Charles A. Beard to write an introduction for a reprint of John B. Bury's analysis and to edit a new volume on the idea of progress to coincide with the fair. Beard wrote to the fair's Exhibits Department seeking its approval and cooperation. Its representatives responded by inviting him to visit Chicago and discuss the book project. Undoubtedly, they received Beard's interpretation of the idea of progress enthusiastically. His view included the Bury elements of incremental improvement and optimism, but it moved beyond that to articulate progress as philosophical "calls to action, to research, to planning, to conquest."[7] America's democratization of material benefits, making manufactured goods available to all classes, influenced Beard's Americanization of the idea of progress. For him, the United States excelled at the elements necessary for progress to continue—"respect for industry and labor, a preoccupation with secular enterprise, and a spirit of experimentation and invention."[8] Beard did not believe that capitalism, communism, or any other economic system provided the means to progress. Rather, he found the key to advancement in science and technology, specifically in their American rationality. Warning the fair exhibits team that the public was weary of mechanical shows, Beard recommended that they gear the exposition to "the central theme of the civilizing process" to create a new direction that would draw families to the fair.[9]

World's fairs are the offspring of the industrial revolution. Fittingly, England sponsored the first international exposition—The Great Exhibition of the Works of Industry of All Nations, popularly known as the Crystal Palace—in 1851. Those who organized the Crystal Palace, Prince Albert among them, used the fair to assert Great Britain's scientific and technological dominance, its prosperity, and its desire for peace. Organizers of this exposition and others staged through the end of the nineteenth century attempted to illustrate the idea of progress by integrating the arts and sciences. For instance, nineteenth-century fairs often featured monumental fountains as examples of the successful combination of art and engineering. The Crystal Palace's fountain, located at the central intersection of the exhibition hall, represented progress by demonstrating the efforts of industrialized people to conquer nature and to use it to improve the quality of life. Organizers believed, perhaps overoptimistically, that the fountain's melding of aesthetics with hydraulic technology embodied both traditional cultural accomplishments and scientific triumphs.[10]

New York City's 1853 Exhibition of the Industry of All Nations, the second world's fair, imitated the Crystal Palace in that it filled its halls with examples of scientific and technological triumphs. Horace Greeley, editor of the *New York Tribune*, noted in his remarks at the opening ceremony that Great Britain had "aggrandized her own manufacturing industry at the expense" of the rest of man-kind.[11] Greeley then spoke of the Americanization of progress. American industry, he boasted, had actually democratized progress by making its scientific discoveries accessible to the general population and had thus raised the standard of living. That, more than anything, defined real progress.

The 1853 fair's centerpiece made a powerful statement about America's under-standing of progress. Rather than a fountain, organizers selected a bronze statue of George Washington. The statue, sculpted by Baron Marochetti, towered high above the podium from which Greeley spoke. It captured a triumphant Washington astride his horse. Marochetti's statue depicted Washington as an average, modestly dressed American, and in so doing it bridged the shifting ideology of native-born white men's identity. It broadcast a powerful message that American white men—heads of households, dutiful soldiers, and triumphant rebels—now saw themselves as potent activists and self-made men who had proven themselves in the public sphere of a nation of progress.

Chicago's Columbian Exposition of 1893 coincided with an era of rapid indus-trialization, technological transformation, corporate expansion, urbanization, and immigration. The massive White City, as it was popularly known, used a perfectly ordered urban model to showcase technological achievements. Imre Kiralfy's drama *America*, presented during the fair, expounded upon the contemporary view of the idea of progress. The pageant character named Science recited: "Deep mysteries, once deemed forbidden, the daring mind of man reveals, He brings to light what once was hidden, and from the sun his glory steals." In other words, the journey from darkness to light, from the mysteries of the Dark Ages to the Enlightenment's brilliance, was the path of progress taken by the protagonist Science. This embodied the moral and spiritual notions of progress inherent in Progressive era ideology.[12]

Frederick MacMonnies's *Columbian Fountain*, centrally located in the Grand Basin, embodied a spectacular vision of the 1893 idea of progress. An electric gen-erator churned water around a monumental vessel depicting progress. Above the vessel was seated a watchful Columbia. With Father Time at the helm, figures per-sonifying Music, Architecture, Sculpture, Painting, Agriculture, Science, Industry, and Commerce rowed the vessel seemingly toward the new worlds to be conquered through technological and military triumphs, through adventure and action. Fair organizers used the fountain's imagery to make clear their understanding that art and industry propelled progress.[13]

The intersection of science, industry, and progress at the 1933 fair included a distinctively new notion of progress for a world traumatized by economic crisis. Following the expansion of big business and World War I, the concept of progress shifted from one that was socially driven to one that was materially driven. Now many Americans, who fully embraced the twentieth century as the new age of science and industry, saw the machine itself as a symbol of progress and social promise. For example, women stopped wearing corsets and rode bicycles, drove automobiles, and even flew airplanes. Further, art reached far beyond traditional subjects to celebrate production and consumption. Fair organizers drew experts from around the nation to stage the fair and rescue capitalism in its economic crisis.

Fair officials gave the responsibility of executing the fair's pivotal artistic endeavor—the representation of progress—to a local woman sculptor, Louise Lentz Woodruff. The sculptor and her banker husband, George Woodruff, were socially prominent in Chicago's elite circles. She served on women's boards of artistic and civic organizations, and he was treasurer of the 1933 Chicago world's fair's board of trustees. These social connections, combined with the fair officials' efforts to integrate exceptional women into selected positions within the fair organization, resulted in Woodruff's commission. She included a woman in her composition and positioned her equal to the male figure, representing women's struggles to assert new and equal roles in American society.[14]

Visitors to the 1933 Chicago world's fair could not help but be awed by Woodruff's glorious *Fountain of Science*, placed at the focal point of the fairgrounds, the open-air rotunda of the main entrance at the Hall of Science. The fountain could be viewed from the outdoor terrace on the main level, from the rotunda on the ground level, and from the Sky Ride rocket cars gliding high overhead.[15] A promotional flyer explained, "The theme of this fountain—Science Advancing Mankind—is represented by the great robot-like figure typifying the exactitude, force, and onward movement of science, with its powerful hands at the backs of the figures of a man and a woman, representing mankind." The robot, man, and woman stood on a pedestal surrounded by pools of water. Each basin featured a relief panel on the fountain's base, indicating which of the basic sciences it represented: astronomy, mathematics, physics, chemistry, botany, zoology, medicine, or geology. The sculpture and the panels provided fairgoers with an interpretive vision of the origins of science and the role of science in modern American society.[16]

Perhaps the most conceptually daring of Woodruff's design ideas was her portrayal of Science as a robot. In the decade preceding the Chicago fair, science fiction, the arts, and expositions all featured performing robots, often as symbols of out-of-control technology. For instance, the Czech playwright Karel Čapek's play *R.U.R.* and Fritz Lang's film *Metropolis* used robots in this way. Woodruff conceived her anthropomorphic mechanical figure as a male, and as such it reflected the American identification of science and technology with masculinity. Unlike Čapek's and Lang's robots, however, Woodruff's robot, with its clean, geometric lines, suggested the strength, precision, and reliability of science. This five-hundred-pound symmetrically ordered form, which she cast in white bronze, brilliantly complemented the architecture of the Hall of Science. Both sculpture and building were centrally located, massive, and created with precise geometric planes. The robot bends forward and "advances" with slow, automated steps. Its powerful hands gently nudge the male and female figures on to a fuller life. Head and shoulders lowered, the robot appears to shield itself from those who fear and criticize scientific research and its applications.[17] Science, it seems to suggest, understood that more obstacles awaited progress, a reality underscored by conditions in the fair's host city during the Great Depression.

The facial features of the man and woman in the statue are European, but the pair wear Egyptian clothing. Many scholars questioned Woodruff's decision to link Egypt with the origins of Western science. They pointed to Greece rather than Egypt as the wellspring of Western science and progress. Inspired by the opening of Tutankhamen's tomb in 1922, however, Woodruff saw Egypt as the cradle of Western civilization and Egyptians as the first group to further science.[18] Her statue announced that just as the cradle of civilization gave rise to science, so too would the fair give birth to a new understanding of science and progress.

Woodruff's figures embodied the fair's thematic motto: Science Finds, Industry Applies, Man Conforms.[19] This slogan represented a shift from the earlier rhetoric concerning progress, in which humankind was the focal point.[20] The Enlightenment's aggressive conqueror of nature had become a modern, passive, conforming participant in the capitalist world of science and technology. Science now constituted the autonomous force of progress, continually advancing humanity in economic, social, and cultural ways, and as a result scientific authority was firmly established and scientific determinism ruled.

The mark of the previous century, Rufus Dawes believed, had been that man had conquered the forces of nature and put them to his own uses. Specifically, humankind had learned to use steam, electricity, and chemistry to reduce burdens and increase comforts.[21] In the previous forty years and especially after the Great War, Dawes pointed out in an address, the bond between science and industry had spawned many new industries and scientific discoveries. By promoting that angle—applying scientific knowledge to industry and agriculture—the fair could mark not only Chicago's hundred years of progress but also that of the entire world. The past, present, and future of science's applicability to society and of its benefits to humanity would thematically tie together the noncompetitive exhibits as well as the fair's architecture. To this end, Rufus Dawes and Lenox Lohr met with their staff, business people, and experts from universities to find new ways of exhibiting the progress of industries, sciences, and arts.

Creating a New Vision for a World's Fair

A Century of Progress would be a new exposition for a new era. Along the lakefront, the already familiar Field Museum, planetarium, aquarium, stadium, art museum, and Rosenwald Museum offered visitors permanent structures with exhibits reminiscent of the old-time exposition. Fair organizers sought to incorporate them into a fresh, new experience rather than construct more of the same. Museums alone would not draw the crowds, but people would flock to see a show.[22]

Further, the organizers wanted to shift away from the old model that used separate buildings to showcase industrial wares from each individual state or nation. Given the depressed economy, the old model would surely fail if only due to lack of funds. This left the door open for Dawes and his staff to develop their radically different vision based on shared space and cooperation. They hoped that the various states and other nations would use this cost-saving approach as an incentive to participate.

The situation demanded far more than developing a plan. Rufus and the fair promoters had to sell the plan to a community with many doubters. Some skeptics feared that the fair could never be completed on time. Others felt that the international fiscal crisis made the timing problematic, dooming the fair to failure. The cruel truth: Chicago was bankrupt. To counter, promoters repeatedly reminded citizens of Chicago's "I Will" spirit and of the Dawes brothers' impeccable credentials in banking, politics, utilities, diplomacy, oil, and the military. They also publicized that foreign countries and a majority of states planned to participate, advance ticket sales were strong, and hundreds of corporations had signed contracts for exhibit space.

Cynics grumbled that the time of world's fairs had passed. Transportation, Rural Free Delivery, mail-order catalogs, radio, and public education all brought the modern world to the doorstep of people in even the most remote rural areas, and so there was no longer a need to travel to a fair to experience new wonders. Fair enthusiasts countered with statistical evidence of who attended expositions and how often, plus an explanation for the success of Baltimore's 1927 Fair of the Iron Horse, the Baltimore and Ohio Railroad exhibition. Exciting visual displays attracted more visitors to the Baltimore fair in three weeks than the Philadelphia Sesqui-centennial International Exposition had drawn in three months the previous year. Visits to expositions and museums in Europe had convinced fair organizers further that noncompetitive exhibits presented in an entertaining and educational spirit could effectively showcase each industry. Despite naysayers, they pushed plans forward. Their Chicago, which had risen on the swell of scientific advancement and its application to industry, agriculture, and social organization, could successfully present its determined spirit to the rest of the world.

The fair management developed a vision for A Century of Progress that diverged radically from that of the White City. The organizers of the 1893 World's Columbian Exposition had used the "trade fair" concept and its competitive exhibits to display the progress of industry and the advancement of civilization. Dawes, Lohr, and their team, on the other hand, revolutionized the trade fair concept. The idea of cooperation, not competition, underlay their vision, and they saw the very *idea* of progress itself as the fair's thematic centerpiece. During the first decades of the twentieth century, businesses had discovered that cooperative action could actually advance their own industries, and fair organizers believed that this same concept could be used to demonstrate the collective progress of all industries. Cooperation would also save money for industrial exhibiters by eliminating display duplication. Surely this fact alone would attract wide-ranging corporate participation, thus supporting the fair financially. Further, organizers believed that A Century of Progress would distinguish itself from all earlier fairs by underscoring the reality that science and technology serve the public interest by improving the everyday lives of each and every person.[23]

Architecture Experts House the Exposition

Once they had agreed upon a vision, fair managers turned to professionals from a variety of fields to design and create A Century of Progress. Architecture, color, illumination, exhibits, and landscaping—each must excite the public, and each demanded an expert's skills. From architects and the Science Advisory Committee, for instance, fair management eagerly solicited advice but insisted on retaining control of its vision. Management also wanted to stay within its budget and meet deadlines.[24]

Identifying a subject or skill specialist was not difficult for fair organizers. The number of middle-class professionals had increased significantly early in the twentieth century. Some eagerly joined the fair staff as paid employees; others willingly volunteered to garner prestige or accepted fair bonds that would be payable after the success of the event. Many of these experts had earned academic credentials, joined professional organizations, and adhered to modern management styles. The difficulty arose in developing working relationships with these specialists because, fair organizers discovered, along with the effort expended to achieve professional expertise came a certain possessiveness of one's creativity. Consequently, experts sometimes found it difficult to align their own ideas with those of fair management.

Ten nationally recognized designers comprised the Architecture Commission. The commission was to develop an overall design for the narrow 425 acres of undeveloped park along Lake Michigan. Rufus Dawes selected Raymond Hood of New York and Paul Philippe Cret of Philadelphia to help bring together a team of architects who were not only accomplished designers but who could cooperate well with one another. Anticipating difficulties and jealousies, Dawes first secured architects who were not Chicagoans and only then asked for three additional nominations to include locals—a maneuver to ensure that fair organizers maintained responsibility to achieve the vision.[25] In addition to Hood and Cret, the team included three Chicagoans, Edward Bennett, Hubert Burnham, and John A. Holabird; a New Yorker, Ralph T. Walker; and Arthur Brown Jr. of San Francisco. Harvey Wiley Corbett of New York would lead the team.[26] A multifaceted challenge confronted them: the fair's architecture was to represent the idea of progress through structures intended for short-term use and a high volume of foot traffic;

the buildings would be constructed on unsettled landfill along an asymmetrical waterfront landscape; the interiors should be flexible enough to accommodate changing needs; and construction materials should have salvage potential as officials intended to raise additional funds by selling disassembled units at the close of the fair. Finally, the commission must work within a limited budget.[27]

The architecture committee's vision stressed a sharp, clean-cut break with the past. To emphasize the idea of progress, the fair's architecture must broadcast a dramatic illusion of hope and project an optimistic course to the future. Members of the commission wanted "sky-piercing piles of night-lit stone and steel that will thunder the message of this modern age."[28] The 1925 Paris exposition with its crisp Art Deco lines had fired many imaginations, and Chicago's organizers wanted the simplicity that Art Deco created by employing unbroken lines, zigzags, pure colors, and new materials.[29]

The modernistic architectural style finally selected by the commission embodied the fair's principal theme: the idea of progress. The commission definitely considered other designs, all based on symmetrical plans. Most who submitted designs had been trained in the classical mode of architecture, and the first sets of plans reflected the Beaux-Arts traditions of past American expositions. Fortuitously, the tight budget pushed commissioners to visualize other possibilities. Raymond Hood's trip to Paris in 1929 proved pivotal. There he brainstormed with a group of French architecture students about asymmetrical designs. Their enthusiasm encouraged him further. Eager to share his idea to shift from a balanced composition to an asymmetrical one, he met with the commission. His radical and futuristic vision caught the architects off guard, and commission members immediately realized that this simple, modernist style truly captured the fair's spirit better than any other.[30] Though some would criticize the architecture as atrocious, many believed that the fair's streamlined, modernist designs—often termed Classic-Modern—offered a futuristic vision and were "the first example of pure expositional architecture in America" that created "harmony between appearance and purpose."[31]

Budget demanded innovation, and science found the solution. Unrestricted by Chicago's building codes, the committee looked for building materials that could reduce costs for both raw goods and assembly and would have post-fair market value. Laboratory tests produced an inexpensive, strong, and fire-retardant wallboard that replaced staff, the plaster compound used for structures at the 1893 White City. Designers first used the new material to construct the 1933 fair's Administration Building (E. H. Bennett, H. Burnham, and J. A. Holabird, architects), and this building served as the test model. It offered designers and carpenters alike the opportunity to assess the new material, which was composed of asbestos, gypsum, cement, and pulverized wood. Certain other innovations kept actual construction costs to a minimum. For instance, designers decided to eliminate all windows, which cut costs and assured total control over interior lighting; spider-web truss joints replaced solid steel I beams, providing lightweight yet strong support and framing; and a system of clips that hooked together reduced the need for nails, which reduced both construction and demolition costs.[32]

The Hall of Science (Paul Philippe Cret, architect), the fair's largest building, served as the centerpiece of the entire design. Identified in the planning stages as the Temple of Science, it covered eight acres and featured a 175-foot tower topped by a 25-note carillon.[33] A dramatic shift away from applied ornamentation, the building's clean lines emphasized its simplicity and its three-dimensional massing. A monumental approach afforded by the Avenue of Flags walkway dramatized the building's asymmetrical composition. Visitors approached the grand structure via numerous ramps on various levels, all of which led to exhibit areas and provided continuous circulation of viewers. Terraces staggered at various levels offered sweeping panoramic views of the lagoon, fairgrounds, and Lake Michigan. Railings, recessed lights, and details on the building's exterior emphasized strong vertical and horizontal lines as neon lights formed abstract branch patterns. On the water side, an outdoor theater accommodated up to 10,000 persons for the nightly lighting of the grounds. Later it was used for scientific stunts and called the Theater of Miracles. The circle of pylons leading to a great hall 260 feet in length was perhaps "the high spot in the entire Exposition."[34]

The Hall of Science articulated Paul Philippe Cret's aesthetic vision. That vision, coupled with the ideas of collaborating fair engineers, concretely portrayed a harmony that captivated fairgoers. A designer of public buildings, Cret understood the goals, interests, and values of the institutions for which he worked—museums, libraries, or courthouses.[35] He thought of world's fair architecture as a stage on which to create a festive atmosphere. His early, simple sketches for the Hall of Science depicted freestanding pillars with emphasis on verticality and multiple heights.[36] He believed that the 1933 fair theme—progress and scientific achievement applied to industry—justified his decision to abandon recognized architectural forms in favor of modern, experimental designs. Further, he felt that the decision to avoid glazed openings, so popular in some futuristic designs of the time, fit his personal doctrine that "the essence of Modernism is a frank acceptance of certain conditions without compromise with aesthetics or traditions."[37] He was most excited about the fair's use of materials that had previously never been used for construction purposes, including asbestos board and plywood for walls and a variety of metals such as aluminum nickel for structural and decorative elements.[38]

The dazzling facade of this revolutionary structure brought wide-eyed visitors to a standstill. At a time that everyday life seemed harsh and bleak, the building's brilliant colors lifted downtrodden spirits, inviting people to escape, to play, and even hope again. Joseph Urban, director of exterior color and a consultant on lighting, used two shades of orange, two shades of blue, white, and a touch of red to create the building's arresting appearance. Further, he used a palette of at least twenty-four brilliant colors to create contrast and variety among all the fair's buildings.[39] Besides the lighthearted feelings they stirred, the colors thematically grouped buildings situated at different sites across the fairgrounds. This innovation stirred an enthused Paul Cret to remark that he witnessed "conservative people gasp at the violent pigments covering a whole facade, and then, when they left the Fair grounds, wonder why the streets of the city were so dreadfully grey and drab."[40] Thanks to the brightly painted exterior surfaces, all of laminated five-ply Douglas fir sheets, the fair earned its nickname "The Rainbow City." The nickname underscored the contrast between the fair's colorful modernist architecture and the 1893 Beaux-Arts White City.

Urban visualized the exposition as a huge stage setting, which was not surprising given that his background included designing for theatrical productions. He undoubtedly used the theater as a conceptual device when creating the fair's dramatic light displays. He had designed sets from palaces to public works, from opera houses in Europe and America to the Florenz Ziegfeld Follies.[41] Shepard Vogelgesang, one of his employees, remarked that Urban "visualized the Exposition Buildings as a background for moving crowds. He selected his palette for the effect that would be produced by people moving before the masses of color. He tried to get life into this most colossal of all his settings, blood, warmth, texture and motion."[42] An artist of unquestioned skill, Urban succeeded in melding his plans for vibrantly colored buildings, the fairgrounds, and lagoons with the work of members of the architecture commission, landscape architects, and a sculpture consultant, Lee Lawrie.[43]

Urban insisted on artistic freedom when he began the fair project, but reality forced him to compromise. He initially asked that he not be sent any color schemes developed by the fair organizers as he did not want to be influenced by their ideas. The contract, however, defined his position as "advisory." It stipulated that, as owners of the fair, the fair organizers would make the final decision in all matters of construction. There was a good reason for this: if one of the architects did not agree with Urban's color recommendations for a building, that architect could create his own color scheme for his building. This would reduce the time and expense of asking Urban to make several further studies until one was acceptable to all parties.[44]

Fair organizers restricted Urban in other ways. One constraint, determined by the fair's budget, required that Urban create colors that could be mixed for casein paint. Because the labor unions required that oil paints be applied with brushes, water-based casein paints that could be sprayed would save time and labor.[45] Fair officials negotiated with several paint manufacturers before finding one that would mix the colors to order at a reasonable cost. The manufacturer also had to guarantee that the casein paints mixed with the tints needed to obtain Urban's colors be tested to ensure durability. They needed to retain their intensity over the duration of the fair.[46]

Light displays created yet another revolutionary way in which to showcase the fair's architecture, dramatically changing the environment without actually altering fixed units. Urban began his work by painting on colored glass, which he illuminated with different kinds of lamps. This experiment disclosed the ways that various lights changed his colors. It also guided his advice on how best to show off the colors at night. While fair organizers would take Urban's suggestions into consideration, they would base the final decision on the recommendation of the committee of electrical illumination experts, chaired by E. W. Lloyd, vice president of Commonwealth Edison Company.[47]

Over eight miles of dazzling gaseous tubing illuminated buildings throughout the fairgrounds, a testimony to Urban's inventiveness. The Hall of Science provided one example. The final, glorious display on the building's exterior did not appear without considerable scrutiny by the committee, however. When Urban suggested using neon lights for the lighting effect he desired on the Hall of Science's pylons, Otto Teegen, his liaison at the fair, expressed budgetary concerns.[48] Teegen did agree to researching costs on the two or three colors for the neon that would give the proper effect on the pylons' color orange #6.[49] In the end, over 1,200 feet of red neon tubing enhanced the pylons, creating a spectacular effect. Vertical lines of neon tubing placed at three-foot intervals wrapped the carillon tower to offer another captivating view of the hall. The tower's fins and coves created an indirect lighting effect that reflected on the painted surface while hiding the tubes from view. Two sides were lit in orange-red neon and two in a soft blue created from a combination of gases, filling 2,700 feet of tubing. To complete the effect, floodlights and motion searchlights lit the building on all sides. All together, 4,760 feet of gaseous tubing lit the Hall of Science's exterior.[50]

In accordance with organizers' goals, the fair's pioneering use of gaseous tube lighting—as distinguished from the neon used in advertising signage—illustrated one way that modern science enriches everyday life. A Century of Progress was the first exposition to use neon, kryton, helium, and mercury vapor tubes as floodlighting. This was also one of the earliest widespread public usages. After experiments in the fair laboratories, installations on individual sites varied from 200 to 5,000 linear feet of tubing. Special-effect lighting at the fair, undertaken jointly by General Electric and the Westinghouse Electric and Manufacturing Company, included color-shadow effects, color transparencies, electrical fireworks, electrical cascades, luminescent and iridescent features, and a scintillator that projected multiple arc searchlights with interchangeable color filters often into steam clouds.

Because of illness, Urban made few trips to Chicago during the fair's planning stages. He stayed in New York, working from his office there and then from a hospital bed. He relied on fair contacts, photographs, and sketches to make his decisions. He had planned to supervise the final phases of color application and work at the fairgrounds, and had requested an open automobile so that he could view construction without walking. As his health declined, he cancelled his plans to travel and requested that his representative Otto Teegan speak for him and make decisions for him. Unfortunately, Urban died during the opening month of the fair without ever having seen his captivating color palette in daylight or illuminated at night. He never experienced the total visual effect or witnessed the bright and memorable atmosphere that he had created for fairgoers.[51]

When buildings needed repainting in 1934 for the second season, Vogelgesang reduced Urban's scheme to ten colors, now including turquoise and red-orange. He continued using color to unite buildings thematically, but he used white as the transitional paint. Thus, the automobile buildings all related to each other: the Ford building was white with accents of dark green, blue, and yellow; the General Motors building was white; and the Chrysler building was white with accents of yellow and lavender. He changed the Hall of Science color scheme to predominantly white and green, with one side emphasizing blues and greens and the other side yellows.[52]

The fair's architectural structures and their innovative decorative elements articulated the organizers' visions: the idea of progress and the application of scientific research to industrial production. Louis Skidmore, assistant to the director of exhibits in charge of design, later concluded that the exposition architecture—modern in style and featuring new and synthetic construction materials, prefabricated construction, brightly painted windowless walls, and neon lighting—had been a successful testing ground for new materials and new design approaches. It also demonstrated that a balance could be achieved with high-quality effects at an acceptable cost.[53] Daniel H. Burnham, director of works, felt the exposition architecture expressed "an honest reflection of the actual function of the building" through its dramatically colored and lit planes and surfaces rather than through embellished plaster.[54] Fair officials relied on experts to develop an exposition layout and to design the structures necessary to house the exhibits. The nation's economic woes made staying within budget a critical element of planning, and designers did so. Their ingenuity solved the problem that had troubled John Stephen Sewell, one of the exhibits directors: "to devise suitable housing for the exhibits in the simplest and most inexpensive manner possible" so that the exhibits themselves would be the most important feature.[55] Experts from other disciplines would be consulted to help decide what to exhibit and how best to do so.

National Research Council and Science Exhibits

The issue of what to exhibit in the Hall of Science and how best to do so demanded professional guidance. Fair organizers recognized this, and they immediately approached the National Research Council for assistance. Established during World War I to mobilize the nation's scientific production and national defense, the National Research Council organized approximately four hundred scientists from all disciplines to serve on A Century of Progress committees. They worked with fair organizers to identify exhibit classifications and to articulate the exposition's philosophy through the science exhibits. These committees made their recommendations in thirty-four committee reports. Fair organizers intended that the highly publicized joint venture with the National Research Council would advance public enthusiasm as well as establish credibility among members of the scientific community.

The Science Advisory Committee of the National Research Council recommended that the Hall of Science house exhibits that chronologically dramatized the major discoveries and developments of the scientific fields: biology, chemistry, geology, mathematics, physics, and others. They suggested further that industrial exhibits displaying the application of science should be divided into three groups: physical sciences, biological sciences, and earth sciences. Though the Hall of Science itself should be the focal point of the exposition, science exhibits should be located throughout the fairgrounds. They suggested a giant mountain range to accommodate the earth science exhibits. The replica Mayan Temple could house an exhibit on the development of man in the Americas quite effectively. Having submitted its recommendations, the committee expressed its desire to continue acting as a link between scientists and the fair exhibit planners, to serve on scientific congresses, and to act as a court of appeals when the fair organizers could not carry out the plans of the subcommittee reports.[56]

Fair authorities avoided allowing the National Research Council to extend its authority beyond its advisory role. As always, they wanted overall control of the exposition. Charles Dawes believed engineer-statesmen, not consulting experts, solved problems, and he had demonstrated this repeatedly throughout his career. As the fair organizers finalized plans for science exhibits, they agreed to follow the National Research Council's proposals. Its suggestion to organize important discoveries of the basic sciences sequentially rather than geographically—a design element employed at previous international expositions—appealed to them. By creating five sections of basic sciences—astronomy; physics and mathematics; chemistry; biology, including psychology; and earth sciences, geology, geography, and geodesy—fair organizers planned to demonstrate society's indebtedness to science. They also planned a publication with articles by known scholars that would expand this theme.[57] Although a large number of the scientists were disgruntled that they were not more frequently consulted after the submission of their reports, Dawes, Lohr, and their loyal staff had the absolute control and understood the need to execute and operate the fair with "the cold-blooded drasticness of military organization."[58]

When complete, the Hall of Science's exhibits emphasized fundamental facts of the basic sciences rather than the applications of science. Instructive displays featured phenomena and life processes rather than scientific instruments and animal or plant specimens. Upon entering the hall, awed visitors craned their necks to study the muralist John Warner Norton's *Tree of Knowledge*, which soared to forty feet above the great hall's east entrance. To illustrate his concept, Norton had superimposed an abstracted, geometric tree over a leafy silhouette. The names of the basic sciences radiated as roots of the tree while fourteen applied sciences, including six in engineering, formed the limbs.[59] Surrounded by walls bearing other murals, inspirational inscriptions by famous scientists, and lists of scientific achievement, the great hall also showcased an underwater bathysphere, a stratosphere gondola, a geological time clock divided into one hundred million-year sections, a model of a molecule of table salt, a gyroscopic compass, and a display of all chemical elements. Eight acres of scientific exhibits lured visitors to learn about the latest research on cosmic rays, light waves, neon glow tubes, television, and atoms.[60] Visitors could go on to study human embryo specimens, examine a life-size transparent man, listen to a talking tooth, visit a house made of the new plastic Vinylite, or view George Washington's wooden teeth. Finally, the Hall of Science offered medical science exhibits that dramatized the cause, detection, treatment, and prevention of diseases, including cancer.[61]

The idea of progress inspired the fair organizers as well as the architects, designers, and scientists who worked together to stage a new style of international exposition. The architecture and science exhibition, however, told only part of the story of progress. Exhibits showing how scientific research had revolutionized industry also had to be designed, and fair organizers sought sponsors from the business world to develop and finance those exhibits.[62] Organizers grouped industries thematically and then decided which specific manufacturers to solicit for participation. Fair organizers applied certain criteria when selecting industries for inclusion. The mere fact that an industry had used scientific research to improve its product did not justify its inclusion in the exposition. For instance, Sewell's own industry—the production of marble for interior design—did not qualify. Though it had incorporated into its production process a product developed through scientific research, the product had not improved the lot of mankind. Fair organizers definitely sought industries that had used scientific research to produce a product that advanced society's well-being. The electrical engineering industry, based on the discovery of electric magnetic induction, as well as the telegraph, telephone, radio, television, and transportation industries fit naturally into the vision. Organizers' selectiveness served another purpose: to restrict the number of exhibits and therefore stay on budget.

Organizers also planned that corporations operating within a shared industry—automobile production, for instance—cooperate to stage exhibits showing progress within the industry rather than progress solely within an individual business. This would, they believed, highlight the ways research within an industry had improved the population's daily life. Further, corporations would finance and construct pavilions based on industrial themes, yet another strategy for restraining the fair's overall expense.

Shedd Aequarium and Entrance to the
Chieago 1933 World's Fair

General Manager Lenox R.
Lohr (left) and President Rufus
C. Dawes view a diorama of
the second Chicago world's
fair during its planning stage.
Chicago History Museum,
ICHi-37698.

Strategically located near the
north entrance and across
from the fair Administration
Building, the Sears, Roebuck
Building became "the nation's
meeting place," with a visitor
information center and exhibits about the mail-order and
direct retail company.

Louise Lentz Woodruff's *Fountain of Science* employed a robotlike figure representing the onward movement of science and progress. A Century of Progress Records (COP neg. 39), Special Collections and University Archives Department, University Library, University of Illinois at Chicago.

Paul Philippe Cret's Hall of Science served as the centerpiece of the entire exposition. Occupying eight acres, it featured a 175-foot tower topped by a 25-note carillon. Howard A. Bauman, Photographer; Bauman Family Collection, West Bend, Wisconsin.

The great hall of the Hall of Science, 260 feet long, showcased an underwater bathysphere, a stratosphere gondola, a geological time clock, a model of a molecule of table salt, a gyroscopic compass, and a display of all chemical elements. Howard A. Bauman, Photographer; Bauman Family Collection, West Bend, Wisconsin.

Sinclair Refining Company's seventy-foot-long brontosaurus could swing its head and tail while hissing and roaring, reminding visitors that millions of years ago nature produced the crude oils for 1933's best automobile lubricants. Howard A. Bauman, Photographer; Bauman Family Collection, West Bend, Wisconsin.

The Sky Ride, the iconic engineering feat of the fair, carried about six million people during the 1933 season.

The facade of the Social Science Hall resembled the design of a radio. Howard A. Bauman, Photographer; Bauman Family Collection, West Bend, Wisconsin.

While many corporations tied their vision and products to streamlining and modernism, International Business Machines (IBM) exhibited more than seven hundred of its machines in a setting of classical architectural elements to emphasize a transition from the past to a future of efficiency and progress.

Visitors waited in line to enter General Electric's House of Magic, eager for details of scientific discoveries made in the GE research laboratory. A Century of Progress Records (COP neg. 16-265-487010), Special Collections and University Archives Department, University Library, University of Illinois at Chicago.

Inside the House of Magic, General Electric
engineers demonstrated lighting an incandescent lamp without using wire connections
and popped corn kernels with electric "microwaves," to the amazement of fairgoers. A
Century of Progress Records (COP neg. 16-
265-487027), Special Collections and University Archives Department, University Library,
University of Illinois at Chicago.

The Goodyear Tire and Rubber Company's
blimp landing field was just south of the
Chrysler Motors complex and the Travel
and Transport Building with its outdoor
train exhibits. Goodyear Tire and Rubber
Company, Akron, Ohio.

Electric lights illuminated the Firestone Tire and Rubber Company building and the Sky Ride. Howard A. Bauman, Photographer; Bauman Family Collection, West Bend, Wisconsin.

The House of Tomorrow gave visitors a utopian glimpse of the future in home construction and appliances. Howard A. Bauman, Photographer; Bauman Family Collection, West Bend, Wisconsin.

Haeger potteries displayed the traditional potter's techniques by featuring the renowned Pueblo Indian potter Maria Martinez of San Ildefonso, New Mexico. Howard A. Bauman, Photographer; Bauman Family Collection, West Bend, Wisconsin.

Neon lights drew attention to the pillars, vertical bands, and display windows of the Chrysler Motors Building.

In the General Motors Building, Chevrolet assembled parts from the parallel Fisher Body line demonstrating the final twenty-four operations to build a car while visitors watched from the balcony.

The Ford Motor Company marketed its corporate image through entertainment, drama, and style by simplifying and romanticizing the message to impress consumers. Howard A. Bauman, Photographer; Bauman Family Collection, West Bend, Wisconsin.

4

The Vision on Display

The Century of Progress is ahead of us
and not behind us.

—William Randolph Hearst,
   Previews of Industrial Progress in the Next Century

It was the evening of May 27, 1933. Opening day at A Century of Progress had enchanted over 120,000 spectators. The sun had set, shadows were long and gray, and the time neared 9 P.M. In hushed anticipation, tens of thousands of visitors flowed toward the Hall of Science's great courtyard. Something truly miraculous was about to happen, and they would witness it. They understood that astronomers, scientists, and other geniuses had somehow captured the light of a far, far distant star named Arcturus and converted its light to electrical power. Incredible. Soon the power would trigger a switch, and the whole fairgrounds would glow.[1]

The fair organizers had coordinated scientists and university astronomers with General Electric (GE) and Westinghouse Electric to produce the astounding light show. Truly amazing at the time, the collaborative team had captured light from Arcturus and then lit the fair arena with it. The electric companies had provided the research and equipment to transmit electrical impulses from the star's captured light via revolutionary photoelectric cells and Western Union lines to the fair arena. Light that had left the star forty years ago, during the time of the 1893 Chicago World's Fair, had traveled 186,000 miles a second through space to reach Chicago just in time for the 1933 opening. With the final contact of the master switch, relays operated both a visual and audible signal so that colored lights flooded the exposition buildings and searchlights reached for the stars. Fairgoers found the display so fantastic that it was repeated nightly thereafter.[2]

Fair organizers aimed to captivate exposition visitors by showcasing inventive ways in which science applied to everyday life. They also wanted to exploit the genius of diverse technological fields to produce unique exhibits while working within the confines of a Depression-era budget. The wizardry that created the light show proved they could definitely do it. Cooperatively produced displays such as the Arcturus show severed ties with past exhibitions that built on competitive exhibits, and fair organizers predicted that this innovative approach would establish a new model for designing and financing twentieth-century fairs. They used personal contacts to convince key business leaders to help support the fair by sponsoring exhibits—that is, designing, coordinating, constructing, and actually paying for their displays and the space they occupied. As it turned out, efforts to develop exhibits through joint ventures met with mixed success. Some industries cooperated to produce displays staged in "theme" buildings. Others preferred to produce their own exhibits and so built individual corporate pavilions, many featuring technological innovations that tapped into visitors' desires for products reflecting a higher standard of living. Business leaders used corporate pavilions to showcase their products, recapture public trust and respect during an era of economic strife, and promote a corporate image.[3]

The Idea of Cooperative Progress

The challenge to create engaging, enlightening exhibits tested fair organizers and culminated in new design techniques. In the process, the craft of showmanship preoccupied fair organizers.[4] Simply displaying artifacts as had been done at past fairs did not satisfy their vision. They wanted exhibits to educate and engage viewers. They struggled to identify strategies, instructing staff members to prepare comparative studies of sites, attendance, finances, and exhibits of previous world's fairs. Some organizers—Rufus Dawes among them—sought inspiration by visiting foreign exhibitions. After a trip to Europe, Dawes noted that movement alone in an exhibit did not hold viewers' attention. He observed that exhibits with movement but a weak story lost viewers sooner than stationary objects and images that followed a strong story line with clear explanations. He consequently insisted that an exhibit tell a story that illustrated a principle.[5] Thus, showmanship reigned over motion for the 1933 fair.

Early in the planning stages, organizers invited key leaders of earlier fairs to share their experiences and thoughts on creating exhibits and financing a fair. Ernest T. Trigg, a paint and varnish businessman who had chaired the executive committee of Philadelphia's 1926 Sesqui-centennial Exposition, spoke to the Chicago committee in 1928. Fifteen fair organizers and several members of the local press attended the session. The importance of an exhibit's educational value, Trigg stressed, should not be underestimated. An exhibit should plainly highlight for fairgoers the great differences between their everyday lives and those of earlier generations. To accomplish this, he urged fair organizers to engage the nation's most modern industries, especially those that had so obviously reshaped American life—the automotive industry, aviation, radio, and telephony. Recalling his Philadelphia experience, Trigg warned of the problems that internal bickering and clashes with a mayor and local politicians could create.[6]

Trigg pointed out that competitive exhibits failed to satisfy current needs, especially when economic pressures threatened to keep exhibitors from participating. He offered a better idea: create exhibits based on trade and professional associations rather than rivalries. A joint venture, he believed, would lower costs and almost certainly yield a more engaging end-product. He also felt that steering away from competitive exhibits served the public interest. Cooperatively staged exhibits organized around the idea of industrywide progress made good sense and could help defray construction and exhibit expenses for the fair management. Created purely for their educational value, such exhibits could effectively illustrate the industry's "hopes and ambitions" as well as its economic importance to the nation.[7]

Trigg's ideas proved pivotal to plans for A Century of Progress. They clearly inspired Rufus Dawes, who now conceptualized the fair in radically new ways. He moved to transform plans by establishing cooperation among industries as an organizing principle. He used that principle to visualize and promote thematic pavilions which would tell an exciting, expansive story rather than feature individual products in competition. When his idea of thematic pavilions failed to appeal to all potential exhibitors, fair organizers moved to devise an alternate plan. In the end, three types of exhibit space proved most practical: fair-sponsored pavilions, theme pavilions, and corporate pavilions.[8]

Efforts to persuade trade organizations to coordinate cooperative exhibits met with limited success. As a result, emphasis shifted to leasing space for individual exhibits at a cost of ten dollars per square foot, or, another option, allowing individual corporations to build and pay for their own pavilions. In the end, A Century of Progress sponsored several exhibit halls, including the Hall of Science and the Travel and Transport Building. Both of these halls displayed state-of-the-art technological achievements organized to demonstrate progress within the field as recommended by experts from the fields of science and transportation. The U.S. Government Building, the States Building, and the Illinois Host House functioned under government sponsorship. Fair management also coordinated industrial exhibition theme halls that leased space according to specific classifications—agriculture, electricity, and radio and communications, for instance. The five theme halls of General Exhibits showcased mineral industries and industrial engineering, graphic arts and paper products, furniture, office equipment and sporting goods, jewelry and cosmetics, and textiles. The Home and Industrial Group included industries that produced building materials. It featured a series of model homes—including the House of Tomorrow with its garage for an airplane—and new building materials and fresh ideas for use of brick, glass, enamel, steel, and masonite.[9] Finally, major corporations such as General Motors (GM), Chrysler, Firestone, and Sears Roebuck sponsored individual pavilions to promote their own interests.

Telling a widely cast story became the guiding principle for illustrating the transformative power of science. With this in mind, the Science Advisory Committee suggested that scientists envision more than exhibit arrangement. They should challenge themselves by asking how each individual could contribute "a word picture of his conception of each exhibit to move the story forward one step."[10] After thoroughly scrutinizing the science reports and the divisions the reports suggested, the fair's experts sketched a floor plan for the Hall of Science that arranged exhibits into logical groupings. An engaging narrative would naturally guide viewers through the hall, effortlessly telling a story of scientific progress and the ways it had reordered everyday life.[11]

Fair organizers accepted some but not all advice regarding the application of science to industry. In this they revealed their resistance to using women's everyday lives as a conceptual framework. This became more than clear in their dealings with Seabury Colum Gilfillan. They approached Gilfillan, who had written his dissertation on the sociology of invention and had served on the President's Research Committee on Social Trends with the sociologist William F. Ogburn, for exhibit recommendations. He prepared multiple lists of functional groups with inventions and discoveries that could be used to organize industrial exhibits. Fair organizers warmed to his conceptual framework using transportation, architecture, agriculture, health, communication, and household inventions as primary categories. On the other hand, his lists for social sciences that used the city or women as conceptual themes were not well received. Gilfillan suggested, for instance, an exhibit on the social and mechanical inventions affecting women. He highlighted labor-saving and leisure inventions from birth control, household appliances, and synthetic fabrics to the bicycle, player piano, and cigarette machine.[12] Organizers commented that exhibiting these products in the context of women's daily lives did not fit into their vision for the fair. They claimed that many of these products would be displayed in the General Exhibits Group, which would house corporate exhibits that did not fit into the themed pavilions. These exhibits would use corporate-defined conceptual frameworks designed to advertise products to consumers, often women, but their message would be industry-based rather than woman-based.

Business Reasons to Support the Fair

A Century of Progress financially benefited the city of Chicago and corporate sponsors. The 1933 fair attracted nine million visitors who spent approximately $400,000,000 in hotels, restaurants, theaters, and department stores in Chicago. Conventions, timed to coincide with the event, brought a new world record of

1,478 meetings with an attendance of 1,596,000 participants. The fair created more than 22,000 new jobs on the fairgrounds for construction and exhibit building and many more in the city. As a result, Chicago became a leader in the nation's effort at economic recovery.[13]

Since organizers determined to operate without government financial support, it was crucial that big business back the fair. Fair organizers and staff used the Exhibit Department's handbook, *The Exhibit Salesman's Primer,* to court corporate participants. Businesses initially resisted paying for rental space because space at earlier, competitive fairs had been cost free. They ultimately accepted the fair organizers' rationale that collective use of space and the elimination of duplicative exhibits ensured a quality investment. Once they agreed to this principle, businesses rushed to reserve prime exhibit locations. In the end, exhibit frontage extended more than eighty miles. Amazingly, in the midst of the Great Depression, American industry invested $32,000,000 as exhibitors in the fair—$20,000,000 in 1933 and an additional $12,000,000 the following year.[14] Industrialists recognized A Century of Progress as a spectacular showcase for their new products as well as a way to impart optimism and confidence in an economic recovery. Eastman Kodak's Oscar Holbert had alerted businessmen to this potential when he claimed, "The Fair should be a tremendous vehicle for advertising the great comeback of business with the new products that have been designed and discovered in this era of depression."[15]

Advertising new products and thereby generating revenue was only one advantage of corporate participation at the fair. Some industrial leaders saw the exposition as a symbol of reviving prosperity. Charles W. Fitch, who became exhibits director when John Stephen Sewell's health failed, convinced corporations that by contracting for space and paying for it in advance they would help lead the nation out of the Depression.[16] Still others defined participation in even broader and more lofty economic terms. For instance, Edward H. Sniffen, Westinghouse's representative to the fair, believed that the exhibits would supply vision, courage, and "the setting up exercise to revive [America's] spirit and restore its confidence," an exercise that could generate a new wave of clear thinking and industrious action to the country.[17] General Charles Dawes put it differently, reminding participants that confidence generated a demand for durable goods, which would mark the beginning of restored prosperity. In other words, nothing succeeds like success.[18] Convinced, the leaders of General Electric and General Motors, along with others, understood the extraordinary opportunities A Century of Progress offered. Seizing the fair's modernist style of architecture and the theme of progress to project optimism and confidence, they "banded together in defiance of the pessimists" proving that "when the crucial test comes and cooperation and money is needed to sell America to the entire world, they stand shoulder to shoulder in the front line of offense."[19]

Optimistic rhetoric aside, the fact remained that the Great Depression had the nation in a vise, and big business feared regulation. Manufacturers struggled every day to survive by cutting expenses, lowering wages, and laying off workers. So why—besides wanting to promote a sense of optimism and the opportunity to publicize and market products—did industrialists commit so much money to A Century of Progress? Col. J. Franklin Bell, who coordinated industrial exhibits, offered fellow business leaders three reasons: confidence in the exposition management, confidence in the exposition theme and purpose, and confidence in the exposition staff and policies.[20]

Sewell offered one of the most straightforward explanations of why industry would spend so much on exhibits and advertising in the peak year of the Great Depression. He argued that scientists and industrialists recognized A Century of Progress as an unparalleled opportunity to tell their stories of service to the public, and consequently they committed exceptional amounts of money to seize this opportunity. He encouraged each industry to use its exhibit to tell its story in an entertaining but instructive way. He relied on the common sense of Americans to grasp the message. Simply put, he believed that if extraordinary exhibits could demonstrate to average Americans the ways that scientific research and its industrial applications had improved their everyday lives, those citizens would then be more sympathetic and supportive of industrial causes and needs, including self-regulation. After all, while enjoying the comforts and luxuries made available to them through mass-produced goods, Americans would acknowledge that they depended on industry to supply those goods.

Goodwill and gratitude factored into Sewell's reasoning. He believed that, although many people condemned big business and its greed for causing the Depression, feelings could be changed by their attending corporate exhibits at the fair. He argued that if society could "be made to realize the difficulties that have been overcome and the benefits which they have derived there from, their sense of fair play will cause public opinion to become a great asset to industry for years to come."[21]

Sewell anticipated that exceptional exhibits would enlighten viewers by alerting them to contemporary political and economic alternatives, such as a self-regulated economy, socialism, or communism. In other words, he believed that exhibits could shape public opinion. American capitalists, fearing another workers' revolution or extreme government controls, recognized that they must regulate and thereby revitalize the economy or face the consequences. Sewell saw three alternatives for the future of businesses: legislation would be passed to allow business to regulate itself; government would regulate all business as it had the railroads and public utilities; or "the country will go bolshevik" and the government would completely control businesses. Without doubt, public opinion would be an important factor in influencing political decisions that would favor self regulation. The historian Charles A. Beard reinforced Sewell's position when he wrote that, by exhibiting the achievements and working methods of technology, "what was once utopian becomes actuality. What appears to be impossible may be surmounted."[22] Exhibit designers sought to emphasize technology's dynamic character and its potential to raise public awareness of the idea of progress in business, politics, and society.

Showmanship

Fair organizers brought very strong ideas about how best to translate the fair theme of science and progress into exhibits. Tours of exhibitions in Stockholm, Dresden, Barcelona, Antwerp, Liege, and Paris as well as the Deutsches Museum in Munich, Germany, helped shape their ideas. They suggested first that designers contrast the old to the new to highlight progress over time; second, they suggested that designers consider using a new method of display: the diorama.[23]

Dioramas captivated Lenox Lohr. The level of detail achieved by British diorama experts simply amazed him. That they cost less to produce than full-scale displays made them particularly appealing. He engaged Edward J. Ashenden, a London artist who had prepared diorama exhibits for the British Empire Exhibition at Wembley, to set up a diorama workshop on the fairgrounds and to train a staff in the art of making miniature models and dioramas.[24] Ashenden employed more than a dozen men and two women to learn the skills. Their backgrounds ranged across the fields of engineering, architecture, decorating, advertising, publishing, and commercial and fine arts. They learned to craft miniature models that, when fixed before painted backgrounds, created a sense of perspective and an illusion of the third dimension. For the United States, it would be a new field of commercial art.[25]

Ashenden's team promoted A Century of Progress by creating dioramas for the American exhibit at Paris's 1931 International Colonial Exposition. To contrast the old with the new and Chicago's remarkable growth over the past century, they prepared a diorama of Fort Dearborn to represent 1833 and a diorama of the proposed modernist-style Electrical Group buildings to represent 1933.[26] They also created a seven-foot diorama of the entire fairgrounds as if viewed from a low-flying airplane. These three amazing examples could also be displayed in the Administration Building to demonstrate the effectiveness of dioramas to businesses preparing exhibit plans and also to impress visitors to the fairgrounds before the official opening. Besides the Chicago-related dioramas, Ashenden's workshop created two others for the United States government, also displayed at the Paris exposition. They illustrated life of the Plains Indians and of Native American cliff dwellers.[27]

The diorama studio prepared a wide variety of displays for cooperative as well as individual corporate exhibits at the fair. Three Alaska dioramas, sent also to Paris, depicted Mount McKinley with gold mining, farming, timbering, salmon canning, shipping, and rail transporting. Other dioramas represented a diamond mine, a rubber plantation, a glass-manufacturing plant, and hospitals. The Galapagos Islands biology diorama illustrated the various types of animals in the single habitat and their evolution in an environment different from other locations. The island-scene diorama illustrated Charles Darwin's visit to the Galapagos Islands and his observations that led to his theory of evolution by natural selection. It included sea lions, boobies, gulls, penguins, cormorants, iguanas, and red-rock crabs. The diorama studio's real showstopper, though, was the ninety-foot-long ideal city and countryside landscape diorama. Created for the Electrical Building at A Century of Progress, this miniature urban and rural setting depicted the generation, transmission, and distribution of electric current for private, municipal, and industrial use.[28] This idealized technological portrait of the future, illustrating the advantages of an electrical world, would profoundly influence visitors and future fair designers.

The fair's diorama workshop did not produce all the dioramas at the fair even though it did influence the extensive use of this form of showmanship. Rufus Dawes asked Ashenden to provide technical support for the construction of a full-size brontosaurus. A small model at a scale of about two inches to one foot would serve as a guide for the building of a full-size scaffold of wood, metal, wire mesh, burlap, and plaster of paris. This eighty-foot-tall creation could then be treated against the weather and painted. Two outside firms built animated dinosaurs for fair exhibits. Messmore and Damon of New York designed and built the concession called The World a Million Years Ago, with prehistoric creatures including a brontosaurus, saber-tooth tiger, mammoth, sloth, bear, shovel-jawed elephant, and woolly rhinoceros moving and roaring in a natural setting. To complete the comparison of the old with the contemporary, dioramas featured the evolution of "man" living, moving, and talking as he might have from the Ice Age to the present.[29] Hollywood's dinosaur maker, P. G. Allen, created the mammoth life-size dinosaurs for the Sinclair Refining Company exhibit. There a tyrannosaurus rex engaged in deadly daily combat with a triceratops to remind fairgoers that Sinclair used the oldest crude oils to make the finest lubricants for their automobiles.[30]

The Cooperative Display Experiment

Just as the Eiffel Tower and the Ferris Wheel had captured the imaginations of earlier generations of fairgoers, the Sky Ride, a cooperative engineering masterpiece, thrilled the 1933 fairgoers. It became the fair's most visible symbol and was both an exhibit and a theme ride. About thirty-five thousand people took the Sky Ride each day, totaling almost six million passengers in the first year of the fair. For twenty-five cents, a sightseer rode double-deck elevators to the observation deck of one of two 625-foot steel towers, the highest human-built structure erected west of the Allegheny Mountains. Suspended two hundred feet above the lagoon with thirty-five other adventurers, the sightseer traveled at six miles an hour on the world's second-longest cable track. From there the visitor beheld a breathtaking panorama of the fairgrounds surrounded by three states. Admission included a one-way ride in one of the ten skyway cars to or from Northerly Island, a thrill for the many who had not yet flown in an airplane.[31]

It took five months of planning and designing and seven months of construction to create the Sky Ride, unquestionably the ultimate thrill ride of the fair. The Goodyear-Zeppelin Corporation built the streamlined rocket-shaped aluminum and glass double-decked sightseeing cars, lightweight and reminiscent of airship design. The Otis Elevator Company designed, built, and maintained the eight automatic, signal-controlled, high-speed elevators that transported fairgoers to the rocket-car stations or beyond to observation platforms high above the fairgrounds. Inside each elevator, twenty to thirty passengers could study the progress of vertical transportation in photographic murals that depicted the shift from stairs in brownstones to elevators in skyscrapers. At the top of the shaft, visitors were invited to look down for a thrilling view in the first elevator hoist-way with vision panels that revealed elevator operations. Uniformed attendants offered tours of the elevator machine rooms at the top of the towers, boasting that it was the highest exhibit at the fair.

The Sky Ride symbolized the fair management's role as liaison among cooperating corporations. Besides the Goodyear-Zeppelin Corporation and Otis Elevator Company, five other corporations joined the fair organization in this collaborative venture to create the Sky Ride. Together they financed the construction and operation, employing subcontractors and over 1,650 employees at a cost of 1,400,000 Depression dollars.[32]

An experiment in both exhibit financing and production, the Sky Ride was but one instance of cooperation among industries to stage exhibits. Fair officials persuaded manufacturers in complementary areas to take advantage of their similarities—which might ordinarily force them into competition—to create exhibits. These joint ventures sometimes succeeded, but other times they failed. Unexpectedly, some failures provided big business with the opportunity to control exhibit environments and public image through technological showmanship.

The very idea of cooperatively staged exhibits for each industry appealed to many business leaders, especially if the fair sponsored the themed pavilions. Enthusiasm inevitably waned when big-business executives learned they would have to coordinate and finance these displays from company budgets. They still saw the value of participating in the fair, but as one fair official explained, "Since they are paying for it, they expect to determine what it is."[33] Many industries had no representation on committees such as the Science Advisory Committee that influenced exhibit plans. Therefore, corporate giants such as GM and American Telephone and Telegraph (AT&T) wanted to engage their own designers, boost their own products, and even use exhibits to make subtle political statements or to promote a corporate image. By refusing to finance collective exhibits, big business unwittingly forced a rethinking of its public relations and corporate imagery, a shift that resulted in the realization of their quest for what Roland Marchand identified as the "corporate soul."[34]

In the end, only a few industries staged cooperative exhibits, including a group of agricultural businesses that collaborated to create an exhibit linking science to dairy products. Major electricity producers cooperated on special entertainment projects and exhibits, but they also emphasized their own corporate research in individual exhibits. Finally, the automotive industry, composed of major rival firms, rejected collective exhibits in favor of individual corporate exhibits.

The dairy exhibit served as a model of the collective exhibit concept. A committee from the dairy industry, representing eighteen hundred sponsoring firms, thoroughly grasped the joint venture concept and made it happen. The committee collaborated to finance the Dairy Building, stage a pageant, and create an impressive and educational exhibit. The exhibit, bearing the slogan "Dairy Products Build Superior People," celebrated the cow both historically and scientifically while telling audiences how dairy products promote health. An ingenious mechanical bovine revealed the cow as a chemical laboratory that manufactured milk. Contributors boasted in their literature that "the dairy industry is one of the few industries which buried its competitive jealousies and succeeded in presenting a collectively supported industry exhibit."[35]

The Electrical Building featured both cooperative exhibits and individual corporate exhibits. In planning their exhibits, power companies clearly articulated two goals: they wanted their exhibits to impart goodwill, and they wanted to increase power usage among individual consumers.[36] Power stations cooperatively produced the electrical city-rural landscape diorama mentioned earlier as well as a highly entertaining musical-comedy puppet show entitled *What a Night*. Both exhibits satisfied their goals. In the puppet story, Mr. Pettigrew angrily pulled the electric meter off the wall to protest his high electric bills, only to have scolding electrical appliances confront him in a dream that night. Naturally, he awoke better informed and happy to pay the modest costs of his electric bill.[37] The air-conditioned theater in which the power stations staged the puppet show ingeniously became a display in itself that created goodwill. Weary fair visitors, often from rural areas without electricity, could gratefully sink into comfortable seats in the dark, cool theater. Relaxing there, they could only wonder at the modern comforts and conveniences that awaited them once the electric wires reached their homes, and, understandably, they eagerly anticipated the arrival of electric services in their neighborhoods.

While large corporations usually sponsored numerous displays to highlight their progress, small companies often sponsored only one. The Hudson-Essex Motor Company's sole exhibit in the Electrical Building display was perhaps the most thrilling of all displays in that location. This exhibit gave many spectators their first glimpse of a television. The riveting demonstration took place in a small theater. After setting up the equipment, the spokesman asked for volunteers, whose images would be captured and then televised in front of a completely astonished audience.[38]

General Electric and Westinghouse displayed their state-of-the-art products. GE showed products and processes for commerce, industry, and the home. A talking kitchen explained the latest electrical kitchen appliances, and in the House of Magic, engineers offered explanations of discoveries from GE's research laboratory. A demonstration that lit an incandescent lamp without using wire connections and another that popped corn kernels with electric "microwaves" truly astounded fairgoers.[39] Like GE, Westinghouse exhibited its most recent research and modern products. Its model kitchen awed viewers with examples of scientific management and domestic engineering. For instance, it showed visitors that the 50 processes and 143 steps once required to make a cake could be reduced to only 24 processes and 24 steps in a modernized kitchen. Other popular Westinghouse exhibits included an X-ray machine that showed the bones in a viewer's own hand; Willie, a smoking and talking robot; and a microphone that allowed a person to use voice commands to pilot a model of the airship *Macon* as it soared overhead.

While leaders in a few industries managed to cooperate, others clashed and refused to pursue joint ventures. Those corporations preferred renting space in a fair-owned theme building and designing their own exhibits. Leaders of the communications industry, for instance, simply could not agree on the radio's place in their field. Efforts to develop a Radio Building devoted to the sphere of radio science therefore failed even though a plan for the building had been drawn. The building proposal caused a turf battle within the communications industry. James Harbord, chair of the board of the Radio Corporation of America (RCA), agreed with the fair authority that a separate pavilion for the radio industry would be logical and economical, but Dr. Frank Jewett, vice president of AT&T, protested the separation of radio from communications, arguing that radio was part of telephony.

Jewett, who chaired the fair's influential Science Advisory Committee, contacted the presidents of Bell Telephone, Western Union, and International Telephone and Telegraph (IT&T). They decided unanimously not to participate unless the communications exhibits included radio exhibits. Fearing that wire communications would not have drawing power without radio technology, they would agree to a separate Radio Building only if fair organizers limited its scope to broadcasting exhibits. Their demands conflicted with both the fair's plan for the presentation of scientific exhibits—that is, nonduplicating exhibits telling a story that unfolded consecutively and was not subdivided into corporate-focused displays—and its architectural plan, which grouped buildings thematically.[40] Harbord, in turn, feared that RCA exhibits would be dwarfed by the "tremendous exhibits of the old line communications companies," a fear exacerbated by rumors that the three firms had monopolized all of the space in the Communications Building and had relegated only a corridor for RCA's exhibit.[41]

Since plans fell through for the Radio Building, the Communications Building housed all radio and telecommunications exhibits. AT&T dominated the building, its brilliantly crafted displays intentionally promoting an image of AT&T as a public servant by impressing visitors with the telephone's social benefits. AT&T's president, Walter S. Gifford, had articulated the organization's governing policy and purpose in 1927, describing AT&T as providing "the most telephone service and the best, at the least cost to the public," and the company used the fair to advance Gifford's vision of AT&T as a nationwide, unified, and dependable telephone service.[42] The fair exhibit not only promoted that policy but further solidified the company's domination of the industry.

American Telephone and Telegraph Company and twenty-four regional operating companies made up the Bell System. The system handled four-fifths of the seventy-seven million daily calls made in the United States in 1932. Fair exhibits showcased a national Bell telephone network system through dynamic and interactive exhibits. Following fair organizers' general instructions, AT&T exhibit designers set out to tell the story of the application of pure science to industry in two-way communication, to highlight the fair's progress theme by contrasting the old with the new, and to avoid static exhibits. While following these broad instructions, they also insisted on controlling the content of their exhibits. Rather than creating dioramas that illustrated telephone operations, AT&T designers created dynamic exhibits such as one in which some fairgoers could listen in while others talked. Another exhibit allowed people to interact with company employees trained to highlight the human element of the communications industry. These workers provided concise explanations and demonstrations of complex equipment from dial phones to switchboard operations.[43] The message was clear: telephones had made progress but the essence of telephone service was people, not machines.[44] In other words, AT&T served the public good.

For many visitors, AT&T's most thrilling interactive experience was the long-distance telephone call. Crowds thronged to watch as a lucky visitor entered a glass telephone booth to make what might be his or her first long-distance call. After the operator asked "number please" and the caller gave a number, a streak of light flashed across a gigantic map from Chicago to one of fifty-four cities ready to receive the instant transmission. The sight mesmerized spectators. About twenty guests, who were fitted with head receivers, could listen in on the private conversation, often reacting to the theatrics with laughter or awe. The rest of the hushed crowd hung on every word as friends and relatives spoke freely, sharing joy and tears. Rufus Dawes had opened the exhibit by placing a long-distance phone call to James A. Farley, the postmaster general, ironically using the newer telecommunications technology to confirm Farley's opening-day visit rather than mail him an express letter. Over a thousand long-distance calls were placed each week from the exhibit, mostly by out-of-town visitors.

In AT&T's most popular attraction, Oscar, a mechanical man with microphone ears, sat in a glass room surrounded by visitors wearing head receivers. Amazed, they heard exactly what Oscar heard. Flies buzzing, footsteps, or whispers all seemed to surround each listener. Embarrassed participants turned to see who was speaking to them while this astonishing and entertaining auditory illusion highlighted the complex telecommunications devices and research laboratories that were necessary to provide optimal phone service. Forty-four percent of AT&T visitors listened along with Oscar, making him by far the most popular attraction in the exhibit. Twenty-two percent watched and listened in on long-distance phone calls, and only one percent actually interacted with a dial-service assistance operator.[45]

In addition to long-distance telephony demonstrations, AT&T and Bell System exhibits included demonstrations of delayed speech transmissions, inverted or scrambled speech to ensure privacy in calling, teletypewriters for commercial clients, and oscilloscopes that created visual wave forms with changes in pitch and volume so that visitors could "see sound." To control crowd flow and gauge satisfaction, exhibit specialists continually changed signage, language, and procedures. The first to do so, Bell Telephone Laboratories installed a motion picture camera to gauge attendance, estimating that more than six million persons viewed the telephone exhibits—nearly three-quarters of 1933 fair visitors.[46] Clearly, the Bell System had progressed in technology and exhibiting since 1876 when Alexander Graham Bell demonstrated his new invention by speaking over a single phone line from one phone to another at the Philadelphia Centennial International Exhibition.

Corporate Pavilions

Fair organizers had invited the nation's leading automobile makers to finance a collaborative exhibition that would highlight the automotive industry. Charles Kettering, head of General Motors Research Laboratories, chaired a committee to develop a plan for such an exhibition. However, when fair organizers asked Kettering to implement the plan, he refused. He used his technical assistant F. O. Clements to convey a message to a fair exhibits representative, J. Parker Van Zandt, saying he could not commit the time to it. Further, Clements relayed a question to Van Zandt, "what is your proposed method for financing and completing the exhibit, ready for the public's consideration?" which suggests that Kettering's enthusiasm had waned when he realized that the fair would not actually administer and finance the exhibit.[47]

Determined to negotiate an agreement with Ford and GM, Van Zandt visited Detroit in spring 1931. The visit shed some additional light on the situation. Fred Black, assistant to Henry Ford, proposed that some leaders at Ford had "in mind a separate building with an assembly line as their central exhibit."[48] That would, after all, be fitting since it was Henry Ford's ingenuity that first had implemented assembly-line production. Black told Van Zandt that more than 150,000 people a year visited Ford's Michigan plant just to see the assembly lines, and this confirmed the appeal of such an exhibit. All they needed was Henry Ford's go-ahead to finalize a contract.

But Ford dragged his feet, leaving the door wide open for GM to stage a coup. GM jumped at the chance. William Knudsen, who had left Ford to preside over GM's Chevrolet Motor Company, agreed to finance sponsorship of half of the expenses of a corporately owned GM pavilion—the GM umbrella corporation to sponsor the other half—if he could use an assembly-line format for Chevrolet's exhibit and if the fair barred all other automobile assembly lines. Costs would be significant, but Knudsen reasoned that "the advertising merits of a heavy investment" would more than justify the plan.[49] Fair officials, eager to secure a contract for their first private display pavilion and to use Chevrolet's participation to woo other corporations, hastened to seal the agreement. They rationalized that Ford had other ways to display progress, including the processes for manufacturing glass and gauges. Within two weeks they had wrapped up the deal that gave exclusive rights for an assembly line to GM.[50] GM had surpassed Ford in automobile sales by 1927. Much to its satisfaction, it now coopted Henry Ford's idea of the automobile assembly line and put it on display under the Chevrolet name. In the end, Ford decided not to participate in the exposition in 1933 though the company would take part in 1934.

Knudsen enlisted the architect Albert Kahn, who had designed automobile plants for Packard, Hudson, and Ford, to draw plans for the fair's GM building.[51] The building stood strategically at the Thirty-first Street entrance, near the transportation group. A streamlined structure that reflected the modernist vision of the architectural committee, the GM building resembled a giant lighthouse on Lake Michigan's shore. Its 177-foot-tall futuristic central tower, dominated by GM's huge, neon-lighted logo, soared above the fair's other privately financed buildings. Red, blue, aluminum, and bright orange by day, the tower became a luminescent rainbow of colors after dark.[52] The building below was a block and a half long with a semicircular concrete terrace and gigantic plate-glass display windows for showcasing GM's flashy new cars.

Starting with a floor plan to "glorify" the assembly line, Kahn had designed the building's interior space before its exterior. GM promotions boasted that the imposing entrance hall had "the beauty and dignity of a medieval cathedral."[53] Kahn had persuaded the Mexican muralist Diego Rivera to paint a fresco in the entrance hall after giving him a tour of a GM foundry and plant in Detroit, but GM cancelled the commission after Rivera and Nelson Rockefeller had a political dispute over mural content in New York City.[54] Throughout the hall, though, educational exhibits displayed automotive products alongside aesthetic arts—a sculpture depicting a skilled workman, murals made of inlaid wood, woodcarvings, and dioramas. GM's research laboratories featured science as entertainment in the form of Chief Pontiac, a talking mechanical Indian, and the spectroscope, a projector capable of producing a super-rainbow of color to tell the story of steel. Above, on the assembly line room's viewing balcony, forty murals depicted contributions made by all the states to the automotive industry.[55] However, more people thronged to the assembly line than to all the other corporate exhibits.

While general admission tickets gave visitors access to the scientific, educational, and corporate exhibits, concessions often charged additional fees. This ticket for the Fort Dearborn replica contrasts the log fortress of 1833 with the modern fair buildings and night lights.

Chicago's spirit of determination, "I Will," dances on the international stage to show how, in only one century, progressive Chicago transformed itself into an industrial and cultural world leader. Goes Lithographing Company, Chicago, Illinois.

The concession Streets of Paris did not represent France's official participation at the fair. Rather, it offered an exciting cabaret and peep show experience that many Americans thought typical of the "City of Lights" and its red-light district.

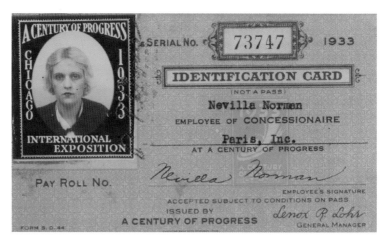

Young women seeking work could find it in the risqué concessions and cafés lining the Streets of Paris.

While the courts debated jurisdiction over appropriate attire by fan dancers and women working in sideshows, fair police kept order as merrymakers stayed after the exhibits closed and drank in the nightclubs until early morning. Edwin R. Evans Collection, Barbara S. Evans, Urbana, Illinois.

For twenty-five cents visitors could visit the Midget Village to witness a wedding, visit the Town Hall and Midget Village Grocery, or see a show in the Tiny Theater.

Superlatives reigned at the fair, including the world's largest thermometer. Neon light tubes represented mercury in Havoline Oil's 218-foot-tall thermometer, registering the temperature in the shade at the base of the steel shaft.

The Hall of Science *(below)* served as the centerpiece of the fair and as the fair's largest building. Exhibits underscored fundamental facts of the basic sciences. Corporate exhibits typically emphasized the applications of science to industry.

WF.5   HALL OF SCIENCE, CHICAGO WORLD'S FAIR

3A-H338

The modernistic architectural style of the Hall of Science embodied the fair's principal theme: the idea of progress.

WF-36 INTRA-MURAL BUS WITH HALL OF SCIENCE IN BACKGROUND, CHICAGO WORLD'S FAIR

3A-H336

General Motors built more than sixty buses for Greyhound Lines to transport visitors throughout the fairgrounds. Cast-iron bus toys became the prized souvenir for youth attending with their parents.

587:—Gigantic Fountain, Chicago World's Fair.

Evening activities included the Arcturus ceremony, which activated the exhibition's night lights, plus fireworks and a water show at the lagoon's fountain. The fountain featured forty searchlights in five colors.

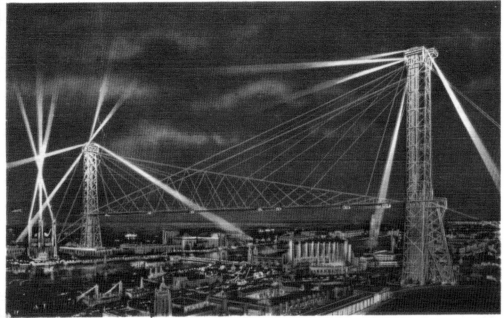

3A-H8

In 1933, the Sky Ride, the fair's engineering masterpiece featuring two 625-foot steel towers, provided a panoramic view of the fair and neighboring states.

36A34   ROCKET CARS CROSSING LAGOON, CHICAGO WORLD'S FAIR

Suspended two hundred feet above the lagoon with thirty-five other adventurers, the sightseer traveled in skyway cars at six miles an hour on the world's second-longest cable track.

3A-H581

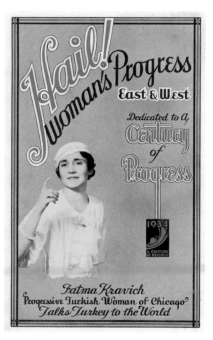

Fair visitors could collect over a thousand complimentary brochures, many of which employed the rhetoric of progress. This example extolled the progress of Turkish women immigrants and the need for women to unite worldwide.

Railroad companies emphasized their progress through diorama displays and full-scale equipment. Exhibits contrasted pioneer locomotives with modern engines that transported passengers and freight on a national network of tracks. Many Americans saw the machine itself as a symbol of progress and social promise.

The Post Office Department issued postage stamps that contrasted Fort Dearborn with the modern Federal Building to suggest Chicago's old and new federal government. Months later, a special U.S. zeppelin postage stamp offset operating costs of the *Graf Zeppelin*'s visit to the fair.

Exhibits pointed to the future with mechanical innovations such as robots and television. To relieve traffic congestion, the Nash Auto Tower showcased an inventive way to self-park more cars and conserve space.

Exhibit designers incorporated movement with a strong narrative in exhibits to illustrate industrial progress and to hold the visitor's attention. This bacon-slicing process offers one example. Demonstrations and assembly lines often included souvenir samples such as hosiery, tin cans, and beverage and food products.

THE WILSON & CO. CERTIFIED BACON SLICING EXHIBIT IN FULL OPERATION DAILY AT THE WORLD'S FAIR, A CENTURY OF PROGRESS

The Travel and Transport Building, with its suspended dome, displayed state-of-the-art technological achievements in both its architecture and in its exhibits of ships, trains, automobiles, and airplanes.

Rather than scatter government buildings and exhibits throughout the fairgrounds, planners created a triangular complex to house the Hall of States and the Federal Building. The three fluted towers of the Federal Building represented the branches of government: legislative, judicial, and executive.

In the Electrical Group complex, corporations told their stories of modern energy with demonstrations of the latest technological research and products in radio, communications, and electricity.

ELECTRICAL GROUP

The streamlined General Motors pavilion, with gigantic plate-glass display windows for showcasing GM's flashy new cars, resembled a colossal lighthouse on Lake Michigan's shore. Albert Kahn designed the building's interior space before its exterior to showcase the Chevrolet assembly line.

GENERAL MOTORS BUILDING, CHICAGO WORLD'S FAIR

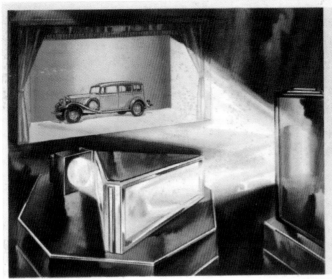

Corporations emphasized research to shift the focus from a socially driven notion of progress to a materially driven notion of progress, as illustrated in this demonstration of a prism spectrum linked to the analysis of steel in motor cars.

The Ford Rotunda suggested the giant cogs on a gear wheel, and each evening roof-mounted searchlights produced an amazing light beam that pierced the heavens, promising prosperity and magnifying Ford's visibility and dominance.

FORD MOTOR CO. EXHIBIT

The stylized-comet logo of Chicago's second world's fair represented the dynamic speed at which the fair organizers envisioned humankind conquering nature's forces, from harnessing the energy of the star Arcturus to penetrating the stratosphere by balloon.

COLOR
AND
PROTECTION

Chicagoans hailed the 1893 world's fair as "the White City" because of its classic monumental white buildings. The brightly painted buildings, colorful neon lights, and multicolored spot and beacon lights of the 1933 fair identified it as "the Rainbow City." Joseph Urban, a color specialist, created a color scheme that emphasized the modernist architectural embellishments and reinforced the notion of optimism. American Asphalt Paint Company developed paints in twenty-eight colors to meet Urban's specifications as well as the requirements of building materials and weather conditions. The company's brochure *Progress in Industrial Color and Protection at "A Century of Progress"* brings the modern architecture, color scheme, and themes of the 1933–34 Chicago world's fair into harmony, as have the memories of fairgoers. Reproduced with permission of Lockheed Martin Corporation.

FEDERAL
Group

A massive gold dome and three stately white pylons, rising to a height of 150 feet, which represent the Federal Government in this exhibit, constitute the base of a triangle, the sides of which represent the states. A dramatic picture is created by the reflection of these pylons on the lagoon to the west.

The three pylons and the statues at their bases, symbolize the three major branches of government — judicial, executive, and legislative.

The design is modern in feeling, yet has a trace of the classic proportions.

The Federal Group and the Hall of States may be reached either from the ground level or from a ramp which extends to the Agricultural Building in one direction and to the Electrical Group in another. This same ramp extends across the lagoon at 16th Street to the Hall of Science on the mainland.

The main entrance is approached by water as well as by land, there being an elaborate embarcadero at the water's edge, directly before the entrance.

The Court of States, wherein each Commonwealth is represented by its shield and flag, affords a picturesqueness and gaiety such as is seldom seen.

A partial view of the state flags and shields as seen from the Court of States.

HALL of SCIENCE

This massive structure lies directly across the Leif Erickson Drive and extends down to the edge of the lagoon. The northern front is a graceful circular arc of high pylons, fittingly terminating the Avenue of Flags. The building itself covers eight acres.

Two floors are used for basic science exhibits, such as physics, chemistry, biology, etc. The ground floor is devoted to industrial applications of science and to medical exhibits.

The roofs of the northeast and southeast pavilions afford excellent observation with stairway leading up from the court.

Rising high above, the great 176-foot blue and white tower, with its network of neon lighting, is impressive either by day or by night. The upper tower contains carillon of bells.

It is in the huge U-shaped court, with a seating capacity of 19,000 people, that a panel of apparatus energizes the rays from the star Arcturus, setting the entire exposition ablaze nightly with gloriously colorful light.

Interior view of the great hall showing the grand staircase and balcony.

SKY RIDE
AND HALL OF SCIENCE

The super-sensation of "A Century of Progress" — this all-steel structure which spans the lagoon between Northerly Island and the mainland. It will be to the 1933 Fair what the Eiffel Tower was to the Paris Exposition of 1899 — what the Ferris Wheel was to the World's Columbian Exposition of 1893.

The giant towers which rise to a height of 688 feet, stand 1850 feet apart. Atop of each, observation floors, higher even than the observation platform of the Washington Monument, afford a wide view not alone of Illinois, but of some adjacent states as well.

Double deck, 36-passenger, steel rocket cars ride at a 210-foot level, suspended from tracks supported by a steel cableway which has a breaking strength of 290,000 pounds per square inch of cross section . . . with one exception, the longest suspension span in the world.

Contrary to general belief, the towers do not alone support the Sky Ride span. They merely act as a fulcrum for the massive supporting cables which extend on behind and down where they are deeply and securely imbedded in massive concrete anchorages. It is from these main cables that the intermediate network of cables carrying the Sky Ride is suspended.

The rocket shaped cars give an unobstructed view in all directions.

One tower of the Sky Ride as it appears from the court of the Hall of Science.

TRAVEL
AND
TRANSPORT
BUILDING

One of the most unusual examples of architecture throughout the exposition grounds. The main structure has a massive suspended dome, 300 feet in diameter — larger than the dome of St. Peter's or that of the capitol in Washington — the largest unobstructed area enclosed anywhere under a roof. It is here that the newest and oldest vehicles are exhibited side by side.

Through an ingenious method, allowance has been made for expansion and construction of the dome due to temperature changes and other climatic conditions.

Twelve trussed towers and a system of tension cables which support the suspended dome, produce a spiderlike effect to the exterior. Rather than conceal this feature of construction, a direct and definite attempt was made to incorporate it in the architectural scheme with the most ultra-modern result.

In addition to the dome, this exhibit group includes a steamship exhibition hall, a long two story structure with acres of space wherein countless travel and transport exhibits are housed.

Interior of the suspended dome as seen from the large circular exhibition hall.

ELECTRICAL
Group

EXTERIOR

As you walk southward from 12th Street on Northerly Island on the shore of the lagoon you will come to a great circular court. Above this at night there is a brilliant fan of light that is visible for miles.

The great building itself, in semi-circular form behind the court, connects with the Radio and Communication Building. It is 1800 x 300 feet, 80 feet high and of striking modernistic design. It is embellished with hanging gardens, artificial cascades, and colored fountains.

On either side of the central neon cascade there is a bas-relief panel 40 feet high. On these, figures are sculptured in mammoth size suggesting the enormous forces they symbolize — "Light" and "Energy."

At the north end of the circular court there is a great water gate marked by two pylons, each 100 feet high. This leads directly into the great circular hall.

The beautiful fountain of water and colored lights in the center of the Circular Court.

ELECTRICAL
Group

INTERIOR

Within this hall numerous companies have exhibits, many of which are spectacular, such as the electrical equipment exhibits which show the progress made in this department of applied science.

In a scene animated with changing lights, running stream, spinning turbines, and the movement of a busy countryside, is revealed the manner in which electric power is produced and distributed.

Leaving the great hall of the Electrical Building and entering the Radio and Communication Building, you are mystified and fascinated by the wonders of the radio world.

Other exhibits in the Communication Section show you the mysteries of the dial telephone and the history of the development and progress of the telegraph system.

Hours of fascination and delight may be spent in this great building. Perhaps you will be awed by the fact that in less than a century all these miracles have come to pass.

GENERAL EXHIBITS GROUP

Just south of the Hall of Science and across the lagoon from the electrical group is the General Exhibits Building.

Its five pavilions and unusually large number of terraces and ramps present a very interesting and unusual architectural composition.

The 18th Street Entrance Bridge connects directly with the Second Floor of the north end and a semi-circular bridge structure joins the building with the south end of the Hall of Science.

The large U-shaped courts, the sides of which are formed by the respective pavilions, abound in fountains and beautiful reflecting pools with brilliant lighting effects.

The building is especially striking at night when a myriad of colored lights play on the horizontally fluted chromium metal towers located at the east end of each pavilion.

The great halls house exhibits of the steel, oil, paint, and office equipment industries. A diamond mine in operation, the manufacture of shirts, hosiery, and printing displays constitute some of the extensive exhibits which may be seen inside the building. Each group of exhibits tells a story . . . not a story of yesterday . . . but a story of today and tomorrow.

West facade of the Administration Building.

Ticket windows at the main Twelfth Street entrance.

The rotunda of the Hall of Science.

Circular Court of the Electrical Building.

Communications' gardens of the Electrical Group.

The children's theatre — Enchanted Island.

DAIRY
BUILDING
EXTERIOR

This building, located at the extreme northern end of Northerly Island, is one of the most interesting of exhibit buildings. The beauty and simplicity of the modern, windowless architecture, combined with its unusual plan, color and illumination scheme, produces striking effects day and night.

A mural painting at the left of the main entrance to the building adds a note of individuality to the exterior.

The tower and fin at the south end of the building form a dramatic feature of the composition.

A dairy restaurant overlooks the lagoon. Adjacent to the restaurant on the same level are club rooms for members of the Century Dairy Club.

The proximity of this building to the Agricultural Building again emphasizes the close association of the dairy and agricultural industries.

A view of the 23rd Street lagoon bridge and fountain.

DAIRY
BUILDING
INTERIOR

You enter into a large lobby. Beyond is a cyclorama on which play streams of color, flowing over it in waves or in startling, yet subtle shade contrasts. At an organ console, a player's hands finger the keyboard, causing the variations of color. The instrument is the Clavilux, or color organ, designed to play with color as musical instruments play with sounds.

With the color music for accompaniment, a spectacle is presented in the darkened amphitheatre in several episodes, showing the trek of civilization westward, and today's highly organized dairy industry with its scientific preparation, distribution, sanitation, and refrigeration of milk and milk products.

In Industry Hall, transparent figure groups show the four ages of humanity . . . childhood, youth, prime, and maturity . . . and the effect of dairy products' diet on the physical and mental powers.

In Commodity Hall, you may see the preparation of ice cream, cheese, butter, milk, and dry milks.

The entrance to the Dairy Building.

AGRICULTURAL
BUILDING
EXTERIOR

The Agricultural Building, a vast structure 658 feet long, which in plan somewhat resembles a three-toothed key, lies midway between the Twelfth and Sixteenth Street bridges on Northerly Island.

The northern end of the building terminates in a huge semi-circular dome-like design.

The long and spacious terrace along the west provides a perfect vantage point for a view up and down the lagoon.

A fin or light trough on the roof, which runs the entire length of the building, is equipped with neon tubing and at night presents a brilliant glow of color.

Numerous metal ornaments, flagpoles, and stepped terraces adorn the exterior.

The Second Floor is connected by a bridge to the Second Floor of the Federal Group to the south.

A semi-tropical garden in the open spaces to the west of the building shows us foods and flowers new and wondrous.

A detail of the northern end.

AGRICULTURAL
BUILDING
INTERIOR

Here may be seen some of the most interesting exhibits. A comparison of the primitive handmade implements used a generation ago, with the modern power equipment of today, marks one of the most rapid strides of any industry.

The interior is gayly painted, and with the aid of beautifully colored vertical cloth strips surrounding the columns, a dramatic effect in lighting is achieved.

The story of the production, distribution, and preservation of foods is told with the use of dioramas, models, and actual processes.

You see coffee and tea prepared, salt brought up from mines, and purified; a model biscuit factory; a miniature brewery showing how beer is made; how sugar is processed; bees at work in a glass hive, honey being prepared, and illustrations of its uses.

An exterior view looking north.

BELGIAN
VILLAGE

This unique and picturesque concession occupies a rambling site just
south of the Twenty-third Street Entrance.

Here has been reproduced a group
of buildings which could have been
found about the Squares of Antwerp
or Brussels in the 16th Century.

It abounds in Old World atmosphere
with its cobblestone streets, moats,
milk carts, pigeons fluttering about,
and men and women in native costumes.

There are approximately 65 buildings,
covering an area of two acres. An
old church, cafes, markets, medieval
homes, and a town hall comprise this
superb exhibit.

Although these buildings were constructed for the World's Fair, one of
the remarkable features about them is
their genuine 16th Century appearance. This was made possible by
expert workmanship in applying the
finishes, even to the creation of the
very antique slate roof effects, as
well at both interior and exterior
appearances.

The bridge and tower from the court yard.

MODEL HOMES

The architects and decorators have
presented, in this group of model
homes, new designs, new structural
and surface materials, new uses for
old materials, which have never been
attempted before.

An attempt has been made to intro-
duce the factory-built home with a
definite objective in mind—to reduce
home building costs and to create
houses which can be erected quickly.

Space-saving devices have been
worked out, standardization has been
accomplished, style standards and traditional architecture have been dis-
carded and a modern functional design has been created.

The pantry has been entirely eliminated, kitchens have been planned for
step-saving by placing equipment in
proper order, hence they are smaller
than the old-time kitchen.

The dining room is almost extinct,
being replaced by the dining alcove.

Some of the houses have air-condi-
tioning equipment, and in most cases
the heating and laundry equipment is
located on the First Floor and not in
the usual dark basement. In fact, the
basement has become a thing of the
past.

A step forward in tempo with the
theme of the exposition . . . progress.

Roxtone, Inc.

Chicago Lumber Institute

General Houses, Inc.

COLOR

PROTECTION

"A Century of Progress"

was undoubtedly the beginning of a new era of more intelligent use of color for both
home and industry. Twenty-eight distinct colors were selected with which to decorate "A Century of Progress." The masterful handling of these colors, directed by the
late Joseph Urban, created an expanse of beauty never seen anywhere. Note the
distinct color schemes for individual buildings, as shown in the pages of this book,
which when combined produce a panorama of color harmony never before witnessed by the human eye on such a tremendous scale! Color is important to our
life and industry, but the correct use of it is of more consequence. Color is reactionary.
When used intelligently, it can induce happiness instead of sadness. It can produce
alertness or drowsiness, comfort or discomfort, perfect vision or indistinctness. Because of appearance and shape, color can be lost to sight, and the result is a cloudy
effect, one of obscurity and darkness, instead of clarity and vision. Color amuses,
fascinates or annoys, inspires or disheartens, excites or repels, exaggerates or under-
values. Yes, a color scheme can even determine to some degree the failure or success
of production, product, or a business.

It may interest you to know a few of the interesting facts about this gigantic "color
and protection" assignment given us by "A Century of Progress." It was the largest
single paint contract of its type ever awarded. It was our responsibility not only to
manufacture and supply these "VALDURA" paint products to match Mr. Urban's
difficult palette, but also to apply the "color and protection" to over 10,500,000
square feet of surface. This required the services of as many as 350 skilled painters
a day. The first undercoats of VALDURA ASPHALT ALUMINUM PAINT were
applied during the late months of 1932 to serve as protection for the surfaces through
the severe, cold, icy, wet, winter months. The high corrugated fence alone has over
236,500 square feet of surface protected with VALDURA ALUMINUM, and
78,500 square feet additional with VALDURA Oil Paints. The Sky Ride alone has
1,200,000 square feet of metal siding, in addition to 2548 tons of steel construction
protected with VALDURA ALUMINUM and VALDURA Oil Paints. As final color
coats, more than 25,000 gallons of VALDURA Oil Paints and Casein were used. The
flat color effects were especially designed to conduce the gala colored lighting effects
which made the nights at this Fair so outstandingly spectacular. Not alone the exterior,
but also the magnificent interiors were a notable achievement in the art of decorative
color. Even many of the murals created by world-famous artists were painted with
VALDURA Oils. Truly, this "Century of Progress" was the world's greatest paint
task.

For more than twenty years we have been selected to furnish "color and protection" for the most severe industrial and decorative uses in practically all parts of
the world. We produce paints to protect the bridge against corrosion, coatings to
keep the roof from leaking, compounds to resist severe acid attack, and quality
preparations to preserve, beautify and extend the life and usefulness of metal, wood
and other surfaces subject to rust or decay. At "A Century of Progress" we were
required to finish most every type of surface; many known as resistant to usual paint
coatings. The exquisite interiors of many model homes, the steel of the 628-foot high
towers of the Sky Ride, and smooth surfaces of galvanized iron or composition boards,
subjected to sun, rain, heat and lake waterfront conditions. And our products did
not fail. Therefore, if you have a "color or protection" problem, may we suggest
that you select a "VALDURA" product? You will find it a true economy. We or our
dealers shall gladly assist you with service or product for "color and protection."

AMERICAN ASPHALT PAINT CO.
Makers of "the World's Supreme Waterproofings"
CHICAGO

The assembly line proved simply sensational. In the assembly-line hall, spectators could watch from a balcony as two parallel factory lines actually built about one car per hour, or twenty-five Master Six coaches each day. While some of the parts—engines, for instance—had been assembled elsewhere, viewers could observe the final twenty-four steps of the process that pulled the product together. The Fisher Body line was timed so that when finished, its body arrived at a designated point, ready to be mounted on the Chevrolet chassis. Each week, GM gave away one of its $580 Master Six models to a lucky visitor.

In 1933 GM spent over two million dollars on its building and grounds at the fair, adding another million in 1934 for new exhibits and additional features. Knudsen's heavy investment for advertising had paid off. Many believed the 1933 GM exhibit attendance to be the largest crowd ever attracted to a single exhibit. One estimate put attendance at about 230,000 visitors per day. It was almost certainly the most popular exhibit site at the entire fair. Many of those fairgoers took home one or more of the complimentary printed brochures that would remind them of GM's progress in automotive comfort, beauty, safety, performance, and research.[56] Perhaps a few fairgoers took home the words of wisdom inscribed on the walls of the entrance hall, including Kettering's Depression-era advice: "No one ever would have crossed the ocean if he could have gotten off the ship in a storm."[57]

Other automotive giants staged their own promotional extravaganzas. Chrysler Motors' building and exhibit covered seven acres of fairgrounds. The company displayed over twenty-five thousand automotive artifacts and products, including a disassembled Plymouth sedan on a single 145-foot table and a 60-ton forge hammer producing steering components. Barney Oldfield, a daring racecar driver, demonstrated hill-climbing and maneuverability of Chrysler automobiles on its quarter-mile test track. Nash's auto showroom was a glass-enclosed tower designed to park nine cars stacked one above the other. With each car in its individual parking platform, an electric motor rotated the parking spaces as if they were the cabins of a Ferris Wheel.[58]

The largest crowd pleaser in 1934 was the new Ford Rotunda exposition building designed by Albert Kahn architects. The complex embodied the shift from fair-sponsored theme buildings to individual corporate pavilions that reflected the visions of industrial design specialists. Walter Dorwin Teague, an industrial designer, conceived the complex's monumental machine-aesthetic photomurals, and he organized the display of Ford products. He felt that the world's fair with its impermanency, nonfunctional standards, and carnival spirit gave him the chance to experiment. The opportunities to create such fresh and unexpected architectural designs as the Ford pavilion liberated his imagination, and the results certainly awed fairgoers.[59] Industrial designers such as Teague shifted the importance of the Ford pavilion from the architecture to the exhibits. They sold the motor company's corporate image through entertainment, drama, and style by simplifying and romanticizing the message to impress consumers.[60] For Teague, world's fairs offered an opportunity for corporations "to meet the public face to face, explain the social value of their operations and justify their existence."[61]

The Ford complex's domed, circular pavilion represented the giant cogs on a gear wheel. Inside the ten-story rotunda, twenty-foot-tall photomurals illustrated the workings of Ford industrial sites. Ford's historical transportation collection—ranging from ancient chariots to the latest Ford V-8 model—was arranged around a center court. A display of Henry Ford's first workshop, engine, and automobile highlighted his pioneer status in the industry. One Ford exhibit focused on the social implications of agricultural-industrial progress. It predicted revolutionary uses for agricultural products such as soy beans that would bring American farmers new independence while reducing industry's reliance on natural resources. And Ford's "Roads of the World" replicated worldwide road construction from early civilizations to America's latest concrete highways, providing visitors with a four-minute ride in a new V-8 Ford. After touring the complex, fairgoers could relax at Ford's outdoor symphonic orchestra shell and gardens, which trailed along the picturesque lakeshore. Each evening a light show featuring roof-mounted search-lights produced an amazing light beam that pierced the heavens with a promise of bright prosperity, magnifying Ford's visibility and dominance.[62]

Automotive leaders, including GM's corporate leaders, pronounced participation at A Century of Progress an indisputable success. R. H. Grant, a GM vice president, believed the fair had served as an impetus to the nation's economic recovery. GM's president, Alfred P. Sloan Jr., like the exhibition's director, John Sewell, saw the fair as even more significant. Sloan viewed the public space of the fair as a political platform from which he could address and influence national recovery issues that affected big business, particularly government regulation of industry.

President Franklin D. Roosevelt's industrial regulation policies troubled Sloan. He disapproved of the role that the national government had assumed. Sloan felt that federal control of labor, wages, and production through New Deal legisla-tion threatened corporations by reducing competition and by giving government bureaucrats power to determine how businesses should be run.[63] Under Sloan's direction, GM sponsored a public forum at the fair on May 24, 1934, intended to promote optimism and to unify big business and universities against govern-ment restrictions. Sloan used the forum to increase his own visibility as well as to broadcast his opinions. Hundreds of prominent citizens received invitations to the affair, and the invitation left no doubt about Sloan's opinions.

> For some time past I have been concerned with the thinking of many who believe that our progress in this world is finished, that we must retrogress, that there are no worthwhile possibilities ahead. We must live merely by dividing up all avail-able jobs and that we must accept a lower standard of living. Contrariwise many believe that the amount of available work can be continually expanded, that pro-gressively higher standards of living will result through broadening the activities of industry by developments of science and industrial research. In my judgment

this question is exceedingly important at this time on account of its influence in the determination of many of our national economic policies vitally affecting the future of us all. Because of the importance of presenting a representative and authoritative viewpoint on this question at this time and in the hope of contributing toward a better understanding of the problem, I am giving a dinner to a group of forward looking leaders in science and industry. . . . We want this conference to look into the future. We feel positively that industry is on the threshold of great achievements.[64]

Intending to shape public opinion, Sloan asked in his invitation that the recipients, whether or not they could attend, provide a brief statement on significant future developments in their fields. Over seven hundred replied, echoing Sloan's views that big business should be free of government constraints in research, development, and technological advancement through production.

Sloan's conference, attended by approximately four hundred leaders of science and industry, garnered considerable positive press for the "calm, unshaken confidence in the future which was presented by men of knowledge and imagination."[65] It also attracted an immediate rejoinder from FDR, who requested that his response be posted at the GM fair pavilion.[66] Sloan included FDR's reaction in GM's published booklet of speeches from the conference: "The nation will remember those who are helping. It also will remember those who believe that our progress in this world is finished and who make no constructive contribution in the present emergency. I count with confidence on the loyalty and support of the nation's industrial leaders."[67] FDR's message was sandwiched among speeches by scientific and industrial leaders and statements from nearly one hundred fifty representatives of business, academe, and journalism offering optimism for recovery while rejecting government interference in the process. Big business had not only assumed a major role at the fairgrounds through corporate exhibits and pavilions, it was ready to exert more force in determining how government would alleviate the economic woes of the country.

Cooperative exhibits fulfilled fair organizers' goals to offer visitors innovative educational exhibitions illustrating the application of technology to everyday life, but so too did exhibits sponsored by individual corporations. The success of the GM, Ford, Chrysler, and other independent automotive exhibits illustrates this. Lenox Lohr eventually decided that collective exhibits were not as practical as had been imagined.[68] Nonetheless, by promoting cooperation among industries and by coordinating private and public institutions, fair organizers established this exposition as one of the prototypes for collaborative undertakings among military engineers, industrial leaders, and academics for large-scale civil engineering projects, an idea later identified as the military-industrial-university complex.

The greatest legacy of A Century of Progress is that it provided the first showplace in which corporations could vie solely for the consumer's attention rather than industrial prizes. With the world traumatized by economic crisis, the fair created and widely broadcast a pioneering notion of progress, which set the trajectory for future fairs and expositions. Futuristic exhibits displayed in colorful, ultramodern structures used ideas of progress to generate dreams of technologically efficient homes, workplaces, and America. Not all of the fair leaders' attention, however, focused on developing and financing exhibits and nurturing hope, optimism, and trust in corporate institutions. To build a broad base of local community support, which was crucial to recruiting volunteers and repeat attendees, organizers also worked with leaders of the city's diverse ethnic population to put the world in the world's fair.

5

Women's Spaces at the Fair

A Century of Progress drew no line between the sexes. There was no Woman's Building. Special exhibits and amusements were not planned exclusively for women. For this fair, in glad defiance of pre-conceived ideas and customs, presented a dramatic spectacle of the age, assuring, and, as events prove, rightly assuming, that men and women are equally interested in the services which science has offered to the lives of people.

—Helen M. Bennett,
  Woman's World: The Magazine of the Town and Country

The Chicago Woman's Club organized a 1933 lecture series entitled "Woman's Contribution to Civilization" as one component of women's limited role in A Century of Progress.[1] The series fittingly stressed women's contributions to the nation's development. Speakers were to focus on the accomplishments of women in their respective fields. When the historian and women's rights activist Mary Beard, wife of Charles A. Beard, spoke, she offered her insights in an address entitled "The Social Role of Women in History." The presentation lambasted historians for falsifying the record by failing to acknowledge women's vital contributions to world progress alongside those of men.[2] Beard referred to Henry Adams's understanding of the "new woman," noting Adams's observation that the industrial revolution had freed American women to rebel against the past's restraints—the cloister, the home, good works or even bad works—and to recreate themselves. Women had since fashioned diverse opportunities for themselves while also contributing to the nation's progress.[3] Beard pointed to Adams's remark in his autobiography, *The Education of Henry Adams*, first published in 1918, that "all these women had been created since 1840; all were to show their meaning before 1940."[4]

The 1933 Chicago world's fair presented a unique opportunity for the nation to acknowledge women's revolutionary, twentieth-century identities and to applaud their contributions to American society. During the Great Depression, Beard continued, women filled a variety of domestic and public roles, but wholly inadequate historical accounts recorded only the accomplishments of individual women—most of them white and educated—rather than underscoring broad-based contributions made by women as a population group.[5] She reiterated that women had always helped shape the course of history, and then she brought her critique home to those attending the meeting by pointedly criticizing A Century of Progress management. "Thus even in the Century of Progress," she remarked, "we got a fuller history of man without getting a comparable history of women."[6]

Mary Beard's observation that historians and the 1933 Chicago world's fair failed to tell women's story adequately draws attention to some very important questions, specifically those of gender relations, leadership among women, allocation and use of space in the fair's buildings, and some women's resolution to find a voice and heighten respect at the fair by creating a unique place for themselves. The fair's thematic centerpiece—progress—makes these and other, even broader questions loom large. Thoughtful attention to the way that gender, leadership, and space-related issues played out at the 1933 fair forces those broader questions, specifically those asked by the historian David Noble: Progress for what? What kind of progress? Progress for whom?[7]

Women's Spaces at Earlier American Fairs

Fair organizers' conceptualization and officially sanctioned plans for A Century of Progress all but closed doors to opportunities and exclusive spaces for most women. Some women conformed to the plan, but this affront pushed others to attempt to create a unique, women-centered arena of expression at the fair. They achieved some of their goals, but not without class-related conflict and struggles over concepts of womanhood. Previous generations of women—that is, white women—had encountered exclusions of various kinds at world's fairs. Often the position women held in fairs reflected the prevailing narrow concept of woman's appropriate role in society. Further, it reflected the fact that, despite their gender's national campaign for greater freedoms, many women accepted that role.

When Congress first discussed Chicago's 1893 World's Columbian Exposition, Susan B. Anthony and the wives of cabinet officers lobbied to establish and fund a Board of Lady Managers for the fair. They wanted to secure more for women than had been granted for the Philadelphia Centennial of 1876. The 1876 fair organizers, while including a women's building and a female board of managers, had not given women official committee status, nor had Congress or fair organizers dedicated funds to support women's fair activities. Anthony and her fellow lobbyists convinced Congress that women deserved more, and so the national commission appointed one hundred fifteen women to the Board of Lady Managers for the Columbian Exposition. Included among them were physicians, temperance workers, suffragists, business women, lawyers, artists, writers, community leaders, and wives of prominent men. Bertha Palmer, a member of Chicago's social elite, chaired the committee. Determined to demonstrate the talents and visions of women, the Board of Lady Managers organized and staged the women's events at the Columbian Exposition.[8]

The Board of Lady Managers used fair activities as a forum to publicize women's concerns, most of them relating to white women. The congresses, one of its projects, brought together hundreds of speakers to explore women-focused topics, especially progress. The press aggressively covered the event. Women—especially native-born white clubwomen—used the congress and other fair activities to make public statements that advanced the causes of suffrage, women's rights, and recognition for women into the twentieth century. Congress attendees could go to any number of the thirty-one sessions, all devoted to the theme of "Woman's Progress." Prominent speakers and members of panels read papers and discussed education, industry, literature, art, moral and social reform, philanthropy and charity, civil law and government, and religion. Other sessions explored health issues, women's legal status, and socialization of women. The list of topics and its diversity clearly reflected the expansion of women's role in society, including dress reform, suffrage, and the woman's sphere.

The neoclassical Woman's Building made a bold statement about the board's ability to organize on a grand scale. By isolating women's exhibits in a "woman's building," the Board of Lady Managers attracted more participants and far more attention than if there had been no separate space. That crowds thronged to the Woman's Building indicates that the public recognized women as capable of many and diverse accomplishments at home and in the business world.[9] The very fact that the building existed and that its exhibits featured women's wide-ranging accomplishments suggests that women understood their place in society as an expanding one. They strained against the confines of the Victorian ideal that defined women solely as mothers and homemakers. Clearly, those who actualized a distinct women's space at the Columbian Exposition wanted to illustrate this. They also used the building to gain individual and group recognition. Displays highlighting the arts and products of women underscored the board's ability to plan a women's space and then follow through with the vast number of details necessary to make it happen.

Historians have differed in interpreting the 1893 Woman's Building and the board's activities. Some see them as revolutionary and pivotal to the women's movement; others disparage them as a grand display of mediocrity by elitist white women. There are elements of truth in both. Despite any aspirations of inclusiveness, the image of women projected through and at the Woman's Building was limited by the creators' own experiences and worldviews. Though the board's ideal for the building was broadly cast to include women from different countries and races, of different social status, and with different social and political concerns, in reality the Woman's Building failed to actualize the vision. Why? While forward-looking, those who planned and sponsored the building were still products of their own time. Those who sat on the Board of Lady Managers were white, extremely wealthy clubwomen. They occupied a niche in society that most women never even imagined. And their prestige gave them power. Understandably, these realities played themselves out in the way they selected and illustrated women's accomplishments. Though they imagined an egalitarian representation that underscored women's strength, they fell short, sabotaged by their own social rank.[10]

One must not assume, though, that the 1893 Woman's Building materialized without tension and even hostility among interest groups. Indeed, a negative undercurrent flowed around and beneath the grand structure. That Bertha Palmer and the socially elite Board of Lady Managers determined the building's final form and the image of women it radiated testifies to the power the clubwomen's wealth and social prestige afforded them. Another group of women, however, had vied for leadership, and if they had prevailed, the Woman's Building would have undoubtedly cast women in a different, more powerful light. These women—not necessarily club members or members of the city's socially elite—were all suffragists and most were businesswomen. They called their group the Queen Isabella Association, a reference to Columbus's sponsor, Spain's Queen Isabella, whom they saw as independent and powerful in her own right. Throughout the early 1890s they battled the Board of Lady Managers for a women's pavilion that would cast women as equal to men. They raised needed funds, planned the pavilion space, and employed an architect only to find that, in the end, they had no real power. The Board of Lady Managers would officially represent women at the fair, and that representation would not, despite rhetoric, veer too radically from prevailing ideas about women's appropriate role in society. Unfortunately, the strained relationship of the board with the Isabellas and the outcome of the tension anticipated struggles for leadership, control of space, and representation of women that surfaced in plans for A Century of Progress. As the Chicago Woman's Club would do in the 1930s, the Isabellas ultimately located activities outside the formal exposition grounds.[11]

Women's autonomy, representation, and presence in leadership roles steadily diminished at male-organized world's fairs following the Columbian Exposition. Interestingly, clubwomen saw this as a statement about their equality with men rather than as a restriction.[12] Each subsequent world's fair—the 1901 Pan-American Exposition in Buffalo, the 1904 Louisiana Purchase Exposition in St. Louis, and Philadelphia's 1926 Sesqui-centennial International Exhibition—saw the American male's idea of women's appropriate place in society defined more narrowly until, by 1933, male organizers relegated women primarily to the role of social hostess. In contrast, women had organized four Woman's World's Fairs, local women's exhibitions held in Chicago from 1925 to 1928. The leaders of these exhibitions sought to empower women by stressing independence, waged employment, and professional accomplishments, including those "in Science and in Industry."[13]

The space that women controlled at male-organized world's fairs suggests the relentlessly constricting idealized role men imposed upon them. Though women had enjoyed impressive galleries and lecture space in the Columbian Exposition's Woman's Building, they found the space they controlled at the 1901 Pan-American Exposition restricted and far less impressive. In 1901 organizers saw a converted country club as sufficient for the Woman's Building. Rather than housing exhibits and lecture spaces, the building functioned as a social space, a reception area where women served as hostesses, and an office space used by women's clubs and organizations.[14] Women found their space further constricted at the 1904 Louisiana Purchase Exposition in St. Louis. Organizers there provided no separate building for women's exhibits but rather offered a social space within the larger complex in which women would feel at home and could act as hostesses to the nation. Women's exhibits competed directly with those of men in the main exhibits. Organizers acknowledged, though, that "the really distinctive work of women as women in the highest and broadest sense" could not be exhibited. They presumably referred to domesticity.[15] By 1926 and Philadelphia's Sesqui-centennial International Exposition, men outspokenly articulated the role they expected women to fill. Though organizers boasted that women sat on the fair's Governing Board, they went on to reveal that "women will have preponderant or exclusive responsibility for features more distinctly within the sphere of women"—child care, rest rooms, emergency aid, and hospitality to female visitors.[16] The Women's Board also supervised a group of historic houses and arranged historical walking tours. As in 1901 and 1904, management provided no separate women's exhibit space. They integrated women's exhibits with those of men. Fair organizers used the rhetoric of "women's equality" to justify their decision to integrate exhibits rather than to provide a distinct woman's space. They pointed to progress made by women since 1893: the vote in some states, admission to more professions, more access to education in a variety of fields, the acceptance of motherhood as a profession, and the availability of electrical appliances to reduce household drudgery.[17] Fair organizers at A Century of Progress would continue this course.

Chicago's four Woman's World Fairs, held in 1925, 1926, 1927, and 1928, diverged significantly from expositions organized by men. The all-women boards of directors for these fairs cast aside the limitations male organizers had imposed on women at other world's fairs. The woman's fairs, organized primarily by politically active women such as Helen M. Bennett, celebrated working women. They threw their exhibit spaces wide open to honor "the multiplicity of occupations in which women have scored successes."[18] The fairs' hundreds of booths, most under gaily colored awnings, highlighted the fairs' openness, celebratory spirits, and carnival atmospheres. While organizers certainly did not slight exhibits focusing on the domestic sphere and traditional arts, they cast their vision far more broadly to emphasize women's persistent push into politics, business, and the sciences. Elizabeth Bass, chair of the 1927 fair, went so far as to speculate about the demise of women's domestic sphere and to wonder at the challenges for women presented by such a revolution. She envisioned the woman's fairs as providing women with the tools to shape their own futures in that strange new world.[19] Interestingly, Vice President Charles Dawes spoke at the 1927 opening gala. He obviously failed to internalize the fair's woman-focused dynamic as he did not push to incorporate it into plans for A Century of Progress. In fact, remarks made during his presentation reveal that he had completely missed the fair's thrust. One can only imagine organizers' thoughts when he stated that a woman's "greatest contributions to society are made [in the home] and there her greatest success . . . is achieved."[20]

A Few Exceptional Women

A Century of Progress organizers recognized the abilities of those who had planned the Chicago Woman's World's Fairs, and several committee members proposed including women in leadership positions as plans for the 1933 fair took shape. As early as 1926, Louise deKoven Bowen, an organizer of the woman's fair, had recommended a woman's department for the 1933 world's fair, and she had offered the services of her Woman's World's Fair committee. She assured organizers that her committee "would be very well equipped to take over this branch of the work" if organizers wanted them to do so.[21] In September 1927, the *Daily News* announced fair organizers' intentions to include women with a range of abilities. An article headlined, "Women to Share in Plans for Fair . . . Asked to Give Leadership and Help with Burdens" quoted one fair organizer, Charles S. Peterson, as saying, "We see women in positions of trust in the business world, proving their capacity for leadership as well as for detail, and so some of the members of the [fair organizing] committee feel that it is advisable that the women . . . should be given place on many committees that will be created to carry the fair through to success." Within a few months, though, the emphasis moved away from those women whom Peterson had pinpointed for participation. By April 1928, fair organizers spoke of "society and club women" as their preferred female participants, a shift that forecast future developments and did not bode well for those who desired a dynamic separate woman's space at the fair.[22] What had happened to trigger the shift? At the December 13, 1927, meeting with Mayor Bill Thompson, Peterson had nominated Rufus Dawes, a conservative man who saw woman's proper sphere as the home and her role as gracious hostess, to presidency of the fair. Dawes had assumed the position one week later, and his acceptance virtually guaranteed that society women would dominate whatever prominent place women would enjoy in fair management. This set the stage for conflicts between Dawes's wife, Helen, who occupied the prestigious position as the fair's official hostess, and Martha McGrew, Lenox Lohr's very capable administrative assistant. It also pitted socialite women against proponents of a women's building at the fair.

Unaware of what Dawes's ascendancy meant for women long-term, Congresswoman Ruth Hanna McCormick, who had served as general director of the Woman's World's Fairs, solicited female leaders from women's organizations to serve as leaders for the 1933 fair. She invited twenty-one to serve on a permanent committee, several of them bringing experience from their days on the board of directors of the Woman's World's Fairs.[23] Seeking inclusiveness and as broad a range of experience as possible, she also invited twelve women representing national ethnic groups and twenty-two others from organizations such as settlement houses, labor organizations, service clubs, and professional groups. When McCormick lost her bid for the U.S. Senate in 1930 and subsequently moved to New Mexico, these proposed groups lost her guidance. By the time the fair opened, few of these women remained active in the exposition's organization. What's more, the male fair leadership decided and sustained the decision not to feature women's culture as a separate entity, and women occupied few key leadership positions on A Century of Progress organizing committees.

Fair organizers invited several elite society women to join them as fair trustees, including women from the McCormick, Palmer, and Swift families. One example of an elite society woman, the social reformer and philanthropist Margaret Day Blake—married to the *Chicago Tribune* editorial writer Tiffany Blake, who objected to a woman's building—worked with the committee that coordinated the Art Institute of Chicago's A Century of Progress Fine Arts Exhibition. Over the course of the fair, forty-three galleries exhibited 744 paintings and 131 pieces of sculpture, many of which Americans had never seen.[24] Janet Ayer Fairbank was the only woman trustee to serve on the executive committee. Prominent in many clubs, she was a social and civic leader in Chicago and was married to an attorney, Kellogg Fairbank. She had used her social prominence and fame as a novelist to raise funds for hospitals and military defense, and as a fair trustee, she used her fundraising skills to solicit donations from Chicago women.[25] One political activist on the board did not fit the profile of society woman. Agnes Nestor, who had founded the International Glove Workers' Union of America, was president of the Chicago Women's Trade Union League.[26]

By far the most telling appointment of a woman to an influential position—and one that would shape the way A Century of Progress featured women—was that of Helen Dawes, wife of the fair's president, Rufus Dawes. Not surprisingly, his feelings about woman's proper role in society led him to appoint her official hostess and chair of the Social Committee, charged with entertaining visiting dignitaries. This truly significant and powerful position situated Helen Dawes as coordinator of numerous key committees, each headed by yet another socially powerful woman, always identified by her husband's name. For instance, Mrs.

Potter Palmer and Mrs. Chauncey McCormick chaired the Art and Artists Committee; Mrs. Joseph M. Cudahy chaired the Club Women Committee; and Mrs. Charles H. Swift chaired the Music Committee.[27]

Both Ohio natives, Rufus and Helen Dawes married in 1893 and had six children. As one of Chicago's most powerful society women, Helen Dawes wielded considerable influence among the city's clubwomen. She had served as president of the Woman's Club of Evanston and board member of the General Federation of Women's Clubs, to which over three million women belonged nationwide. During World War I, she was Illinois's vice chair on the Board of Food Conservation. Without doubt, Dawes saw herself, her lofty position in society, and her role at A Century of Progress as deserving complete deference from all female fair management, regardless how influential. That she was Vice President Charles Dawes's sister-in-law further solidified her opinion.[28]

Fair authorities, particularly Rufus Dawes, prioritized the comfort of important visitors, and so organizers invited other society women to work with Mrs. Dawes to ensure a flawless reception in every situation. Rufus Dawes certainly did not court outspoken women such as Ruth Hanna McCormick for the Social Committee. A letter written to his brother made that more than clear. He criticized Congresswomen McCormick's boldness, noting "in a time of great excitement the female of the species is rather more belligerent than the male." Referring to McCormick's opposition to Wilsonian imperialism in her 1928 and 1930 campaigns, he noted that many "women are so convinced of the incapacity of the American statesmen to meet foreign statesmen in negotiation, that they would prefer war to the creation of any agencies for the maintenance of peace."[29] Clearly, women with such strong opinions could not be trusted to politely entertain foreign dignitaries and other important guests.

General Manager Lohr, whose mother and wife were professionals, valued powerful professional women and included two in the fair organization, both of whom came with him from places other than Chicago. Unquestionably the most powerful woman managing fair activities, Martha Steele McGrew worked hand-in-hand with Lohr as his administrative assistant, often representing him in meetings. Born into a solidly middle-class family from Pulaski, Tennessee, McGrew was no match for the socialite clubwoman Helen Dawes. Nonetheless, these two women held key positions within the fair management structure.

A 1920 graduate of George Washington University, Washington, D.C., Martha McGrew was noted for her intelligence, leadership abilities, and hard work. The university's yearbook editor playfully memorialized her dedication and highly developed work ethic, writing, "Whenever there is anything to be done, Martha is always on the job." When Lenox Lohr first met McGrew in 1922, she worked for a Washington, D.C., publisher. Clearly impressed, Lohr persuaded her to join him in resurrecting the *Military Engineer*, which at the time faced almost certain demise. She accompanied him to Chicago when he assumed his position as the fair's general manager. He trusted her without reservation to satisfy many very serious responsibilities such as reviewing expenditures, publicity, payroll, and employee relations, and she thereby acquired a reputation as Lohr's right-hand woman. Devoted to Lohr, McGrew worked day and night—reportedly at least four hours on every shift—while in the manager's office to keep every detail in order.[30] At one point, Daniel H. Burnham, director of the Works Department, interrupted a prospective exhibitor who had referred to McGrew as Lohr's secretary, correcting her by saying that McGrew was Lohr's assistant and that in Lohr's absence "the rest of the staff was glad to get their orders from Miss McGrew." Burnham continued, confirming that McGrew outranked *him*.[31]

Barbara Haggard Matteson was another office worker loyal to Lohr. She had worked at the fair's London office, and it was there that she and Lohr first met. After touring with him to European exposition sites and museums, he arranged for her to travel to Chicago to work in the Administration Building Exhibits Department.[32] Interestingly, as one who valued strong women, Lohr remained open to the possibility of a woman's building even though fair organizers had publicly announced that they would neither financially support a woman's board nor sponsor a woman's building themselves. Wanting to endorse women's goals, he initially supported a building if it operated as a concession funded by outside promoters who would return a percentage of profits to the fair.

Fair organizers hired Helen M. Bennett, a suffragist whose idea it was to stage the Woman's World's Fairs, to coordinate women's social science exhibits and activities at A Century of Progress. An exceptional woman, she had left her family home in Spearfish, South Dakota, to attend Wellesley College, graduating in 1898. Always active professionally, she had worked as club editor of the *Chicago Record-Herald* before going on to manage the Chicago Collegiate Bureau of Occupations (1913–23). Both her education and professional positions reinforced her understanding of women's concerns and accomplishments, which she built upon to plan the fairs. A personal friend of Ruth Hanna McCormick, she worked with McCormick to stage the fairs, and she also managed McCormick's senatorial campaign. Her responsibilities as managing director of the Woman's World's Fairs—coordination of exhibits, events, and foreign participation—coupled with her political contacts made Bennett a highly desirable candidate for the position at the 1933 fair. Fair management's salary offer and the scope of the position delighted Bennett, as did the fact that she was to remain out of the political fray. Lohr considered hiring Bennett an achievement. He was also pleased when the fair trustee Janet Fairbank agreed to "take the backfire" if the women's organizations complained about Bennett's allegiance to the fair organizers' visions. Women organizers obviously hoped Bennett would lobby for a "Woman's Fair" within A Century of Progress.[33]

Bennett started work in the Administration Building until the social science division began functioning. When Fay Cooper Cole left his position as chief of the social science division, he wrote to the fair president that "whatever success we have had is in a large measure due to the untiring efforts of Helen Bennett. She is capable, resourceful, and above all loyal. Whoever picked her in the beginning 'knew his woman.'"[34] Bennett did not throw her support behind plans for a separate woman's building when they were discussed. Rather, she focused on arrangements with the National Council of Women to stage activities and exhibits at A Century of Progress. She believed in the fair organizers' plan to present men and women equally in exhibits.[35]

As it turned out, important women who served fair organizers in various capacities did not unite around their female identity and notions of empowerment. They clearly failed to develop a defining feminist agenda.[36] Rather, they united with the male fair organizers to promote a vision that denied women a distinctive space. Far more important, perceptions of societal rank and privilege clashed in very disagreeable ways with professional position and realms of authority. Behind the scenes, tensions among certain powerful women ran rampant in a turf war that was aggravated by notions of propriety and deference. They reached a crescendo in March 1934 when Helen Dawes wrote a scathing letter to Martha McGrew, warning in no uncertain terms that she expected proper respect and decorum during the 1934 fair season.

As Lohr's confidant and gatekeeper, McGrew knew which decisions to make in the management office without consulting the general manager. Lohr needed someone who would make the same decisions as he would and understand the reasons behind them. He trusted McGrew implicitly. She saw her own role as crucial to the success of the fair, and it probably was. Other women, however, sometimes failed to appreciate McGrew's influential position, and they resented her independence and condescending style. In fact, clubwomen such as Dawes characterized it as blatantly rude and disrespectful of their social rank. Helen Dawes had witnessed McGrew's lack of deference far too many times in 1933, and she refused to allow McGrew's disrespect for social prestige to tarnish the second season as well.

In March 1934 Dawes wrote a letter to McGrew detailing McGrew's professional failings, social faux pas, and lack of deference "toward the most important and influential women in Chicago." The letter criticized McGrew for inappropriate behavior, for making out-of-line comments, for misrepresentation, for overstepping authority boundaries, for not following social decorum, and for being condescending to society women, who deserved the utmost respect. To Dawes, McGrew was an outsider—a naive, young, boastful professional—who had neglected to learn who actually controlled Chicago socially. "If you had taken the trouble when you first assumed your duties in Chicago," Dawes bitterly complained, "to inform yourself as to what organizations in Chicago have real weight," a more congenial atmosphere might have prevailed during the 1933 fair season. Further, she felt that McGrew had unabashedly overstepped her boundaries by boasting about her power over male managers, including Dawes's husband, the fair president. McGrew's bravado embarrassed Helen Dawes publicly, particularly since she was sensitive about her husband's image vis-à-vis that of his brother Charles. She felt that Rufus deferred too easily to Charles and that he lived in Charles's shadow.[37] Further, Dawes saw the situation as more than a reflection on fair management. She believed that McGrew's exultant comment disparaged Dawes's relationship with her husband. "It is hardly wise to boast to any man's wife," she steamed, "that he moves when you pull the strings." Dawes fumed on with a veiled threat, writing, "It is particularly regrettable that you would speak so of a man in Mr. Dawes' position."[38]

What indiscretions—besides insulting Helen Dawes's domestic prowess and being socially ignorant—had McGrew committed? Specifically, she had failed to consult society women when making decisions about personnel in the Trustee's Lounge, a space in the Administration Building used by Dawes's Social Committee for entertaining. Then for Women's Day, McGrew used her own contacts to make arrangements rather than calling on women of the board of trustees—all society women. Further, she tried to control the spending of the Social Committee, which Dawes saw as outside the management office's responsibilities. She wrote, "It is not for you to presume at all to direct activities of the Committee on Social Functions." But these many perceived insults paled in comparison to the way McGrew handled Eleanor Roosevelt's first visit to the fair. McGrew had treated the First Lady's visit as a fair event, not a social event, and so McGrew had not informed Dawes and her committee of the visit. Stunned and enraged, the Committee on Social Functions learned of the plans from newspaper reports. When one committee member phoned the manager's office, she was told that "Mrs. Dawes knows all about it." In fact, Dawes knew nothing about it since she had not even been invited to the meeting that planned Roosevelt's visit. Dawes's letter revealed the greatest indiscretion of all when it protested, "I was amazed and indignant to find that my name had been signed to a telegram to Mrs. Roosevelt without my knowledge." McGrew had rationalized this by saying that, if the telegram had not solicited a response, she would have wired a follow-up message under the name of President Dawes and General Manager Lohr.[39]

Helen Dawes concluded her inventory of McGrew's offenses by pointedly reminding her of her committee's experience and social prominence. "The part of our Committee," she wrote, "may seem to you to be of slight importance, but it is our opinion that on account of your youth and lack of social experience, we are much better judges as to that than it is possible for you to be."[40] To put it another way, McGrew may have had Lenox Lohr on her side, but Helen Dawes had the city's clubwomen and their husbands on hers. McGrew needed to reflect on her professionalism and behave accordingly.

The Temple of Womanhood

The tensions between socialite club members, who claimed the fair as their domain, and women "outsiders" such as Martha McGrew had seethed just below the surface throughout the fair's planning stages. But issues that appeared to be rather straightforward—that is, dictated by budget or the way organizers conceptualized the fair—were not always what they seemed. Another program sometimes played in the background, driven by jealousy, notions of propriety, and concepts of womanhood's social and political status. The battle for the Temple of Womanhood was one such situation. On the surface, the proposal for the building seemed reasonable and even desirable. Why, then, did it fail?

The story began three years before the fair opened, when a woman calling herself Dorthea Goodrich applied for space on the fairgrounds for an officially sponsored women's building. Goodrich called the building the Temple of Womanhood and articulated its purpose as commemorating "the progress made by women."[41] The building would showcase women's accomplishments by providing space for exhibits, meetings, shops, and services for female visitors to the fair, especially club members. Goodrich assured fair organizers, specifically Lohr, that her committee of clubwomen would raise all the funds to construct and operate the building, and they would raise additional funds by selling $1 admission badges. Along with the badge, women would receive special privileges and office space.[42]

Planning to approach the architect Daniel H. Burnham for a design, Goodrich had gone so far as to make sketches of the building. She had also conceptualized her plans quite extensively. Unfortunately, some of her ideas—a network of state temples, for instance—simply replicated existing societies and federations rather than initiating new organizational structures designed to serve new purposes. Nonetheless, she expected the temple to express the ideals of her newly formed organization and to crystallize woman's best ideas.[43] To this end, the building would include a huge convention hall with a domed roof.[44] Further, she had designed a logo for the Temple of Womanhood, Inc., that featured the temple's dome. The logo would remind women of the national halls of Congress. Using the 1893 Board of Lady Managers organization as a model, Goodrich planned that local and state representatives would establish local temple groups to stage exhibits and state pageants representing the progress made by women in those states during the previous one hundred years. Women from countries throughout the world would be invited to participate. Her rhetoric inclusive in every way, Goodrich imagined a temple of service attracting women from every region, race, and economic group in a way that would avoid dissension and dissatisfaction.[45] Interestingly, the architectural design produced by Burnham disclosed a glaring conflict between Goodrich's rhetoric and reality: though Goodrich had characterized the temple as without ethnic boundaries, that did not apply to racial boundaries.[46] The temple would have a separate entrance and separate facilities for African American women.[47]

Burnham's design plans for the Temple of Womanhood basically retained the modernist vision of A Century of Progress. Only Goodrich's desire for a neoclassical dome forced designers to veer from organizers' dictate that fair buildings incorporate a uniquely nationalist style—efficient, simple, and eschewing ornamentation. The floor plans replicated traditional Western religious space in a feminized fashion with the rotunda as the axis of two intersecting exhibit halls.[48] At the center, a fountain represented woman as life's sacred spring. The first floor of the nave showcased women's displays with an auditorium on the two floors above. The transept spaces offered restaurants, lounges, shops, and a beauty parlor. On the other hand, plans made clear that neither Goodrich nor the architects anticipated any form of racial integration.[49]

Having heard Goodrich's proposal, Lohr informed her that "accredited representatives of the various clubs concerned" needed to make the request before the fair could take action.[50] That is, she needed to submit her request through Estelle Northam, the Illinois Federation of Women's Clubs' representative at the fair and, coincidentally, Helen Dawes's friend.[51] Northam served as Lohr's gatekeeper in that she filtered women's clubs' requests to stage fair activities before they reached Lohr's desk. Clearly, though, Lohr had warmed to the idea that the temple would operate as a concession, distinct from fair-solicited exhibits such as those coordinated by Helen Bennett. Goodrich promptly acted to fulfill fair guidelines. She formed a corporation, obtained a charter from the state, and met with Daniel H. Burnham, authorizing his architectural firm to draw up plans for the building, which it did.[52] Unfortunately, the one step that Goodrich failed to take was to consult Northam. She avoided communication with the Illinois Federation of Women's Clubs and continued to address her correspondence to the office of the general manager, Lenox Lohr.

Meanwhile Goodrich's supporters fanned out, distributing promotional materials and collecting signatures of support from Chicago and suburban women. After submitting their petition to the fair officials, Goodrich met with F. R. Moulton, Director of Concessions, who notified her of a contract for the temple by letter a few days later, stating that "we will agree to assign to you sufficient space to erect the building outlined herein, providing you show within sixty (60) days satisfactory evidence of your ability to completely finance this project."[53] Fair officials bought into the idea of the temple. They understood Goodrich's building as a concession—that is, it would in no way function in an official capacity as did the Woman's Building in 1893. The Administration Building and a management-selected social committee, whose members would serve as official hostesses to important guests, would fill that niche. The Temple of Womanhood would, however, display women's exhibits and serve as a gathering place for female fairgoers.[54] Its coordinators would pay all expenses for the building and would return a percentage of its income to fair management.

Feeling that she had the go-ahead, Goodrich and her committee sent letters to women's clubs seeking participation and financial support. They also organized a meeting for Chicago clubwomen to unveil plans for the Temple of Womanhood. Goodrich mailed a postal card to the heads of women's organizations, inviting them to bring their ideas to a meeting at the Congress Hotel on the evening of June 8, 1932.[55] The day before Goodrich could unveil her glorious vision to a room full of appreciative supporters, she received a cruel blow in a hand-carried letter from Lohr withdrawing approval for the temple and informing her that her "efforts in this regard are entirely without any authority from A Century of Progress and must result only in embarrassment to yourself and others as no proposal for a concession of this nature will be considered by A Century of Progress." Shocked and disgruntled, Goodrich refused to surrender her plans.[56]

What had happened? Why the sudden change? Goodrich had fulfilled fair guidelines, raised funds, worked with an official fair architect, and received the nod from Director of Concessions F. R. Moulton. It appears that she had even secured a contract with the fair officials. Further, she had gathered a group of supportive women to help her and to promote the temple. From any perspective, it appeared that Goodrich could anticipate success.

While Goodrich enthusiastically proceeded, the seeds of her downfall had already been sown in Lohr's office. Just a week or so before the meeting, someone who wished to remain anonymous had shared some unsavory information about Dorthea Goodrich with Martha McGrew. Pronouns used by McGrew in subsequent correspondence confirm that the "someone" was a woman. The news: Dorthea Goodrich was none other than Dolly Ledgerwood Matters, a "disreputable" woman who had attracted considerable negative attention in the newspapers nearly fifteen years earlier. During World War I, Matters had married a wealthy and much older gentleman named Fred Matters, who left an estate valued at over $200,000 when he died in 1916. It appears that the heir to Matters's estate was an infant daughter, whose supposed mother—a young woman named Jessie Ryan—had transported the child to Ottawa, Ontario. In a lawsuit Dolly Matters had protested that she, not Ryan, was the child's mother. If proven true, Matters would have had access to the grand estate. The court recognized Ryan as the mother. Determined, Matters traveled to Ontario and staged a dramatic attempt at kidnapping the child, but she was apprehended by the police. Another tidbit: Matters had also reportedly been involved—perhaps unwittingly—in a case of polygamy in 1917, when she married a man named Frederick Fertner while he was also married to a woman named Lola Fertner. That case too garnered some infamy. To escape the scandal associated with her name, Matters changed her name to Dorthea Goodrich and attempted to reestablish her life and contacts within "respectable" society. She joined clubs, including the Illinois Federation of Women's Clubs, and was highly respected by most club members. In 1923 gossip about her notorious past surfaced, but most women just ignored it, calling comments jealous rumors.[57]

But not all federation women had overlooked Matters's reputation. More information surfaced in early June 1932 during an intimate meeting that included Mrs. Willis J. Burgess, executive secretary of the Illinois Federation of Women's Clubs; Martha McGrew; and Estelle Northam. Burgess had called the meeting. Outraged about a woman's space not authorized by the federation, she recalled that some years earlier Dorthea Goodrich—also known as Dolly Matters—had been "ousted" from the federation, and Burgess wondered whether Lohr's office "had anything to do with a meeting called at the Congress Hotel . . . concerning a woman's building at the World's Fair."[58] Alarmed by this powerful woman's objections, McGrew delved further. She found that most women officially attached to the fair—all society women—knew nothing of Dorthea Goodrich until rumors of her sordid past began circulating. That they did not know her is understandable since she had sidestepped the appropriate channels, specifically Estelle Northam. Mrs. Frederick Upham commented to McGrew that she "had never heard such a scandalous lot of talk about anyone as she had heard about whoever the woman is that is running this project."[59]

Clearly, McGrew and other women anticipated a firestorm that would damage the reputations of Chicago's prestigious society women and the Illinois Federation of Women's Clubs and even the fair itself. If constructed, the Temple of Womanhood, the fair's most visible "woman's space," and its management would reflect poorly on them and their lofty station in society, something they found abhorrent. The Illinois Federation of Women's Clubs, with its many wealthy donors and ties to fair organizers, wielded considerable influence with fair management, and it was certainly in the fair's interest to pacify them. Though powerful in her own right, the outsider Martha McGrew may have squirmed under their gaze. Determined that their reputations remain impeccable, those privy to all the distasteful details about Dorthea Goodrich recoiled at any and all association with her. That this woman, whom they had ousted from the federation, had circumvented the appropriate channels when applying for space at the fair angered them further. Their antagonism toward Goodrich, who not only operated outside proper society but, worse still, also slighted it, sealed the fate of the Temple of Womanhood. In so doing, those women formally associated with the fair revealed something significant about their values and identity: they valued prestige, they wanted to control space and the way it represented women at the fair, and they defined themselves in terms of class far more than womanhood. To defend their own power and status, they sabotaged plans for a uniquely woman's space at A Century of Progress. But how did they accomplish it? And how did they justify it?

Representatives of the Illinois Federation of Women's Clubs and Martha McGrew coordinated efforts to terminate relations with Goodrich. Anticipating a lawsuit by Goodrich against the fair for breach of contract, McGrew contacted a lawyer for the fair, Thomas Slusser. On McGrew's advice, Lenox Lohr signed the note to Goodrich that denied any plans to include a women's building in A Century of Progress and slammed the door on further negotiations.[60] McGrew actually prepared a draft for him to sign. Wanting to do damage control—McGrew was very concerned that the fair end its relationship to Goodrich "with the least embarrassment"—she sought strategies to shift the spotlight from fair officials to the Illinois Federation of Women's Clubs.[61] She suggested that the clubwomen announce that the federated clubs had other obligations to the fair and so had "no interest in the proposed 'Temple of Womanhood.'"[62] She then prepared a message to members of the Illinois Federation of Women's Clubs stating that "A Century of Progress would have no distinctly women's building."[63]

Though she had received Lohr's letter announcing the fair's position, Goodrich proceeded with the meeting at the Congress Hotel. Several incidents that occurred at the meeting underscore the power wielded by federation members, especially officers, and the aggression with which they acted. Interestingly, they did not question the appropriateness of their unseemly behavior. Wanting to know what would be said at the meeting, two prominent federation women—Vice President Mrs. A. H. Johnson and Mrs. Ivor Jeffrey—attended. Scanning the room of about a hundred women, they recognized no one from their own circles. They then demanded that Goodrich read Lohr's letter to the group, which she refused. Scrambling to defend herself and the temple, Goodrich announced that about eight hundred women supported her and the temple. At that, Johnson and Jeffrey boldly demanded to see a list of supporters, which Goodrich produced. They recognized only one name on the list, and the unfortunate woman happened to be in the room. Johnson and Jeffrey then interrogated her about her membership, and the woman withered, denying the signature as hers. When Goodrich refused again to read Lohr's letter, Johnson defiantly produced a carbon copy of it and read it to the stunned group. With Goodrich and her dreams for a Temple of Womanhood completely devastated, the meeting ended.

In the aftermath, Goodrich did sue A Century of Progress for breach of contract, and the fair awarded her $1,200. The firestorm over the Temple of Womanhood revealed the sad truth behind the failure of A Century of Progress to highlight women's accomplishments with a specially appointed building. Though male fair organizers made the formal announcement and paid Goodrich for breach of contract, they occupied only the top, most visible institutional layer. In the public's eye, they took the blame. Under it all, though, flowed the steamy waters of female contention, roiled by notions of propriety and class that worked themselves out in a struggle over space. In their triumph, society women denied others of their gender the celebration of progress they desired. How did society women justify this publicly? They pointed to the Nineteenth Amendment and women's accomplishments in the professions and education, claiming that since women had achieved equality, they no longer desired special recognition or separate space at the fair.

This posture reflected one position in the split over women's rights that occurred during the 1920s; the other approach, maintained by members of the National Woman's Party, supported passage of the Equal Rights Amendment as the way to eliminate women's subordination.[64]

Clubwomen Exhibits and Activities

On the same date as Goodrich's meeting at the Congress Hotel, exposition officials issued a press release claiming that "woman's position in the economic and social world has become too important to be isolated in a Women's Building."[65] They also announced that the National Council of Women in New York City would represent women at the fair, which might be seen as a coup pulled on Chicago's women's clubs. The announcement about the National Council of Women raises important questions about allocation of power and women's representation at A Century of Progress. One can only wonder how and why fair organizers selected a women's group from New York City for such a role when so many women's groups from Chicago would have gladly assumed the responsibilities associated with it. Further, how did a prestigious group such as the Chicago Woman's Club react to such a decision?

That the National Council of Women enjoyed tremendous influence over its expansive network of women's clubs certainly appealed to fair organizers, who saw in the council's numbers both donors and fair visitors. The council, founded in 1888 by leaders of the National Woman Suffrage Association and American Woman Suffrage Association, coordinated the activities of hundreds of clubs nationwide. By 1933 the council represented over five million women, "practically all the leading women's organizations in the country."[66] Member groups ranged from the National Woman's Party, which avidly sought an Equal Rights Amendment, to the National League of Women Voters, which took a moderate political stance promoting education in citizenship. Racial, professional, and service organizations found representation through the American Association of University Women, General Federation of Women's Clubs, National Association of Colored Women, National Council of Jewish Women, and Women's International League for Peace and Freedom. Council leaders hoped that by playing a very visible role in the fair they would inspire even more groups to join.[67]

Helen Bennett had been the primary force behind the Chicago Woman's World's Fairs. Recognizing her leadership abilities and her extensive network among capable women, fair organizers employed Bennett to coordinate women's social science exhibits at A Century of Progress. Throughout 1931, Bennett and key leaders of the National Council of Women refined plans for the council's participation at the fair. A deciding force among women at the 1893 fair—something which generated considerable friction with Chicago's women's clubs—the council jockeyed for a dominant role again at the 1933 fair, and Helen Bennett backed its strategies.[68] "There is no one more anxious than I am to see your outline go through," Bennett wrote to the council's acting president, Mrs. Charles J. Reeder, in July 1931. "I am particularly keen," she continued, "that all the organizations affiliated with the National Council of Women should exhibit only through [it]."[69]

What benefit did Bennett see in turning so much control over to the council? The answer lies in her understanding of Rufus Dawes's vision of the fair as a grand cooperative event. A letter from Howard W. Odum, Bennett's supervisor, to Mrs. Lena Madesin Phillips, president of the National Council of Women, articulates the fair's position. "May I say as a prelude," he wrote, "that one of the fundamentals of the Fair is that exhibits should be collective rather than competitive." He concluded with a sweeping accolade, writing, "your organization is the only organization composed of various groups and available for doing this work."[70] Further, Bennett wished to manage the situation as efficiently as possible. She saw that by working with one organization, she could deflect all inquiries regarding women's activities away from fair authorities and direct them to the council. Interestingly, when Janet Fairbank inquired about the council's cooperative exhibit early in 1932, Bennett denied that the exhibit was a *women's* exhibit. "This exhibit," she wrote to Fairbank, "is not to be confused in any way with a 'women's exhibit.' It is . . . an organization exhibit and happens to be put on by women's groups just as an engineering exhibit might happen to be put on by men's groups."[71] Fair management strictly adhered to its stated goal of integrating women's exhibits under the fair's general umbrella. Another way to understand it is that it underscores to what extremes the fair organizer rhetoric would go in order to squelch any notion of women's autonomy at the exposition.

In its role at the fair, the council would plan a display for the Social Science Hall, organize an international congress, and publish a book on women's organizations.[72] Like other sponsors, it was expected to lease the exhibit space.[73] Original plans housed women's exhibits in the Mayan Temple replica, but the social science division finally situated them in the Social Science Hall, a building originally intended to be the Radio Building in the Electrical Group. Inside the Social Science Hall, a sixty-foot mural divided women's progress into ten episodes that began with women confined to the home and ended with their newly acquired freedom. As women's activities expanded, so did the spacing between the iron bars in the background. The bars disappeared after the portrayal of women's suffrage.[74] Missing from the mural were depictions of working-class women and women of color. An explanatory brochure points out that, without an exhibit on organized womanhood, "the story of the machine age would be inadequately told." In fact, "the gradual widening of women's activities until they have become powerful factors in the commercial and civic life of the day is almost as dramatic as the evolution of the machine itself."[75] And with this concept of women as powerful participants in society as a central theme, the council planned an International Congress of

Women to meet for a week to discuss problems and solutions on "Our Common Cause—Civilization." In the midst of the Great Depression, they saw civilization in crisis. No longer limiting themselves to women's issues, they envisioned women "confronted with the task of shaping the institutions of social control."[76]

How did the Chicago Woman's Club, for instance, react to the coup staged by the National Council of Women? Though the National Council of Women and the Chicago Woman's Club defined their spheres of interest differently, both represented women's interests, and both desired a presence at A Century of Progress. While the council focused at least some of its energy on political issues, the Chicago Woman's Club focused its activities primarily on social concerns such as child welfare, which reflected their interests as members of the city's social elite. Founded in 1876, some of the city's most prestigious women—Bertha Palmer, Mrs. Julius Rosenwald, Mrs. Medill McCormick, for instance—had belonged to the group.[77] Neither a political nor a suffragist organization, it did not veer far from fields its members considered appropriate for women, most specifically motherhood and its many applications.[78] Tensions existed between the two groups that reached as far back as the 1893 fair, when the New York group controlled far more exhibit space than deemed reasonable by Chicagoans.[79] Though the council sought the cooperation of the Chicago Woman's Club to arrange music and lecture programs as well as to provide hostesses in the exhibit hall, ill feelings persisted. The tension extended beyond the Chicago Woman's Club to include other Chicago clubs as well.

A petition drive initiated in 1932 suggests the tension. The council sponsored the drive, hoping that a million American women would sign the petition to encourage foreign countries to send representatives to the fair's international congress, planned for the week of July 16, 1933. The petition also increased the council's visibility, another of its goals. But Chicago women refused to cooperate, a reality disclosed by their extremely poor showing in the petition drive. Of the 850,000 names collected shortly before the fair opened, fewer than 30,000 Chicago women had signed—less than 25 percent of the number collected in New York City. Further, the Chicago organizations had both failed to raise funds for the congress and to plan accommodations for congress speakers.[80]

A meeting between Chicago women's organizations and the National Council of Women, held at the Palmer House on March 30, laid bare the root of the conflict: the council had commandeered Chicago women's rightful place at A Century of Progress. Council leaders accused Chicago of failing the national office twice. "We have not been able to diagnose the problem," the council president, Lena Phillips, declared. "Now we are prepared to go ahead without you. . . . We want your help, but we do not propose to make any more futile appeals." Mrs. Henry W. Hardy, president of the Chicago and Cook County Federation of Women's Organizations, countered, "Everywhere we encountered a lack of cooperation. . . . I do not believe [we can organize the women] without headquarters being established here." Soon thereafter the council established headquarters at the Palmer House. This signaled a kind of recoup on the part of Chicago's women's organizations, and it marked "the first move on the part of local clubs to organize to carry on the activities of the women's section of the fair, after the close of the women's congress."[81]

Though it seemed on the surface that Chicago women had agreed to work with the National Council of Women, the prestigious Chicago Woman's Club tried to avoid the council's management by working directly with the fair organizers. In an undated proposal on the possible contributions of the Chicago Woman's Club to the 1933 exposition, Helen Cooley, chair of the Chicago Woman's Club fair program committee, wrote that "realizing that at A Century of Progress there will be no Woman's Building (rightly so, we believe, because the work of women now justly stands with that of man on its own merit) the Chicago Woman's Club asks the privilege of personifying and making vivid the accomplishment of women during the last century . . . by inviting to Chicago the outstanding representatives in each classification who would present . . . woman's accomplishment."[82] The club wanted to create a weekly speakers program at the fairgrounds under the auspices of the fair management. To avoid conflict with the council, there would be no talk during the week of the international women's congress. If it was not possible to hold these lectures at the fair, then Cooley suggested that they be held at their own club building, "a woman's civic laboratory and dedicated to Social Progress."[83] In the end, the Chicago Woman's Club hosted the lectures in both the Hall of Science and in the Illinois State Host Building.

Women did actually find a unique space during the fair. Ironically and somewhat symbolically, it was located immediately outside the Chicago world's fair's main entrance gate at 72 East Eleventh Street—the Chicago Woman's Club building.[84] Members of the Chicago Woman's Club entertained other clubwomen at their building during the fair by providing dining and housing to select visitors. They also prepared an exhibit for the first-floor club room to illustrate the progress of the club and its role in Chicago's education, public health, reform, and culture. A mural painted by Chicago schoolchildren illustrated many of the club's social programs. As a highlight, club members staged a historical pageant in their theater on the evening before the fair's official opening. Written by one of their own members, the *Evolution of Women's Clubs* traced clubwomen through episodes of fear, romance, courage, and freedom. The tableaux featured staging of the Columbian Exposition, reform in the Juvenile Court, suffrage marches, Jane Addams receiving the Nobel Prize, and their building welcoming A Century of Progress.[85] The timing and conclusion emphasized how members of the Chicago Woman's Club envisioned their importance in society and in relationship to the international exposition.

Holabird and Root had designed the space for the self-supporting Chicago Woman's Club in the same year that Virginia Woolf delivered her talks on *A Room of One's Own*, which argued that women need their own money and space in order to achieve intellectual freedom.[86] Reacting to substantial rent increases for their headquarters in the Fine Arts Building on Michigan Avenue, the Chicago

Woman's Club purchased the Eleventh Street property.[87] Its own downtown site established this club as an affluent, independent, equal, and powerful force in the urban center. The appropriation of space was a political act related to social status and power, symbolic of women's changing position in a changing society.[88] "Modern" in style, the six-story building housed a theater, dining room, lounge, library, meeting rooms, offices, and four dozen resident and guest bedrooms.[89] The height and size of the building reinforced the hierarchy of social status that this club held within the city, and the spatial arrangements reflected the significance of social interaction and education for these reformers.

The exterior of the Chicago Woman's Club building integrated granite, limestone, and terra cotta with two entrances framed in nickel metal. The spandrel designs emphasized traditional female imagery in contrast to the more masculine geometric vertical patterns of the Art Deco exterior design, which signified a modern structure for modern women. Panels above the tall windows of the first-floor dining room depicted an ancient earth goddess and, a few floors above, various bounties of Mother Earth. Finally, the repeated relief panels above the top-floor windows featured stylized floral pistils and stamens that bore a striking resemblance to fallopian tubes and a vaginal opening. Above the main entrance was a bas-relief of two winged and caped women kneeling before an urn, suggesting that these women were not only protecting the values of tradition and womanhood, but as modern women they were ready to serve society.[90]

The interior of the club headquarters offered open spaces for social and civic activities. The user-oriented complex merged form with club function. Decorated with soft colors in a modern style, this building provided traditional comforts expressed with new colors and materials for the clubwomen, who envisioned themselves as leaders in the new gendered social order. Designers realized the feminization of the interior space at the Chicago Woman's Club through coordinated chromatic schemes in soft colors: gray with gold, green with silver and maple, peach with jade, salmon pink with blue, jonquil yellow with chartreuse, gray, and plum. The third-floor lounge of the Chicago Woman's Club emphasized light with windows on three sides and stressed modernity through twin violet-veined marble fireplaces placed at each end amid walnut fluted vertical accents. Furnishings were in gold, green, and violet. Gold and brown draperies complemented the parquet floor with its large brown checkered carpet. The ornamental grilles, like other metalwork in the building, emphasized light, organic movement often using ancient feminine symbols such as spirals. Both entrances of the civic-minded Chicago Woman's Club led to assembly halls and a theater designed for intimate lectures, recitals, and performances for an audience of six hundred persons—a perfect location and setting for entertaining clubwomen from around the United States and the globe.[91]

The Chicago Woman's Club's series of lectures, which were finally offered under the auspices of both A Century of Progress and the National Council of

Women, took place on the fairgrounds at the Hall of Science and in the Illinois State Host Building. A visit to the Chicago Woman's Club by the council president, Lena Phillips, had sealed the cooperative arrangement. Nationally renowned women lawyers, politicians, scientists, sociologists, authors, and artists spoke on "Woman's Contribution to Civilization." The chosen theme reflected the club members' vision of women's new role in civilization, a social construct previously relegated to the male domain.[92] To promote interclub friendship, the committee invited presidents of ten other Chicago women's clubs to preside over some of the sessions, including the American Association of University Women, Catholic Women's League, Chicago College Club, Chicago Branch of the National Council of Jewish Women, Chicago Woman's Aid, the Fortnightly, Musicians Club of Women, Woman's City Club, and Woman's University Club.[93] It did not, however, reach across racial and ethnic boundaries to those Chicago clubs that represented, for instance, women of color. Its officers and members, however, focused on extending their contacts with other clubwomen and professional women from similarly privileged backgrounds. When they envisioned themselves in the public sphere taking their rightful position with men, they followed the social hierarchy already in place for race, class, and gender. The *Chicago Woman's Club Bulletin* quoted Anna Steese Richardson in *Woman's Home Companion* as saying "the function of women in connection with the Century of Progress will be to breathe into a machine-made, man-made exposition the fine, spiritual vision of organized womanhood."[94] In other words, these women saw themselves as an opposing yet complementary force to the male-organized construction of the fair. They retained the traditional role of women who were expected to counterbalance and soften the masculine instincts, but now they operated from their new position in society—no longer individuals confined to the home, but as full citizens organized as a societal force operating from their club base.

Women fulfilled Richardson's prediction with dubious success.[95] This was the product of numerous factors, several related to the lull the feminist movement experienced after the passage of the Nineteenth Amendment. Exceptional women who could compete in the male-dominated workplace, such as McGrew and Bennett, did so. Though they accomplished a great deal individually, these professional women accepted the fair's male-dominated status quo and therefore failed to create a collective women's community. Paradoxically, they felt that by backing the male organizers' vision for the fair, they were actually confirming women's equality. On the other hand, society women such as Helen Dawes, who as hostesses controlled space at the fair, maintained traditional ideas of women's proper role and appropriate morality while maneuvering to boost their husbands politically. They actually undermined any chances for a separate women's space at the fair.

Despite conflicts over status and power, women at A Century of Progress promoted their visions of progress and the new roles of women in society as they sought recognition and respect from each other and from their male counterparts.

Although Goodrich failed in her efforts to erect a woman's building at the fair, there was both a woman's space at the gateway and a multiplicity of spaces within the fairgrounds. Members of the National Council of Women and the Chicago Woman's Club carved out their own spaces and controlled them. The Chicago Woman's Club headquarters preserved their women's culture, expressed their identity as modern and visionary women, and enhanced the possibility for their own political empowerment, despite the fact that their power to shape the city and their identity was limited and affected by class, race, and ethnicity.[96] Unlike the 1893 Isabella site just outside the World's Columbian Exposition, the Chicago Woman's Club was not competing with the official and unofficial woman's spaces within the 1933 fairgrounds. Rather, these women sought a cooperative progress in harmony with both male and female endeavors at the exposition, parallel to the cooperative progress between science and industry sought and promoted by fair authorities. While the exposition's Administration Building, located just inside the Eleventh Street entrance, operated as a masculine technological laboratory, the Chicago Woman's Club house was a feminine civic laboratory ironically placed outside the fair's main entrance. In contrast, African American clubwomen created their own space even amid tremendous obstacles.

6

African Americans and the Du Sable Legacy

The Century of Progress should and must also show the progress we have made. . . . Black citizens are advised to go wherever there is anything to be seen or to be learned, if they so desire. Permit no one to Jim Crow you or to discriminate against you.

—*Chicago Defender*

On April 3, 1928, fourteen African American women met at the home of Annie E. Oliver to hear a talk by Robert S. Abbott, editor of the African American newspaper the *Chicago Defender*.[1] Abbott spoke about black men in history and promoted a project to further the recognition of Jean Baptiste Point Du Sable as the founder and pioneer settler of Chicago. Du Sable had established a trading post at the mouth of the Chicago River about 1774 and lived there with his family until 1800. His father was from a French Quebec mercantile family, and his mother was a black slave. Two events in 1928 had raised interest in Du Sable: the publication of new research on his residence and the announcement that the city of Chicago planned to stage a world's fair in 1933. The convergence of the two led Oliver and her group to establish the National De Saible Memorial Society that evening.

Oliver—an educator, beauty culturist, and active clubwoman—sought widespread recognition and respectability for her race and community beyond Chicago's South Side. By founding the National De Saible Memorial Society, she and the other clubwomen created a safe haven where members honed their professional skills while striving to achieve their goal: to create a memorial for Chicago's first citizen and businessman and simultaneously underscore the importance of the African American community to the progress of Chicago. Using the power of place, public conduct, print, and language, Oliver and other members of the society sparked a public dialogue that elevated Du Sable to his rightful place as a key historical figure in Chicago history. At the same time, they reinforced Chicago's African American community's claim to a place in the city's social, cultural, political, and economic future.[2] They succeeded in building a replica of the Du Sable cabin at the 1933 Chicago world's fair when other African American organizations had failed to unify behind a representative project and raise the necessary funds.

African Americans and the World's Fair

Chicago's African Americans needed concrete evidence that the exposition's optimistic claims for the future would include social justice for members of their race. Unfortunately, fair organizers and concessionaires allocated very few resources to them, though a limited number of blacks did secure low-level jobs. Some blacks held visible positions, for example, as policemen, a lecturer at the Illinois Host House, a ninety-year-old former slave in the Georgia state exhibit, jazz musicians, or choir members. Regrettably, businesses used stereotypical images to sell their products. The Rutledge Tavern, just steps from the Du Sable cabin, featured the African American Mammy, a heavy, jovial woman in a headrag, in its advertising to promote southern-style cooking.[3] In the General Exhibits Group, Anna Robinson made her debut as Aunt Jemima. The embodiment of the Mammy icon for packaged pancake mix, Robinson made exaggerated gestures and rolled her eyes while demonstrating how to flip pancakes.[4] Other African Americans held invisible jobs working in lavatories for tips rather than a salary. For instance, Vernell Taylor had paid an employment agency $12.50 for a job as a maid in a washroom, but she earned only forty cents for a weekend of work, and that was to be shared with the concessionaire.[5] Despite pleas from William L. Dawson, Chicago's African American alderman, for more exposition jobs for blacks, fair officials used their "best efforts to avoid" the matter of employment and thereby increase the visibility of blacks at the fair.[6] African Americans consequently visited the exposition in numbers much smaller than their 7 percent of the population of the city.

Experiences such as those endured at the fair and many, many other affronts shaped African Americans' perspective of the idea of progress, the theme promoted by the fair organizers. Their understanding of progress contrasted sharply with that of the dominant Anglo culture. An editorial cartoon in the *Defender,* for example, entitled "A Century of Progress," showed the slave driver's whip and the lynchers' ropes, nineteenth-century tools of punishment still used in the Deep South to maintain the status quo and thwart progress among blacks. Another of its editorials portrayed a black businessman across the table from President Roosevelt "waiting for the New Deal" for his race.[7]

From the fair's early planning stages, officials discussed how to illustrate African American accomplishments, in what location, and under whose authority, but they resisted following through with any ideas. In 1930 the African American architect Charles S. Duke wrote a note to Daniel Burnham suggesting that fair organizers hire some black architects and engineers. A member of Daniel Burnham's staff forwarded Duke's message to Lenox Lohr's desk. With no intention of honoring the request, the staff member cautioned that "the bubble was now about ready to break" and that already there was "a feeling existing among the negroes that race discrimination would be applied throughout" the exposition. That the fair's southern section skirted the city's interracial vice district only exacerbated concerns. The vice district had recently shifted to the economically deprived black metropolis or "black belt" neighborhood that ran parallel just west of the fair.[8] Burnham's staff member suggested approaching influential African American businessmen, requesting they exert "their influence to assist in warding off the possible trouble" and "to keep down the antagonistic feeling."[9]

The *Defender*, a local African American newspaper with a national readership, reported that Charles G. Dawes and Rufus Dawes actually had a "reputation for breadth and progressiveness and freedom from racial prejudice."[10] If the truth be known, however, the Dawes brothers and the fair's general manager, Lenox Lohr, sought active African American participation primarily when it met the needs and goals of the exposition, especially to boost attendance, rather than when it met the needs of the black community. By excluding African Americans from most levels of exposition activity, they limited the fair's credibility with the local black community.

Rufus Dawes and other organizers did attempt to reach the black community with the idea of creating appropriate exhibits and otherwise securing involvement, but they failed. They approached black business leaders such as Jesse Binga, a banker, and Robert Abbott, an editor, during the early stages of fair planning with invitations to participate. They formed a separate temporary executive committee that included twenty African American community leaders drawn from the press, banks, legal and medical professions, as well as some social club officers. Hoping to generate participation at the community level, they contacted groups that might promote local enrollment ticket sales through churches, professional associations, and service organizations. Hoping to stir enthusiasm and secure participation, Dawes also dispatched his administrative assistant and the Administration Building doorman, Adam Beckley, to community gatherings. Beckley, the only African American working in the Administration Building, was a retired postal worker and ex-slave. As a member of the advisory board of the South Side Civic Improvement Association, he enthusiastically promoted the fair in African American neighborhoods.[11]

Why did fair organizers fail to reach the black community? Divisions within the African American population thwarted local efforts to prepare and fund an exhibit. The Chicago Urban League attempted to organize the Colored Citizens World's Fair Council to represent forty community groups and to cooperate with fair officials and the African American clubwomen. Other groups proposed exhibits but failed to raise the necessary funds to stage them at the fair. Three frustrated professionals who had hoped for an exhibit illustrating black progress wrote to President Roosevelt, asking him to intervene by directing that the exhibits of U.S. government agencies housed in the Federal Building include recognition of the "5,876 inventions patented by colored people in this country from 1776 to 1924."[12] Shunning fair participation, one group did mount an African and American Negro Exhibit outside the fairgrounds at the National Pythian Temple in the African American neighborhood.[13]

Howard W. Odum, the early planner for the social science exhibits and an advocate for an African American exhibit, felt that an honest and respectful display "might greatly facilitate this Afro-American problem and would give place for one unit of this Negro participation which would be very important and very interesting."[14] Odum, a sociologist from the University of North Carolina who had researched and published on African American migration and culture, suggested hiring Aaron Douglas, a local black artist, to do some of the interior decorations in the Social Science Hall.[15] In the end, the Urban League exhibit in the Social Science Hall, rather than an official fair-sponsored exhibit, actually realized Odum's vision by featuring the mural *Negro Migration: The Exodus* by the local artist Charles C. Dawson. The center panel depicted the Great Migration of hopeful blacks from all walks of life leaving the rural south for the industrial north. Side panels featured images and statistics to highlight the social issues of health, housing, and employment and the role of the Urban League in addressing those issues on a national scale. Promoting interracial harmony, the league sponsored a panel discussion at the Illinois Host House on "A Century of Progress in Race Relations."[16]

Though Odum was determined to represent African Americans in the Social Science Hall, blacks did not flock to the building. Many exhibits simply did not interest them. Those exhibits that featured blacks—the Urban League exhibit, for instance, and the State of Georgia exhibit, which showed blacks picking cotton—did attract large crowds. So, too, did Ford's automotive exhibits. In the social science educational exhibit wing, though, black visitors were an exception as evidenced by the journal of the Radcliffe College alumnae booth. The attendant wrote in her journal, "to my surprise a large colored woman stopped beside the desk and said that her teacher graduated from Radcliffe." The surprise continued when she realized that "the woman was intelligent, and had a certain charm and a very sweet voice."[17] Except for the African American man who played the piano in that hall, the Radcliffe alumna's fair experience had been with members of the white middle and upper classes—alumnae and relatives, university personnel, foreign visitors, dignitaries on tour, and youth seeking information on advanced education opportunities.

Fair officials debated whether to include an African American component in "Darkest Africa," the Midway's anthropology-as-entertainment exhibit. The exhibit featured tribal leaders brought from Africa for the exposition. It attracted a large African American audience, many curious about their own history. The Nigerian royalty and Belgian Congo pygmies, who performed ceremonies and music, represented extreme Western visions of African tribal peoples and met with mixed reviews from the African American community. Having discussed their concerns, organizers decided against expanding the exhibit to include an African American component. They felt such an inclusion would be "contrary to our adopted policy to feature progress of the Negro in appropriate places alongside progress in general education, business, social work, etc. rather than a race exhibit."[18]

The "Negro" attractions orchestrated by nonblack concessionaires reinforced stereotypical images of African Americans. The attractions drew criticism, but, interestingly, some of the criticism centered on indecency rather than the stereotypes. For instance, singers and dancers in the Plantation Show portrayed a Deep South with happy slaves willing to do anything to please their masters or their audiences.[19] After visitor complaints, the Operations and Maintenance Department sent reprimands to the concessionaire ordering him to have "his colored chorus girls wear some kind of costume" to cover their breasts and loins; to eliminate dancing that appeared exaggerated, vulgar, and indecent; and to delete language that was obscene or misrepresented the facts.[20] Management did force the concession called African Dips, a game of throwing balls at living black men, to close after protests, but such Sky Ride cars as "Brother Crawford" continued to transverse the fairgrounds in "honor" of the exaggerated black characters from *Amos 'n' Andy*, a popular radio program featuring blackface skits.[21]

Though the fair itself maintained a policy of inclusiveness, African Americans definitely encountered racism when they visited the fair. For instance, by offering very poor service, some concessions in the Streets of Paris made it uncomfortable for African Americans to patronize the restaurants, shows, and shops. When fair organizers gave lip service to ending this tactic, concessionaires found another way to insult blacks—one that presumed black males would rush to peep shows to ogle white women. Barkers singled out black attendees from the crowds, attempting to lure them into the shows. Dewey R. Jones, a reporter for the *Defender*, wrote in astonishment that the barkers probably "thought black men would consider it a great favor to be permitted to look at nude white women. How little they know about this!" This practice only reinforced his perception that "the fair was a WHITE MAN's proposition and the white man ran it to suit himself."[22] At a time when the Ku Klux Klan lynched African American men on suspicion of violating the southern white woman's honor, the northern concessionaires encouraged black men to gaze at nude white women in exchange for ten to twenty-five cents.

Discriminatory practices at the fair often culminated in lawsuits. For instance, fair management did not strictly enforce antidiscrimination in restaurants, so many black visitors suffered the humiliation of sitting for long periods of time without service. Such situations provided the Chicago branch of the National Association for the Advancement of Colored People (NAACP) with documentation to handle hundreds of legal cases involving discrimination in Chicago during the fair period. The NAACP did not lose a single case, recovering over $5,000 in judgments from the fair organization and concessionaires for persons denied service in restaurants, theaters, and the fairgrounds.[23]

The Colored Citizens World's Fair Council, a federation of local professional African American representatives, also mediated instances of racism. Arthur G. Falls, a member of the council and of the Chicago Urban League, and his guests experienced discrimination at the Pabst Blue Ribbon fair restaurant, receiving service only after threatening the manager with police action under Illinois's new antidiscrimination law.[24] Although overt racism lessened after the passage of House Bill 114 in 1934, legislation passed in response to organized African American lobbying, not all African Americans had the arsenal of knowledge and experience to confront racism directly at the exposition. The *Defender* encouraged blacks to go wherever they wished at the fair, to "permit no one to Jim Crow you," to have no fear of whites, and to refuse to cringe or apologize for entering an exposition place of business.[25] While fair officials did not condone racism, they certainly did not break new ground in race relations.

Negro Day at the Fair

The organizers of A Century of Progress had high expectations for Negro Day, August 12, 1933. They publicized it as the "Greatest Day in Race History" and used an official list of "White Friends of Negro Day"—composed of politicians, judges, settlement house founders, and civic leaders—to boost their promotions further. Personal and political differences within the African American community, particularly the clash between a newspaperman, Chandler Owen, and Congressman Oscar DePriest, limited the chances of a successful event. Owen chaired the National Negro Day Committee, an advisory committee of African American community leaders that included the black labor organizer A. Phillip Randolph. Owen and Randolph, old friends since their college days in New York City, had coedited the radical labor newspaper the *Messenger*. Owen had supported Randolph's attempts in 1925 to unionize Pullman porters. Congressman DePriest, the key political figure in Chicago's African American community, refused to participate on the advisory committee, made little attempt to promote Negro Day, and publicized his stand in the black press.[26] He objected to the fifty-cent admission to Soldier Field that did not include entrance to the fairgrounds, leaving Negro Day "outside of the fair." He also objected that promotional materials gave no indication of how the profits would be used. What he failed to mention in his critique of the planning was that he clashed with Owen, a socialist whose radical politics threatened his political authority.[27]

The members of the African American community did not support the fair's Negro Day. In fact, they all but ignored it. After a morning parade that ended at the gates of the exposition, about four thousand visitors paid the fifty-cent admission and enjoyed a "full day of joy and entertainment" at Soldier Field. Entertainment included an all-star track meet, featuring Ralph Metcalfe, Jesse Owens, and other African American track stars, and the selection of Miss Bronze America from young, single women from across the United States. The highpoint was the historical pageant *The Epic of a Race,* depicting African American progress from slave revolts and spirituals to Booker T. Washington and the jazz age. The local African American radio star Andrew Dobson wrote and staged the show.[28]

The *Defender* headlined the story: "Negro Day at Fair Flops: Parade Is Worst in History of City."[29] African American civic, fraternal, and business groups had refused to march in the parade. Instead, the six African American policemen stationed at the fair led city police, the Eighth Regiment band, a battalion of soldiers, and a few automobiles. Straggling a half mile behind were a few members of the Elks and the Knights of Pythias, and two other bands. In a city that takes parades seriously, this embarrassing spectacle did not bode well for the day's activities at Soldier Field.

Fair officials thought that targeted advertising and a list of names demonstrating interracial harmony would draw and satisfy crowds, but this approach failed. Two articles printed in the *Defender* offered explanations for the fiasco. First, an article by Dewey Jones reviewed the disappointing pageant and the restaurant discrimination at the fair. Jones expressed his hope that the low attendance would show white fair officials that blacks would not endure condescension on their day off work.[30] A week later, Dr. Dennis Bethea offered another perspective. He maintained that some African Americans appreciated the special day on which to express their racial pride publicly before the dominant Euro American culture. He concluded by chastising those who had opposed and sabotaged the event, saying they had acted unwisely.[31]

Negro Day opened a full week of African American national conventions, all held in Chicago and planned to take advantage of activities at the fair. More than thirty organizations held their conventions that week, including the National Negro Medical Association, the Royal Circle of Friends, the Alpha Phi Psi fraternity, and the Alpha Kappa Alpha sorority.[32] Delta Sigma Theta sorority representatives convened later in August. After Mayor Edward J. Kelly presented the key to the city of Chicago and scholarship funds to its president, Gladys Byram Shepperd, the women then listened to music and speeches, took a boat ride on Lake Michigan, dressed in evening gowns for a lavish banquet, and met to address their national issues and concerns.[33] The convening National Association of Colored Women published its thirty-seven-year history, *Lifting as They Climb.* The account's author, Elizabeth Lindsay Davis, employed political and exposition rhetoric to write that a new day and a new deal had arrived for American women and that it was "fitting at this time that the Negro woman should take her part in the Century of Progress and prove to the world that she, too, is finding her place in the sun."[34] Clubwomen from thirty states attended the NACW's eighteenth convention to promote public interest and community cooperation, to protest racism, and to address Depression-era issues.[35]

Only seven days after the poor showing of Negro Day at the fair, African Americans came out in droves to enjoy the *Defender*'s annual Bud Billiken Day. The striking contrast of the turnout for the two events demonstrated the necessity of planning with local organizations and leaders to ensure community support. The newspaper had named the event after a weekly column in its children's section written by Willard Motley. Billiken became a symbol of pride, happiness, and hope for African American youth. The Bud Billiken Day events included free games, music, entertainment, dancing, and ice cream in Washington Park. The Sioux tribe of Native Americans from the exposition entertained the children. Cab Calloway, Earl Hines, and Adelaide Hall added to the musical fun. The parade was viewed by an estimated fifty thousand people, more than ten times the number of persons who bought tickets for Negro Day at Soldier Field.[36]

African American Clubwomen and the Du Sable Cabin

The National De Saible Memorial Society, formed by Annie E. Oliver in 1928, achieved at the fair what black male community leaders could not: a pavilion of self-representation. Because the fair authority sponsored no exhibits of ethnic or racial progress, privately funded groups staged such displays as concessions or as government-sponsored exhibits. Though political infighting and the inability of male organizations to raise funds for a major exhibit limited the black community's representation at the fair, the National De Saible Memorial Society managed to produce a stellar exhibit, a reproduction of Jean Baptiste Point Du Sable's cabin. The society's members worked amid overt discrimination, and their resourcefulness provided continuity in the black clubwoman's struggle against negative stereotypes while at the same time illustrating progress for their race. The women used their fair exhibit to counter gender and racial bias while claiming the African American's rightful place in Chicago history.

Carter G. Woodson, a historian, took up the crusade to reclaim black history when in 1915 he established the Association for the Study of Negro Life and History. Woodson also edited the *Journal of Negro History,* and in 1926 he initiated Negro History Week.[37] His organization motivated professionals, teachers, and ministers to save records and write the life histories of notable black Americans in order to instill racial pride and to correct the historical record.[38] The National Association of Colored Women and its history department reported at Woodson's annual conference on "women's part in popularizing Negro history" and promoted clubs throughout the country to follow its program.[39] Woodson's prolific output of textbooks and studies made him well known among Chicago's African American leaders, including the editor of the *Defender*, Robert S. Abbott. In 1928, when Abbott spoke before the women at the first meeting of the National De Saible Memorial Society, Woodson had not yet written about Du Sable or his role as the founder and first entrepreneur of Chicago.

Recent scholarly recognition of Jean Baptiste Point Du Sable as Chicago's first settler had inspired Oliver and the society members. Milo Milton Quaife had published a document in 1928 that he had found in the records of the Wayne County Building in Detroit, Michigan. Written in French, the original manuscript recorded Du Sable's sale of the property near the mouth of the Chicago River to Jean Lalime in 1800. John Kinzie acquired the property from Lalime in 1804.[40] Other written accounts describe Du Sable as tall, handsome, and well educated. Du Sable had described himself as a "free negro." The bill of sale listed his home at 40' × 22' and referred to a horse mill, bakehouse, dairy, smokehouse, poultry house, workshop, stable, and barn. He also owned lumbering and farming tools plus thirty cattle, calves, thirty-eight hogs, mules, and forty-four hens. This inventory suggested that Du Sable was more than a simple fur trader; he was also a prosperous farmer with several employees. He lived on the banks of the river with his Native American wife, Catherine, and their children, Susanne and Jean Baptiste. Quaife argued that Chicagoans should take pride in Du Sable for his achievements "of commercial importance and assured respectability; . . . even in his mixed blood he truly represented the future city, for where else on earth is a greater conglomeration of races and breeds assembled together? His story is one with that of early Chicago."[41]

Their imaginations heightened, Oliver and her clubwomen determined to make Du Sable's story one with that of Chicago. While the nation's economic crisis prompted African American clubwomen to focus on community aid, the National De Saible Memorial Society also pursued its vision. Members of the society belonged to numerous clubs, and these social networks helped organize a broad base of support for the Du Sable memorial. Clubwomen such as Annie Oliver were middle-class, married, college-educated women with secure incomes from their spouses and leisure time to advance their families' social status while tackling pressing racial and community issues. Oliver, a Baptist migrant from Tennessee who married a Chicago doctor, had served as an officer for many social, fraternal, professional, and religious organizations in Chicago, including matron and committee chair in the Order of the Eastern Star (OES); president of both the Poro Club for beauty culturists and the Henrietta P. Lee Comfort Club; and secretary of the Quinn Chapel Improvement Club. She also belonged to the Royal Eagle Court, Heroines of Jericho, and Forresters.[42]

Martha McGrew, seated at Lenox Lohr's immediate right during a Chicago business-men's meeting with fair officials, was highly influential and often made decisions on Lohr's behalf. Chicago History Museum, ICHi-50682.

Helen Dawes, the First Lady of the world's fair, appeared with Eleanor Roosevelt, the First Lady of the United States, during events honoring Roosevelt's visit to the fair. McCormick Library of Special Collections, Northwestern University Library, Evanston, Illinois.

Dorthea Goodrich, also known as Dolly Matters, in court defending herself against charges of kidnapping.

BROTHERS ARCHITECTS

TEMPLE OF WOMANHOOD

Daniel H. Burnham interpreted Dorthea Goodrich's concept for the Temple of Woman-
hood with a blend of modernism and neoclassical elements. A Century of Progress
Records (COP neg. 181), Special Collections and University Archives Department,
University Library, University of Illinois at Chicago.

The Du Sable cabin souvenir booklet featured a cover illustration by the African American artist Charles C. Dawson of the enterprising black man who had selected the location of the future Chicago.

By the 1930s some African American women had earned college degrees, which opened doors to professional positions in educational and social organizations. African American clubwomen, many of them middle-class homemakers, took on challenges that addressed the dual discriminations that they faced: racism and sexism. They organized their battles around notions of respectability and progress. They fought, for instance, for antilynching legislation; they also attempted to repel negative stereotypes of Jezebels and Mammies, to further civil rights, and to provide humanitarian reform in their communities. One scholar, Floris Loretta Barnett Cash, articulated that "the clubwomen looked to progress and respectability to bring the masses in step with the values and attitudes of the middle class," as evidenced by their desire to educate and bring new levels of respect to their race.[43] These women found themselves questioning whether to strive for interracialism or to focus on strengthening their own institutions.[44]

In the 1920s, the New Negro movement of African American literary and artistic culture had heightened the clubwomen's awareness of history and public image. From songwriters and Harlem Renaissance authors, they had learned the shaping power that words lent to their campaigns.[45] This influence was especially evident in the mission of Oliver and the National De Saible Memorial Society as they worked to create a respectable community identity. For Oliver, the experience of the beauty parlor, where women congregated, had also taught her the importance of a place where members of the community could share ideas. She extended this concept to the Du Sable project. Clearly, creating a public display and increasing public visibility would be necessary to achieve recognition for Du Sable, the club-women, and the African American community.[46] A daunting task all on its own, uncooperative fair authorities only made it more formidable. Further, the African American community overall did not embrace the project. Most people were more interested in finding jobs than in staging an exhibition.

An indefatigable woman, Oliver worked steadily from the time she formed the club in 1928 until she realized her goal of erecting the cabin in 1933. Even then she continued to work, organizing volunteers to enlighten visitors concerning the black community's role in Chicago's history. She worked to increase membership of the National De Saible Memorial Society, she raised funds, she battled for space on the fairgrounds, and she hosted countless visitors in the Du Sable cabin.[47] In the first years of their society, membership grew from fourteen to one hundred twenty-five women, many of them schoolteachers. The educational mission offered members an opportunity to use their teaching abilities outside of the confines of the classroom and the African American community. In addition to Oliver, other officers included Mamie E. Edmondson and Minnie B. Chavers, vice presidents; Lela B. Cannon, recording secretary and vice president; Alice Coachman, recording secretary and treasurer; Lucy Miller, recording secretary; Elizabeth Simon and Cora Brown, corresponding secretaries; Alice J. Neal and Martha B. Mitchell, financial secretaries; Eva Romayne and Ida Bullette, treasurers; C. Finch, parliamentarian;

Margie Hackney, reporter; Blanche V. Shaw, chair of research; Sallie B. Thompson, chairwoman of auditing; Juliette Keith, chaplain; and, Antonette C. Tompkins, chairwoman of music.

The founding of the National De Saible Memorial Society occurred only months after a meeting in the city council chamber resulted in a committee to plan a second Chicago world's fair, the Chicago World's Fair Centennial Celebration. Determined to participate, the politically savvy society members soon launched a letter-writing campaign that alerted politicians and community businessmen to their plan for the Du Sable memorial. They also sought to raise funds for the project. Alderman Robert R. Jackson consequently introduced a resolution to the Chicago City Council for a $20,000 appropriation for a Du Sable memorial. Mayor Bill Thompson, who received strong support in his elections from the African American community, appointed a committee of five aldermen and four citizens—one of them Congressman Oscar DePriest—to fulfill the terms of the resolution.[48] In June 1929, DePriest resigned from the committee, and Oliver took his place. Obviously, Oliver and the black community wielded considerable power at City Hall. That the city of Chicago, bankrupt at the time, funded her society's plan for the Du Sable memorial suggested the power of the plan and the city council's desire for political backing from the black community.

The city's financial backing certainly did not guarantee a smooth road for Oliver and the society. Fair authorities opposed them. Less than a year after the Dawes brothers began planning the city's centennial celebration, Oliver informed fair officials of the society's intention to erect a monument to honor Du Sable. She pointed out that he was not only the first settler in Chicago, but also the first trader, pioneer, and businessman of the city. He built the first house in Chicago, which the society planned to replicate. Oliver requested a location on the fairgrounds for the building and offered cooperation.[49]

Oliver confronted resistance at every turn, but she persisted, contacting various fair officials by letter and by phone.[50] She reminded Dawes's assistant that as members of the Chicago World's Fair Legion, her society had sold advance tickets to assure the financial success of the exposition.[51] She contacted Rufus Dawes and every official that each previous contact suggested for referral. She gathered letters of support from Irene McCoy Gaines, the president of the Colored Women's Republican Clubs of Illinois, and members of the Appomattox Club, Chicago Urban League, and other African American civic organizations.[52] In response, the head of concessions denied the request, stating that, though he could "not discuss in detail the reasons underlining our decision, you may be assured that the matter has been well considered."[53]

Disappointed but undaunted, in 1932 Oliver enlisted the help of Mary McDowell, head of the University of Chicago Settlement, to uncover the reasons for rejection. Through McDowell she learned fair officials' rationalizations: the Du Sable Cabin would replicate the plans for a reproduction of Fort Dearborn, it offered nothing distinctive, its value was questionable, and it would lack popular appeal.[54] Refusing to accept their reasoning, Oliver became more determined, and she used a more forceful tone in her continued letter-writing campaign. Her perseverance paid off. Just four months before the opening of the exposition, fair authorities relented. They granted concessionaire space for her Du Sable cabin as a concession. One fair official later explained that the exhibit represented "one of the few distinct contributions of the negro race to the Exposition" and that the "considerable feeling last year that the negroes were not accorded sufficient part in the Exposition" had led to the concession. The official confided that he did not agree that such feelings were justified, but the decision prevailed.[55]

The Chicago city council's support covered the cabin's $1,500 erection costs. The replica of Du Sable's log cabin, designed by the African American architect Charles S. Duke, sat on the Midway near other pioneer sites, including the Lincoln Group of buildings, the Marquette Cabin, and the Rutledge Tavern. Fortuitously, the cabin's location was near the replica of Fort Dearborn, a popular destination and a site historically linked to the cabin's later years as a trading post.[56] Corn and wheat stalks roofed the 8' × 12' cabin, which was about a third of the original "mansion" size described by one of its later residents, Juliette M. Kinzie, in her book *Wau-Bun*.[57] Animal skins, guns, Native American baskets, cooking utensils, a drinking gourd, and a table and chairs all made the interior seem snug.[58] The replica lacked the numerous outbuildings, fields, and livestock of the successful trader. Next to the log cabin stood a memorial tablet explaining its historical importance, a tablet originally intended for placement at the actual site at the mouth of the Chicago River.

Visitors to the cabin could purchase the society's booklet, *Jean Baptiste Point De Saible: The First Permanent Settler in Chicago*. The cover illustration by Charles C. Dawson, who had painted the Urban League's *Negro Migration: The Exodus* mural in the Social Science Hall, showed the pioneer trader in buckskins with a rifle surveying the original site of his homestead.[59] Dawson gave his Du Sable distinctively African American facial features rather than emphasizing mulatto or French Canadian features. Du Sable's cabin and a canoe dominated the scene's foreground. Just behind and above the eighteenth-century scene rose the Wrigley Building and the Tribune Tower, symbols of the twentieth century. The message was clear: an enterprising black man had selected this place, and his entrepreneurship had launched Chicago as a great commercial center. Certainly, the booklet and the Du Sable cabin validated the African American clubwomen's claim that their race deserved recognition for its contributions to Chicago's past and would undoubtedly share its march into the future.

In preparing the booklet, the committee searched the existing Chicago history literature to find all references to Du Sable. The booklet's footnotes not only pointed out how many scholars had recognized Du Sable as the first settler, but also indicated that this was a scholarly study written by African American clubwomen.

Further, the booklet highlighted the many significant events that had occurred at the site, including the birth of the first white child, the first solemnized wedding, the first election, and the first court in Chicago.[60]

The officers of the National De Saible Memorial Society sent engraved invitations for the cabin's dedicatory services, to be held June 11, 1933, which coincided with the exposition designation of Interracial Day. Speakers included Alderman Robert R. Jackson, who had championed the cause to obtain city government funding, and Irene McCoy Gaines, president of the Colored Women's Republican Clubs of Illinois and vice president of the Northern District Federation of Women's Clubs. They and others honored Du Sable, Oliver and her committee, and the proud local citizenry. On a blistering day the Du Sable chorus performed spirituals in the shade of the cabin for fair officials, politicians, and African American community leaders.[61] The interracial group visibly tied Du Sable to the larger fabric of Chicago society, and it symbolically emphasized the city's progress from this small cabin to the great city that such a diverse population called home. The National De Saible Memorial Society clubwomen were the educators and homemakers who made that house their home just as they had made Chicago their city.

The Du Sable Cabin served as a meeting place in the fairgrounds for African Americans, as an educational site for visitors of all races and ethnicities, and as a symbol of African Americans' determination to represent themselves. Free admission assured that even in a time of dire economic strife, anyone with A Century of Progress admission ticket could visit this concession. Mrs. Charles S. Duke, the architect's wife, wrote in the *Defender* that the cabin was a "wonderland" that provided undeniable evidence of Du Sable's entrepreneurship in Chicago for both white and black citizens.[62]

The cabin was occasionally the scene of racial tension and harassment. Club matrons, who served as educators and hostesses at the cabin, were often caught in the middle and subjected to thoughtless remarks made by visitors who listened with amazement to the story of the first black man in Chicago. These visitors stared at the exhibits, asked incredulous questions, and still in disbelief bought souvenir booklets and cards.[63] Oliver and the other clubwomen handled the curiosity seekers gracefully and respectfully whether they came to marvel that a black man was the first non–Native American in Chicago or to express their disbelief and anger. Extreme reactions often began with "oh!" and ended with loud, angry voices as the visitor stormed out the door. Others commented more politely, "It is hardly believable." One elderly white man exclaimed, "You have no right to claim that the first settler was a Colored man!"[64] Handling the outspoken visitors, the clubwomen successfully demonstrated their respectability and that of their race. The clubwomen were hostesses, not servants, and they understood the importance of representing all African American domesticity through the display of Du Sable's home.

The educational impact of the Du Sable exhibit was far reaching. The press featured the cabin in stories, and schoolteachers left with ideas for teaching local children. Even the fair management, which had been so reluctant to cooperate in the early planning, featured the cabin in a story entitled "Chicago's First Citizen" in its *Official World's Fair Weekly*. The article noted that the cabin expressed "a quiet, dignified pride, indulged in by a people who have something very dear to cherish."[65] Another study released to coincide with the exposition offered a cornucopia of information to educate the uninitiated on black accomplishments. John L. Tilley's booklet *A Brief History of the Negro in Chicago, 1779–1933* listed African American contributions to Chicago's progress: service and sacrifice at Fort Dearborn; the first elected official town crier; the freeman John Jones's efforts to repeal Illinois slave codes; headquarters for the Underground Railroad; businesses and institutions; and medical research.[66]

Oliver and her fellow clubwomen had triumphed by increasing awareness of Du Sable's identity as well as their own. They had nurtured positive self-images of black women and of African Americans for the community hit hard by the Great Depression. They had claimed their place in Chicago history and had insisted on "giving credit where credit is due."[67] They exemplified a statement made by the African American educator Mary McLeod Bethune in her speech "A Century of Progress of Negro Women" before the Chicago Women's Federation that June: "The true worth of a race must be measured by the character of its womanhood."[68] Unexpectedly, the African American clubwomen—well dressed, educated, accomplished, successful, and confident—had become an educational exhibit themselves.

Although not invited to participate at the international exposition, the African American clubwomen found ways to create a space for themselves. By illuminating their community's distinctive heritage, they defined themselves and their community's progress for fairgoers and for Chicago's business and social leaders. Using a key historic figure as their point of reference, they claimed their legitimate place in modern Chicago. Further, they used the power of place through the replica cabin, of deportment through their hosting, and of print through their published booklet to embody black pride and identity politics before such terms existed.

In 1936, the clubwomen campaigned for the renaming of New Wendell Phillips High School as Jean Baptiste Point Du Sable High School, a success that led to the spelling of "Du Sable" still used today. When Assistant Principal Annabel C. Prescott heard the suggestion to name the school De Saible High School, she protested. She feared that the students would be called "disabled." In a compromise, rather than use the proposed spelling utilized by the National De Saible Memorial Society, the spelling used by Milo M. Quaife found favor. In 1936 the society changed its name to reflect Quaife's spelling, evidence of the power of language to further its cause.

Like the courageous members of the National De Saible Memorial Society, Chicago's Italian American community, Mexico's postrevolutionary government, and the fascist leader Benito Mussolini juxtaposed key historical figures and ancient civilizations with their twentieth-century technological progress, optimistically underscoring their rights to prominence among the world's most modern nations. While Chicago's Italian American community touted its relationship to Christopher Columbus and Mexico honored its pre-Hispanic heritage, Mussolini reminded fairgoers of Rome's glory and also exploited Italy's dramatic air display to impress Chicago and the world with Italy's military prowess.

7

Ethnic Identity and Nationalistic Representations of Progress

We are a cosmopolitan city and our population is composed largely
of people who have come here from more than thirty different countries.
They are all Americans, and they are now vieing with each other in
making preparations for this great birthday party.

—Major Felix J. Streyckmans, WGN Radio Address

After parading around the cinder track at Soldier Field, ethnically
costumed immigrants and their families from twenty-seven different nations formed a huge heart at the center of the stadium to symbolize that, in
1928, Chicago's heart was its diverse population.[1] Marchers waved the Stars
and Stripes along with flags from their native lands. Then an entourage of
police, soldiers, and bands escorted the guest of honor, Dr. Hugo Eckener,
commander of the German airship *Graf Zeppelin*, and his crew around the
stadium's field to the roaring applause of fifty thousand spectators. Five hundred people in the stands lifted lanterns bearing twenty-foot-high letters that
together spelled out "Gut Heil," sending good wishes to the fliers who had
just crossed the Atlantic.[2]

With only six days' notice, the Chicago World's Fair Centennial Celebration planning committee and its Committee on Coordination of Nationalities (later known as the Committee on Nationalities), under the leadership
of Major Felix J. Streyckmans, had organized Chicago's ethnic communities
for this colorful pageant.[3] For Streyckmans, a Chicago lawyer active in the
Belgian American community, this pageant was not just a local event or ethnic
celebration. It was an "opportunity for Chicagoans to show that each racial

group was a true integral part of the 'Melting Pot' of the Middle West, in which all prejudicial feelings of race and country were secondary to Americanism."[4] On an even larger scale, Streyckmans and other fair organizers visualized the use of space within the fairgrounds as well as cultural exhibits and demonstrations to clearly illustrate change and progress within ethnic groups and the city itself. Most ethnic groups aggressively sought a role in Streyckmans's design. Mexico and Italy serve as illustrations of the ways these goals and community interests played themselves out.

Ethnic Chicago and the Idea of Progress

Streyckmans's "Melting Pot" metaphor favored acculturation over total assimilation, allowing immigrant Americans to be proud of their citizenship as Chicagoans and Americans while celebrating the cultural bonds of their ethnic heritage. Further, it spoke to the ability of the fair organizers to gain the early support and enthusiasm of the local citizenry for an event of international stature and to gain positive press coverage at a time when skeptics were still vocal about their doubts that a successful exposition was possible.

Chicago's steady increase in European immigration had peaked by 1930. This population, either first- or second-generation immigrants, comprised nearly two-thirds of the city's residents. Germans, Poles, Scandinavians, Irish, Italians, and Russians outnumbered dozens of other ethnic groups. The Chicago world's fair officials, most of whom were Anglo-Americans or Euro-Americans, targeted the European ethnic groups as participants and attendees for the fair. In contrast, though migration of African Americans and Mexicans from the American South and Southwest increased dramatically during the 1920s, fair officials did not pursue the participation of these groups.

Astute observers of the 1920s and 1930s have sought answers to one very pointed question: With the Western economy in shambles and socialist-leaning groups pushing for radical political reform, why didn't Americans—particularly immigrant laborers—follow the example of the Bolsheviks and revolt? European immigrants readily embraced the idea of progress and ethnic pride put forth by fair officials. Not only had they witnessed the progress of Chicago's last few decades, they were part of it and eager to celebrate their role in the creation of the skyscraper city. For them, the idea of progress intertwined with the "American dream," ethnic identity, and success. After all, many of their own families had arrived in poverty and worked hard so that each successive generation could improve its lifestyle. Many had moved out beyond the industrial tenements, acquired new skills and more education, started their own businesses, enjoyed increased leisure time, and expanded their power as consumers. Their newly purchased homes had electricity, plumbing, such labor-saving devices as refrigerators and vacuum cleaners, and the trappings of middle-class America including radios, phonographs, and automobiles.

Chicago's ethnic communities not only enjoyed the material benefits of the American dream. They also found a political voice when in 1931 they elected Anton J. Cermak as the city's first foreign-born mayor. Of Czech origin, he was a strong politician, constructing Chicago's first multiethnic political machine. He reached out to all the city's ethnic communities, stressing the city's indebtedness to each while encouraging participation at the fair. For instance, in 1933, just five days before being assassinated while riding in an open vehicle with Franklin D. Roosevelt, he had honored the city's Danish population by claiming that "Chicago is proud of the Danish blood which courses in her veins and she lists among those distinguished citizens who have contributed to her progress and advancement many persons of Danish blood. It is our sincere hope that Danish people will be well represented at our coming world's fair."[5]

A pronounced shift in immigration occurred in 1924 when federal restrictive immigration laws, designed to preserve northern European dominance, established quotas for European immigrants based on national origins as reported in the 1890 census. Because quotas limited southern and eastern Europeans from entering the United States, a shortage of unskilled labor threatened American manufacturers. These restrictions forced recruiters to entice African Americans and Mexicans to work in the industrial and agricultural Midwest by offering free train fare.[6] Consequently, Chicago's African American population more than doubled, making it the third-largest population group other than native-born whites. At the same time, the city's Mexican population, eligible for unrestricted immigration, increased tenfold. During the Great Depression, even though employers began firing Mexican workers in favor of Euro-Americans and the United States government aggressively deported many Mexicans, Chicago's Mexican population remained sizable. Meanwhile, the city's African American population continued to grow. Nonetheless, fair officials all but ignored these two sectors in favor of the city's more established and favored European immigrant groups.

The Committee on Nationalities

Fair organizers based their outreach to Chicago's ethnic populations on the First World War's "home front model." Felix J. Streyckmans had observed after scrutinizing tabulations that ethnic groups "beat all records in the United States in the purchase of liberty bonds and other patriotic work." He reasoned that the same enthusiasm would ensure success for the second Chicago world's fair.[7] He went on to form the Committee on Coordination of Nationalities by contacting officers and leaders of ethnic societies, professional organizations, and the foreign-language press in addition to working with the consulate offices. He presented a plan in which each ethnic group formed its own committees for religion, society, music, athletics, pageantry, publicity, enrollment campaign, and organization operations. The ethnic group's chair represented the committees at the Committee on Coordination of Nationalities meetings. Streyckmans met regularly with the various ethnic groups, and he published *Progress,* a newsletter with a circulation of twenty thousand, in English, German, and Romanian. In addition to keeping local groups informed of current events, the newsletters featured stories promoting the actions of successful groups and photographs of ethnic leaders, both men and women. This practice not only offered recognition but also helped to create a competitive atmosphere among various groups as they strove to prove their worth to the cause.[8] Besides recruiting volunteers, raising funds, and providing costumed performers for the opening-day parade and ethnic-day celebrations, the committee established foreign press contacts, initiated consulate participation, and facilitated activities for aviation events.[9]

Fair organizers fully recognized the importance of the city's ethnic groups to the fair's success. During a motivational mass meeting for ethnic representatives, Rufus Dawes noted that 75 percent of Chicagoans were either foreign born or the offspring of foreign-born parents, making the city an appropriate venue for a world celebration and deserving of international recognition.[10] Other speakers criticized Philadelphia officials who, in 1926, "failed to sell the Sesqui-centennial" fair to *all* its citizens, including ethnic communities. Chicago organizers, they warned, must not repeat the error.[11] They must seek the participation of all the city's diverse population groups. To accomplish this, the organizers proposed a unique promotional strategy in which all residents of the city would become, essentially, individual financial backers. As noted earlier, the plan saw each resident purchasing a five-dollar enrollment subscription. Organizers reasoned that subscribers, who were each awarded ten tickets with the payment, would create a strong demographic base of enthusiastic repeat customers. Further, purchasers would "form a legion of loyal supporters and workers," pledging allegiance and interest by virtue of the subscription.[12] In addition, their contributions at banks, places of employment, and club meetings publicly demonstrated civic pride, and their collective donations brought positive recognition to their ethnic heritage.

Because it focused on European-born residents, Streyckmans's organization held little interest for Chicago's newcomers, especially African Americans and Mexicans. The one effort to engage more recent arrivals took place in May 1928, five months before the Eckener visit. The Committee on Coordination of Nationalities organized a *Pageant of the Nations of the World,* later retitled *Americans All,* for the first town meeting of the Chicago World's Fair and Centennial at the Auditorium Theatre. This event provided an excellent opportunity for Streyckmans to demonstrate to fair organizers and attending city dignitaries his organizational skills, his committee's potential, and his expressed belief that "the history of Chicago was the history of every nation on earth!"[13] To illustrate this, urbanized Native

Americans dressed in beaded moccasins, buckskin garments, and feathered headgear crossed the stage, followed by a procession of thirty-six representative groups of foreign nations and races, suggesting a "colorful pageant of Americanism."[14] All of these groups had contributed to Chicago's growth and prosperity. Photographs of the pageant's representative groups, many in ethnic costume, illustrated the committee newsletter. It is noteworthy that some representatives, including African Americans and Latinos, wore professional clothing rather than costumes for their photographs. These same groups avoided later committee meetings and events.[15]

The Committee on Coordination of Nationalities encouraged friendly rivalry among Chicago's ethnic groups in order to motivate them to action while contrasting supportive Chicagoans to New York ethnics who, in the committee's opinion, had unfairly criticized the Illinois city's fair project.[16] Streyckmans frequently used hyphenated American descriptors for ethnics and wrote to organizations that "it should be clearly understood that this is an organization of Americans of [fill in the nationality] origin, who, like other groups, are able because of their special knowledge and their ties of blood in the old country, to contribute valuable service."[17] In response, the ethnic committees used their own nationalistic language to further motivate their members. For instance, "Brother Vikings" learned that Swedish Americans must continue their tradition of leadership in relationship to other ethnic groups. The opportunity to lead the procession and to show civic pride went out to those "of Germanic blood." Bulgarians, too, could prove their pride in their cultural heritage and demonstrate their celebratory nature by participating in great numbers.[18]

The fair management had stated initially that the most important contribution of ethnic Chicagoans would be to encourage the intellectual leaders of their countries of origin to participate in the fair. Close contact at the fair of "the greatest men in every nation in every line of science, industry, and philosophy with like men of Chicago and this country will result in lasting benefit to this nation and, of course, specifically Chicago."[19] At the same time, fair officials had limited the ways in which organized groups of foreign nationals or their descendants could participate in fair promotion and activities. Groups were welcome to arouse interest, disseminate "accurate information," volunteer for pageants and festivals, and participate in music and sports. They could send information to the foreign press to stimulate interest and encourage their family, friends, and business acquaintances from their homeland to attend. They were not, however, to do anything that could increase costs for foreign participants, suggest what scientific exhibits should be included, or negotiate with foreign governments. In the end, Euro-Americans furnished large audiences as everyone from local workers to ambassadors from Washington attended on national days for the ethnic programs. That translated into turnstile funds, contributing to the success of the fair.

In 1933 the Committee on Nationalities designated thirty-seven days for events featuring a specific ethnic group or country. Groups that had been active in the committee had a day to celebrate their specific culture. For instance, local foreign nationals and ethnic descendants participated in such festivities as Austrian Day and Czechoslovakian Day. Canadians enjoyed a full week of activities, and the Swedes, Danes, Norwegians, and Finns held consecutive daylong celebrations to create a Scandinavian week. Dutch Americans banded together to organize exhibits and activities, resulting in Hollanders' largest gathering in the United States to date. Speeches emphasized the contributions to the growth and progress of America made by their fellow ethnic immigrants. Several groups published souvenir handbooks to document their role in building a great nation.[20] On the other hand, because the committee did not work with many in the local Mexican population, Mexico Day—not Mexican Day—reflected the committee's and fair officials' desire to attract Euro-Americans with an interest in the country and culture of Mexico rather than Mexicans living and working in Chicago.

Chicago's Jewish population was the world's third largest in 1933, exceeded only by that of New York and Warsaw, and represented various countries across central and eastern Europe. The population's significant presence in Chicago definitely made it a force to be considered when planning the fair. According to Meyer Weisgal, executive director of Zionist activities in the Midwest, fair organizers debated for months whether the Jews were a race, a religion, or a nation, which would determine whether they should be represented by a building, an exhibit, or an event.[21]

The success of the Jewish Day event, held at Soldier Field on July 3, 1933, convinced many skeptics—particularly those from among the Jewish community itself—that unity and solidarity among American Jews was indeed possible despite their differing national origins. A few had worried that some Christians would react negatively to a Jewish Day celebration, a perspective that had been reinforced by anti-Semitic acts in previous decades.[22] In response, the Jewish paper *Sentinel* pushed for a large turnout so that Jews could win respect and admiration in addition to building on "the friendly feelings of the wide sympathy felt for Jews because of what was happening in Germany."[23] Despite its various concerns, the Jewish Agency for Palestine mounted an evening spectacle pageant, *Romance of a People*, that drew one of the fair's largest daily attendances, suggesting that bigotry and intolerance were unacceptable in America. The pageant, tracing Jewish people from their beginning to the present time, was such a success that the *Chicago Tribune* newspaper underwrote a reenactment to be held three days later.[24]

Old European Village

Seeking a colorful, entertaining, and richly textured venue for ethnic participants and fairgoers, fair organizers optimistically envisioned a medieval European village on Northerly Island, just south of the planetarium. They imagined a large, open plaza for dances and entertainment, surrounded by pockets of picturesque reproductions of ancient European structures. Charming streets and waterways would wind throughout, encouraging visitors to explore the shops and dine in each village's restaurants. These visitors, who would come from Chicago's diverse European ethnic communities, would naturally want to learn more about their own heritage, and they could not avoid contrasting the charming, antiquated Europe to the vibrant and modern city of Chicago. The villages would allow foreign governments, struggling with economic strife, to pay their way by selling their arts and crafts and operating ethnic eateries, staffed by natives in ethnic costumes.

The idea of an Old European Village developed further as Rufus Dawes and other fair representatives traveled to Europe to visit and study the success and failures of current fairs. The intention was to raise the village idea "to a more dignified plane than that of a mere amusement concession."[25] For instance, at the Antwerp Exhibition they saw an old Belgian village showing early types of building with people in period costumes while Barcelona featured an old Spanish town. By combining individual national villages into one large setting, an enthusiastic Dawes and other organizers hoped to create a financial blockbuster while at the same time segregating ethnic and social activities from educational exhibits. They believed that the villages would be more profitable than the exhibit pavilions, attract more attendees, and promote tourism for the respective European countries. Further, though they stressed the advantages of the "joint village" concept, they did not discourage individual countries from erecting national pavilions—at their own expense, of course. The Old Europe scheme was an alternative based on a successful prototype with minimal costs and maximum returns.[26] Col. John Stephen Sewell headed the fair's foreign participation division. A West Point graduate, he had organized the Seventeenth Railway Engineers and served as its commanding officer in London during the First World War. A gentleman named Lt. Col. Charles Dawes had served under him.

The plan as originally conceived failed. In the end, foreign exhibits and representation took many forms ranging from villages to pavilions operated by concessionaires, ethnic organizations, and foreign governments.[27] Fair authorities had envisioned more countries participating in the fair with their own pavilions or as part of Old Europe Villages, but the economic crisis limited official involvement on a large scale to just a few countries. Further, in 1931 the International Bureau of Exhibitions, meeting in Paris, decided not to participate. The bureau cited deteriorating economic conditions and Chicago crime as factors in its decision, which reinforced other nations' lack of desire to participate.[28] Although several countries, including Czechoslovakia and Sweden, built individual pavilions, others sent exhibits for thematic buildings. Their disinterest in promoting and emphasizing their historical past or even romantic stereotypes at the fair created a void.[29] Local concessionaires saw opportunity and eagerly stepped forward to fill the gap. Inspired by profit rather than authenticity, they replaced most semblances of true ethnic culture with exoticism from the Streets of Paris to the Oriental Village.[30]

Mexico and Italy offer illustrations of different ways in which countries established a presence at the fair. Though the newly established Mexican Republic sent its presidential train to the fair as a symbol of the republic's progress and forward-looking worldview, it left cultural representation to American concessionaires, who hired dancers, singers, and food venders to create a pretense of Mexican culture. Italy, on the other hand, sponsored its own futuristic pavilion and controlled cultural exhibits, events, and entertainment venues by engaging participants from Chicago's Italian population.

Mexico's Representation at the Fair

While fair organizers snubbed the city's Mexican population, they aggressively wooed representation by Mexico itself. The United States' romance with its southern neighbor grew out of a fascination with postrevolutionary Mexico as an exotic and romantic retreat, which Franklin D. Roosevelt's "Good Neighbor Policy," enacted in 1932, nurtured further. As Mexicans migrated north for work, artists and tourists from the United States traveled south seeking new sources of inspiration, a picturesque retreat, and an idealized, vanishing culture.[31] A cultural exchange emerged in art, books, films, and Mexicana decorative arts produced for the American market. Stuart Chase's 1931 book *Mexico: A Study of Two Americas,* which explored the handicraft age versus the machine age and featured illustrations by Diego Rivera, became a best seller.[32] American industrialists such as Nelson Rockefeller pursued Rivera with mural commissions, and Rivera and his wife, the artist Frida Kahlo, spent time in the United States while he worked on these commissions. Meanwhile, exhibits of Mexican art toured the museum circuit. In 1930 and again in 1936, the Art Institute of Chicago staged two exhibitions, "Mexican Arts" and "Mexican Arts and Crafts," which featured native and regional pottery, jewelry, metalwork, and weaving.

During this time of cultural exchange, Mexico's participation and representation at the fair took several forms in order to appeal to Anglo-American imaginations, captivated by the bright colors and festivities of Mexico during the Great Depression. Most significant, an exact replica of a thousand-year old Mayan Temple from the Yucatan stood on the highest ground of the fair.[33] Rufus Dawes, fascinated with the archaeology of ancient cultures, took a personal interest in the execution of this exact temple replica with its elaborate designs originally carved in stone. Dr. Franz Blom, an anthropologist at Tulane University, had led an expedition to Uxmal, Mexico, to study one section of the Puget site Nunnery and to make casts of the details on the ornate facade: masks of the rain god Chac, serpents, and lattice work. Carlos Contreras, a noted Mexican architect and city planner, visited Chicago as chief of the Mexican government's planning commission to inspect the site and view the reproduction casts.[34] When completed, the replica monument allowed fair visitors to view such "relics of the artistic and engineering genius of the lost civilization of America" as feathered costumes, pottery, forms of currency, jade and obsidian carvings, household goods and tools, drums, miniature masks, and even war trophy shrunken human heads.[35] Because it was an official goal of the fair to promote the progress of social sciences, the fifty-cent fair admission price included admission to the temple.

The Chicago world's fair featured Mexican Villages in both 1933 and 1934, but these concessions did not emerge from a Mexican fair commission and could hardly be called representative. American businessmen established these venues to provide entertainment and produce revenue by drawing fairgoers to the charm of "Old Mexico." For a modest entrance fee, these villages offered visitors a mix of Mexican folklore, educational exhibits, food, music, and dancing. Other events around the fairgrounds also promoted Mexican culture and the village, including the Típica Police Band of fifty-five instrumentalists, singers, and dancers; and the World's Fair Rodeo, performing twice daily and starring Mexican musicians, dancing señoritas, and Gen. Jesus Jayme Quinones and his troupe of famous and daring Charro horsemen from Mexico City.[36] In shops along the charming, recreated village streets, imported workers wove, carved leather, and made tortillas while costumed natives rode around the picturesque cobblestone streets on burro-drawn carts. Mexican potters demonstrated the making of small pots that could then be fired and sold to the tourists. But the major attraction in both years was the Old Mexico Night Club with its orchestra, dancing, and hourly floor shows, some of which strained organizers' ideas of acceptability. A newspaper advertisement in 1933 announced that Old Mexico was "the talk of the fair—and there are reasons!"[37]

Entertainers at the village offered only a hint of true Mexican culture while concessionaires aimed solely at profits. Hot-cha San the acrobatic dancer, Dorreane and Douglass (actually Euro-Americans), and the sensational Rosalia's Fan Dance lured the public to the nightclub.[38] Concessionaires hired Arthur Bublitz and Lenore Felden, who dressed in Mexican folkloric costumes, to interpret the *jarabe tapatío*, or Mexican hat dance, for the fair's white, middle-class clientele. Rosalia provided a Latin version of Sally Rand's fan dance for sensation seekers as the high-heeled brunette danced, deftly maneuvering bright red ostrich feathers to conceal her grease-painted nudity.

Fair authorities wanted to stop what it considered objectionable shows, but their legal counsel advised them to avoid litigation and wait for the South Park Commissioners to take action. Difficult questions included concerns over what constituted covering, how many threads were necessary for a fabric cover to cover, or how to determine the quality of transparency. Although the management of the Mexican Village concession promised to "be good" in its future floor shows, the performances featuring the "sizzling finale" continued.[39]

Despite its "hot" floor show, Old Mexico suffered financially in 1933, so a different concessionaire created the Mexican Village for 1934 in a new, hopefully more profitable, location on the fairgrounds near his financially strapped Hollywood attraction. During the off-season, a barge moved sections of the village from the south end of the fairgrounds to the Midway section of Northerly Island. The Mexican Village offered visitors new attractions, including a replica of the Cathedral of Cuernavaca and the Acatapec church with an Amacameca chapel. A hall, fronting on a public square used for music and dancing, housed government exhibits of modern Mexico's art, industry, and handicrafts. The village featured works by Mexican muralists, including originals by Diego Rivera and photographs of his Radio City murals at Rockefeller Center in New York City. Nelson Rockefeller had ordered the murals destroyed because of the inclusion of the communist Vladimir Lenin's portrait and Rivera's refusal to replace it.[40] Even with special events planned to attract new visitors, the second Mexican Village also suffered financially and the concessionaire filed for bankruptcy.

The festive cultural experience presented by the villages offered one lens through which to view America's southern neighbor. The new Republic of Mexico provided another by dispatching its presidential train carrying recently excavated jewels from Monte Alban, Oaxaca. The intent was to announce the republic as a scientifically progressive and economically successful nation. Positioned in the outdoor railroad exhibit near the Travel and Transport Building, the train promoted tourism by rail to Mexico's many historical sites. The palatial coaches, built by Chicago's Pullman Company, advanced the image of a modern industrial state linked by the latest rail network technology; the jewels of gold, silver, jade, turquoise, and pearl on display hinted of the treasures to be found to the south. The president's private train with its luxurious interiors, including a dining room set for a royal feast, stood with the fast and luxurious British *Royal Scot* and the air conditioned, streamlined American designs. Its presence continued the tradition of Mexico's participation at world's fairs, and it publicized the new republic's place as a modern, successful nation in the Western world of technological progress.[41]

Eugenio Pesqueiro, the Mexican consul general in Chicago, worked with business representatives from Mexico to develop an exchange of ideas with Chicago and fair business leaders. On Mexico Day, July 21, 1934, twenty-six representatives of Mexican industry met with Pesqueiro and the Mexican consuls from San Antonio and New York City; Chicago's Mexican industrialists and civic leaders; and local members of the Lion's International for a luncheon at its headquarters. They then visited the fair's General Exhibits group to dedicate a world time clock and to tour the International Business Machine (IBM) exhibit before hearing speeches and Mexican music. Finally, in the Mexican Village they dedicated the Government of Mexico's exhibit of handicraft works on loan from Mexico City's Commercial Museum.[42]

The national image of Mexico took many forms at the fair, mixing official and unofficial perspectives. The fairgrounds offered a world between Mexico and the United States where government officials, artists, businessmen, scholars, citizens, and immigrants could participate and interact to portray Mexico as a modern country of historical significance with a strong arts and cultural tradition. Ironically, the Near West Side neighborhood, the largest Mexican colony in Chicago, was only a mile west of the fairgrounds. There Mexican immigrants danced the hat dance in their native costumes for the annual Mexican fiesta at Jane Addams's Hull-House settlement complex.[43] Also at Hull-House, local Mexican workers learned English, played music, organized social groups, and made pottery decorated with indigenous designs evocative of their homeland. Concessionaires did not employ these Mexican immigrants, many of whom needed jobs, even though they had experience demonstrating crafts at the Hull-House Shop on Michigan Avenue and would have been more authentic than many of the Mexican Night Club's floor show dancers.

Mexicans in Chicago struggled to survive the dire conditions of their neighborhoods and the workplace, often with limited English-language skills. Many lost their jobs before American-born ethnics did. Because the census records did not find all undocumented workers for an accurate count, fair officials underestimated by many thousands the number of Mexicans living in Chicago by 1930. The Near West Side neighborhood, anchored by Hull-House, teemed with Mexican-owned businesses and Mexican cultural organizations.[44] Many Mexicans arrived in Chicago only to discover that they needed to rethink their own identity when faced with the discrimination of Euro-Americans who saw Mexicans as one homogeneous people of color rather than as a varied people from diverse local regions and cultures.[45] The 1933–34 world's fair simply did not meet the needs for education and amusement of many Mexicans in Chicago, nor did it offer them work. Further, the Mexican Villages presented an anglicized version of Mexican culture that could not compete with the authentic culture that immigrants could find in their own neighborhoods, churches, sports teams, and fiestas.

Italy's Representation at the Fair

Just as Mexico's presence at the fair announced the young republic as a progressive and culturally rich nation, so too did Italy's. The fascist regime, however, intended its presence to make an even more sweeping statement, one that expressed the recaptured military prowess of a nation recently bowed by Western powers. In 1930 and 1931, fair authorities wooed Italian officials in America, including the commercial attaché, the consul general, and the ambassador, before sending fair representatives on two trips to Rome to join American diplomats in meetings with the foreign secretary, foreign office officials, the minister of commerce, and members of the bureau of tourism.[46] The final decision rested with Mussolini, who found the opportunity to show off his accomplishments irresistible. Italy sent so many official exhibits that some had to be housed in the Hall of Science, the nearby Adler Planetarium, and the Museum of Science and Industry several miles south of the fairgrounds. That Mussolini had appropriated air technology as symbolic of his fascist government revealed the power of aviation imagery in the popular imagination. That he saw a need to promote that imagery as synonymous with his government rule was not necessarily a novel idea, but that he had spared no expense to send that message to an international exposition in Chicago during the Great Depression was surprising.

Mussolini's decision to participate in the fair ignited wild enthusiasm among Chicago's Italians, most of them oblivious to or disinterested in Mussolini's politics. A huge crowd stopped all traffic in Chicago on the evening of July 15, 1933, when Mussolini's premiere air navigator, Gen. Italo Balbo, circled his fleet of twenty-four planes over the city. The deafening roar of the crowds lining the lakefront competed with loudspeakers, automobile horns, factory sirens, and military gun salutes as the fleet performed a water landing in Lake Michigan near the fairgrounds. With this extraordinary show Balbo had realized his dream of flying his aerial armada to America, the birthplace of flight and the global leader in technical progress and aviation development. He brought an oral message of a new Italy and eternal friendship from the fascist leader of his home country plus a visual message that Italy was a contender in the future of aviation progress. He provided the proudest moment in the history of Chicago's Italian community, which had suffered from so much negative press regarding organized crime. The press hailed Balbo as the Christopher Columbus of the twentieth century.

Balbo's warm reception translated into permanent honors in the city. Chicago's Italian community unveiled a statue in honor of Columbus in Grant Park near the main entrance of the fair on Italian Day, August 3. Inscribed on the base of the statue was a tribute to Balbo. The Italian ambassador, who had been a passenger in Balbo's plane, Italian American community leaders, and politicians spoke of the friendship between Italy and the United States.[47] To add permanence to the tribute, the city christened the inner drive, which ran through the park and past the fairgrounds, Columbus Drive. Only a few weeks earlier, the city had renamed nearby Seventh Street as Balbo Drive to honor the fascist aviator. During Balbo's visit, the Italian consul general told Mayor Kelly that Mussolini intended to present Chicago with an ancient Roman column, which the city should mount facing the anchorage site of the Italian squadrons. Mussolini believed that this historic artifact would not only symbolize his achievement of bringing the air armada across the Atlantic but would also reinforce fascist propaganda that equated the old and new worlds of Italian government as progressive leaders. Before the column's installation on Italian Day in the following year, Balbo wrote that "eternal Rome will receive in the shadow of the skyscrapers the homage of the builders of the new civilization for this column which symbolized her constructive power."[48]

Balbo's flight, which had originally been planned to coincide with the unveiling of the statue, reinforced the Italian government's already strong presence at the exposition and the message that Italy was vital and resilient despite the depression in Europe and America.[49] Beyond the main entrance and down the Avenue of Flags stood the Italian Pavilion. Designed by a group of Italian architects to represent a giant airplane, it was a dramatic modernist showcase of light, line, and glass suggesting Italy's scientific accomplishments. The architectural designs and details, including furniture, created a sleek, stark, and visually impressive space. *Architectural Forum* noted that the dominating theme of the "fascist ax" returned again and again, reinforcing the force and frankness of Mussolini's new era.[50] Inside, 450 exhibits told the story of engineering feats ranging from the draining of ancient marshes to the building of airplane engines. Around the main rotunda, a global map showed fascist Italy's transportation facilities and routes by land, water, and air. Photo murals promoted the scenic aspects of the country and reinforced the message of progress in both its old and new civilizations through such juxtaposed images as aviation scenes and Rome's Coliseum. In the section of science exhibits featuring model planes and air engines, the text label above the exhibit claimed to show "how Italy contributed to the greatest inventions of this century of progress."[51] Wine displays and a Venetian glassblowing factory sought to lure American tourists to visit an Italy that honored its traditions in the midst of its great renewal.[52]

Many Italians, proud of the pavilion and overcome by Balbo's patriotic deeds, demeanor, and words, celebrated his arrival and followed the fascist protocol without a total understanding of the policies of Il Duce. Although enthralled and enthusiastic over the accomplishment of Balbo and his crew, America did not blindly endorse fascist politics. Critics of the Italian participation in the fair distributed leaflets and wrote letters to the press, but Balbo reported to Mussolini that he found no evidence of antifascism.[53] Under heavy police protection, occupied with receptions and dinners, and surrounded by pro-Italy dignitaries and citizens, he either missed the protests or felt it prudent to ignore them.

Teresa DeFalco, a resident in Chicago's Italian immigrant neighborhood and a cigarette girl at the Italian Pavilion, was proud to be chosen as one of the two young women, one brunette and one blond, to present flowers to the handsome, goateed Balbo. She felt it was a beautiful, joyous occasion with all of the pilots in their dress white uniforms participating in parades and festivities for several days. She joined several crew members at one of their banquet tables and toured the city with them by car. She recalled that everyone wore fascist buttons and learned a fascist song because they were "real proud of being a fascist, but we didn't know what it meant."[54]

An Italian government representative at the Italian Pavilion had prepared people well for the event by implementing rituals and symbols that reinforced the message of the exhibits. The message coupled the old and new Italy in a powerful "invented tradition" that both symbolized the social cohesion of Italian Americans with Italy and legitimized Mussolini's authority.[55] While local immigrants may have admired some of the accomplishments of Mussolini, in Chicago there was massive indifference to his politics, and efforts to establish local fascist groups had failed. Italian Americans found themselves drawn by a nostalgic nationalism—kinship, language, religion, and customs—to the Italian cultural representations at the exposition while at the same time they felt no conflict with their allegiance to their new homeland.[56]

Most of Chicago's immigrant and ethnic groups responded positively to fair activities and displays of their homelands' culture and political aspirations. As will be shown, German Americans, who vehemently objected to Germany's use of the fair to spread Nazi propaganda, provided the one significant exception. Most fair celebrations—the naming of the fair thoroughfare Leif Erickson Drive, the dedication of the statue of Christopher Columbus, and the honoring of ethnic heroes, for instance—reinforced the reality of the United States as "home" by pointing to contributions of their ethnic groups in the building of a great city and nation. Clearly, these commemorations strengthened ethnic identity and social status within a new *American* identity.

In addition, virtually all Chicago's ethnic groups clung fast to America's social, political, and economic systems, which accepted ethnic if not racial multiculturalism and embraced capitalism. They continued to believe in America's changing vision of liberty and the pursuit of happiness. Despite difficulties brought on by the Great Depression, they hoped for a better tomorrow and believed they would find it in America. Along with the broader American population, they rejected revolution and "new and dangerous government experiments."[57] While worker affluence might have been the reason that they did not see radical revolution as the solution to their economic woes or that a society that celebrated individualism could not assume a collective identity, it might also have been that "the ruling myths of security and pluralism renewed popular faith in the state."[58] In fact, the prevailing Horatio Alger myth reinforced by the actual upward mobility of many immigrant groups gave recent arrivals encouragement and offered multigeneration ethnics in America direct evidence that hard work did lead to the American dream of a better life.

Representations of Italy and Mexico at the fair created cultural bonds for immigrants and their descendants as well as for prospective tourists and businessmen. The Balbo flight demonstrated that the Italian military had conquered time and space; the Italian Pavilion reinforced the reputation of Italian architects and futurist artists as designers in the forefront of the modernism movement; and the exhibits identified Italy as a world leader. When the Mexican government offered its presidential train brimming with historical artifacts as an attraction, it followed a long tradition of using the rails to promote its image as one of the world's advanced, industrialized, and progressive nations. In this, Mexico actually highlighted its ties to a fast-fading past. Although in the nineteenth century the iron horse had represented engineering mastery and technological progress, the twentieth century belonged to aviation. International exhibitions have provided a forum for the evidence of this, and the 1933 fair organizers sought to feed the public's insatiable appetite for demonstrations of air power.

The Swiss Village was one of many "Old World" concessions designed to attract fairgoers through replica architecture, folk dancing, craft demonstrations, shops, and outdoor cafés.

The Belgium Village folk dancers performed on an open stage while crowds sat at cafés drinking beer legally for the first time since Prohibition had ended.

Euro-American dancers dressed as Mexicans performed the popular Mexican hat dance in the Mexican village. A Century of Progress Records (COP neg. 190), Special Collections and University Archives Department, University Library, University of Illinois at Chicago.

The Mexican Village concession recreated picturesque cobblestone streets with burro-drawn carts and pottery demonstrations. The major attraction was the Old Mexico Night Club with its orchestra, dancing, and hourly floor shows.

The futuristic Italian Pavilion, designed by Italian architects to represent a giant airplane, was a dramatic modernist showcase of light, line, and glass, suggesting Italy's scientific accomplishments. A Century of Progress Records (COP neg. 100), Special Collections and University Archives Department, University Library, University of Illinois at Chicago.

The Italian Pavilion housed 450 exhibits displaying examples of Italy's engineering feats. The exhibits reinforced the message of progress in Italy's old and new civilizations through juxtaposed aviation murals and images of Rome's Coliseum and other monuments. A Century of Progress Records (COP neg. 98), Special Collections and University Archives Department, University Library, University of Illinois at Chicago.

Crowds lined Chicago's lakefront when General Italo Balbo and his fleet of twenty-four planes arrived, declaring Italy a global leader in technical progress and aviation development. Howard A. Bauman, Photographer; Bauman Family Collection, West Bend, Wisconsin.

The flight of Germany's *Graf Zeppelin* to Chicago demonstrated the era's shift in transportation technology from the rails to the air and the role of politics and nationalism in aviation.

A CENTURY OF PROGRESS 1933

'ZEPPELIN-TAG' CHICAGO, ILL. U.S.A.

At a reception to honor the German ambassador and the *Graf Zeppelin*'s visit, National Socialists sold postcards that illustrated the *Graf Zeppelin*, the Travel and Transport Building, and Commander Hugo Eckener.

A few minutes after 3 A.M., thousands of spectators watched preparations for the liftoff of the stratosphere balloon *A Century of Progress*.

8

Aviation, Nationalism, and Progress

May both our countries continue to contest the heights in every sphere
of science and technique.

—Maxim Litvinoff, cablegram to Lt. Cmdr. Thomas "Tex" Settle

Approaching Chicago at daybreak on September 26, 1933, Commander
Hugo Eckener ordered the *Graf Zeppelin*, a 775-foot-long German airship, to
fly west beyond the city and then circle clockwise, although a northerly route
from Indiana with an approach to Chicago from the east over Lake Michigan
would have been more expeditious.[1] After circling above the city for about
an hour, the *Graf Zeppelin* flew north to suburban Glenview for a brief exchange of passengers and mail.[2] Willy von Meister, the United States special
representative of Luftschiffbau Zeppelin G.m.b.H., the Zeppelin Company,
was in the control car with Eckener during the approach to Chicago. He asked
why Eckener had not taken the shorter circle. "And let my friends in Chicago
see the swastikas?" asked Eckener, who had a doctorate in psychology. Adolf
Hitler, leader of the National Socialist Party, had become chancellor of Germany earlier that year. The German government had required the Zeppelin
Company to paint the National Socialists' swastika banner, which was one
of two official German flags, on the port side of the upper and lower tail fins.[3]
Rather than display the two red billboards featuring twenty-foot swastikas,
Eckener preferred to show Chicagoans the starboard side of the craft, which
featured the traditional tricolor German flag.[4]

While Mexico and Italy each sent symbols of technological progress to
the fair, Germany's *Graf Zeppelin* became the fair's most powerful and divi-
sive emblem of national identity. The flight of the *Graf Zeppelin* to Chicago
demonstrated not only this era's shift in transportation technology from the

rails to the air, but also the role of politics and nationalism in aviation as the German Zeppelin Company sought to establish a global transportation network. The importation of the swastika symbol may have promoted National Socialism for some, but it disrupted the German American community in Chicago and forced it to reevaluate its nationalistic identity. While the Zeppelin Company sought to conquer the oceans with a zeppelin transit system and to further its global respectability, the United States had already moved beyond establishing commercial air routes and looked to establish itself as the progressive technological frontrunner by exploring a new frontier: outer space.

Aviation Technology at the Fair

In the early stages of preparation, fair officials focused on representing the history and progress of train technology as well as that of flight. After all, Chicago had a reputation as the rail hub of the continent, and rail companies were struggling to find ways to entice the traveling public back to trains. Fair officials hired Edward Hungerford, who had staged the 1927 Baltimore railroad Fair of the Iron Horse, to coordinate their train exhibit. He planned and organized exhibits for the Travel and Transport complex and wrote the historical pageant *Wings of a Century: The Romance of Transportation* for an open-air stage.[5] Travel and Transport's main building featured pioneer engines and cars showing the development of the rail industry from steam to electric and from iron to stainless steel. The luxury express *Royal Scot* of the London Midland and Scottish Railway of Great Britain stood near the Chicago and North Western line's mammoth class "H" locomotive.

Many exhibits, such as the Burlington's, placed smaller, vintage engines and passenger cars next to larger, newer models to dramatize the speed and power difference. To emphasize progress, the Pullman Company of Chicago placed its first Pullman car next to its latest design, a triumph of engineering progress, which featured a contemporary décor in brushed aluminum, indirect lighting, air conditioning, and rounded observation windows in the rear, offering greater visibility. For the fair's reopening in 1934, the streamlined, stainless steel Burlington *Pioneer Zephyr* broke long-distance nonstop records when it arrived from Denver, having averaged over seventy-seven miles per hour for more than a thousand miles, to be added to the display in the Travel and Transport complex.[6] Despite the speed and high-tech glass, efforts to modernize and increase rail travel would be challenged as new materials, new inventions, new designs, and a new form of transportation captured the imagination of industry, the military, and the public: air transport.

Chicago's Municipal Airport had more scheduled flights than any other airport in the world by 1930, making Chicago the aviation operations center for the United States and extending its status as the transportation hub of America from rail to air. The exposition's aviation exhibits and events reflected an industry that had captured the Western imagination at a time when America, the birthplace of powered heavier-than-air flight, was experiencing its own golden age of racing, expansion, and exploration in all kinds of aircraft from fixed-wing planes to airships.[7]

As staff of the Smithsonian Institution's United States National Museum prepared federal exhibits, they realized that "the exhibit which would attract the greatest public attention" "would be one visualizing the story of progress in aviation."[8] The exposition therefore featured aeronautical displays in the official cooperative exhibits of the Travel and Transport Building, where United Airlines suspended a Boeing 247, the world's first modern airliner, from the interior dome to advertise the airline's leadership in America's commercial domestic air travel.[9] In addition to aeronautical exhibits interspersed with shows of other modes of transport, a concession exhibit building at the fair boasted exhibits entirely about flight. The Air Show was devoted to developing airmindedness.[10] Here visitors could see pioneer, military, and ultramodern 1933 models of aircraft, plus engines, accessories, and model planes. Cal Rodgers's *Vin Fiz* Wright biplane, which had made a well-publicized transcontinental flight, hung near a Blériot XI monoplane similar to the one that first crossed the English Channel. In contrast, larger and faster commercial and military planes clearly highlighted how far aviation had progressed in the thirty years since the Wright brothers had made their first flight at Kitty Hawk.

In addition to static exhibits of aircraft, fairgoers could see planes and airships in flight. Daily demonstrations of the Adams airmail pickup method showed how a plane in flight could pick up a sack of mail or drop it. These planes carried souvenir mail between the fairgrounds and Municipal Airport. Rides in a kite balloon, a Sikorsky amphibian plane, or a Goodyear blimp thrilled passengers by offering panoramic aerial views for a fee. The Goodyear-Zeppelin Corporation and the U.S. Navy flew the airship *Macon* over the Chicago fairgrounds on its fourth and final test flight to demonstrate the future of lighter-than-air aviation.

The fair's 1933 international Gordon Bennett Balloon Race and Air Races brought participation from several European countries and the United States vying to establish new aeronautical records. The races took place at Curtiss-Wright-Reynolds Field in suburban Glenview, with cash prizes sponsored by the press. The hydrogen-filled balloons lifted off one by one on a windy day, bound for their distance competition. The Polish team outdistanced the American, German, Belgian, and French teams when it landed 846 miles later in Quebec, Canada. Pilots of airplanes competed in speed races for various divisions, with special events for women pilots and parachute jumpers. Flyers from seven countries and from the United States Army and Navy participated. A special guest pilot was Maj. Ernst Udet, Germany's flying war ace. Jimmy Wedell set a new world's speed record for land planes when he broke 300 mph. Interestingly, while the four-day event brought renewed attention to air racing, those who supported the expansion of private and commercial flight believed that air races promoted the image of aircraft for military use and reinforced negative perceptions of air safety.[11]

Aviation as a Powerful National Metaphor

After Wilbur and Orville Wright's first sustained, powered, manned flight in 1903, Americans identified the airplane as a symbol of adventure, military might, progress, and the future. Flight reduced distance and time for travel, mail delivery, industrial shipping, and military transport. For many in the 1920s it became a secular religion, and as Joseph J. Corn has written, people's expectations for "the winged gospel" included enhanced mobility, enlarged prosperity, cultural uplift, and even social harmony.[12] By the time of the 1933 Chicago world's fair, some government leaders had appropriated the images of aircraft and the aviation industry as powerful, futuristic, and symbolic of their political prowess.

Americans and Europeans alike spent the first decades of the century eagerly following the expansion of aircraft technology and applauding each new accomplishment, from Louis Blériot's first flight across the English Channel to the Latin American and transpacific survey flights of Pan American's Clippers. They attended air meets, flew with barnstormers, posted airmail, and decorated their homes with aviation memorabilia. Italians held their share of aviation triumphs during the pioneer era, including the issuance of the first airmail postage stamp and the 1926 crossing of the North Pole by the semirigid airship *Norge*, piloted by Gen. Umberto Nobile. The prestige Charles A. Lindbergh achieved after his 1927 nonstop solo transatlantic flight in the *Spirit of St. Louis* announced to Americans that their status as enterprising entrepreneurs capable of conquering new territory and demonstrating pioneer individualism remained intact.[13]

Germans had been celebrating the progress of zeppelins since Count Ferdinand von Zeppelin flew his first design, the LZ1, on July 2, 1900. The zeppelin had become a symbol not only of German nationalism, but also of the nation's economic resurgence. Zeppelin fever, reflecting the pride and awe of the Germans for these masterpieces of airship technology, ran rampant. German airship technology first linked to nationalism in 1908 when a spontaneous public outpouring of funds followed the destruction of Zeppelin's fourth dirigible, the LZ4. After World War I, the Zeppelin Company and many aviation supporters promoted airships as the vehicles of the future for long-distance travel and transport, connecting the airship routes to local airline routes. Airminded Americans also caught zeppelin fever, a contagious enthusiasm sweeping the country as airships floated overhead.[14]

German Nationalism and the German American Community

The LZ127 *Graf Zeppelin*, completed in 1928, was indeed a technological wonder.[15] Silver-doped cotton and linen covered an intricate duralumin girder framework, which housed seventeen hydrogen gas cells. Designed as a commercial aircraft for long-distance transport with accommodations for twenty passengers and a crew of more than forty men, it could fly ten thousand miles without refueling. By 1933, Hugo Eckener had commanded this zeppelin around the world and to the Arctic before establishing regular commercial service to South America. A Chicago newspaper editorial praised Eckener and the *Graf Zeppelin* visit to Chicago as emphasizing the internationality of A Century of Progress and the kind of progress the fair was designed to celebrate.[16]

As a symbol of Germany and its technological progress, the *Graf Zeppelin* captured the public's imagination and ultimately became an international emblem of goodwill and cooperation. But another symbol, the swastika, broadcast anti-Semitism and Hitler's National Socialist policies. The swastika clearly inspired racial pride and patriotic obedience in Nazi followers, but it antagonized or embarrassed many German Americans, who, in 1933, formed one of the largest ethnic groups in Chicago.[17] Dr. Otto L. Schmidt and Karl Eitel, active leaders of the German Group of the World's Fair, had been spokesmen for German patriotic support in Chicago during America's neutrality phase before the First World War. Despite their gospel of patriotism, when the United States joined the war, anti-German sentiment and overtly hostile acts forced German Americans to downplay their German heritage and language.[18] Through the late 1920s, German Americans gradually recovered from these negative experiences. With an improved image, they reasserted their political power and ethnic pride as they sought political unity among themselves.[19]

The much-anticipated visit of the *Graf Zeppelin* further boosted their revitalized ethnic pride. Eckener's idea of a zeppelin's visiting the 1933 fair can be traced to the early organizing period as well as to the enthusiasm of the German American community and the airshipmindedness of Chicagoans. Besides thrilling fairgoers, especially German Americans, Eckener wanted to promote the friendly international cooperation that would be necessary to achieve his life's goal: world traffic by airship. In the previous year the Zeppelin Company had initiated the first regular transatlantic air service, demonstrating that zeppelins could indeed provide timely service regardless of meteorological conditions.[20] The company negotiated for a zeppelin facility in Seville, Spain, and arranged funding to build a zeppelin hangar near Rio de Janeiro in Brazil. Although Eckener had once selected Chicago as the only terminal in America in an international commercial airship plan, by 1933 he no longer considered a Chicago port feasible for the start of commercial service.[21] Nevertheless, he told the press that he hoped that a Berlin–Chicago line would become an actuality within a few years.[22]

Eckener needed to arrange adequate financing before committing to the special flight to Chicago for the fair, and so he proposed sharing profits from the sale of a special zeppelin postage stamp to be issued by the United States Post Office Department. On August 1, 1933, the Zeppelin Company responded to an official invitation from Rufus Dawes as president of A Century of Progress. Eckener ac-

cepted the invitation, saying that the LZ127 would visit Chicago as an extension of the final trip of the 1933 season to Brazil if the United States Post Office
Department would issue the zeppelin postage stamp. The plan was not unique.
Philatelists had already financed several special flights of the *Graf Zeppelin.* The
post office had issued two postage stamp issues for A Century of Progress in late
May, just before the exposition opened. As a result, postal officials had rejected
the fair management's request for a third denomination.[23] Eager for the flight and
its anticipated goodwill, Meister, the Zeppelin Company representative, traveled
to Washington to meet with postal officials and convinced Postmaster General
James A. Farley of the need for a special stamp.[24]

President Franklin D. Roosevelt's lack of support for the stamp threatened
to bury the idea and create diplomatic problems with Germany. The Bureau of
Engraving and Printing, which designed and printed postage stamps for the Post
Office Department, had prepared three designs of the stamp to be presented to
Roosevelt for his final approval. The president immediately protested that "this
zeppelin is just toddling back and forth across the ocean. I don't see why a stamp
should be issued again for it," and he used his authority to reject the issue.[25] Negotiations followed, and Secretary of State Cordell Hull advised that the breach
of diplomacy resulting from the rejection of the stamp issue would be a disaster.
Rudolf Leitner, the German chargé in Washington, D.C., pleaded with Hull that the
failure of the Post Office Department to carry out its agreement would be entirely
misunderstood in many parts of Germany and that the sensational section of the
press would exploit the entire matter in a way that would be very disagreeable all
around.[26] Eckener had arrived in New York two days earlier to complete flight arrangements. He traveled to Washington, D.C., to discuss with Farley the fact that
the postage revenue was the determining factor in deciding whether the Chicago
flight would take place. In addition, they negotiated the future establishment of
regular transatlantic airmail service.[27]

Further negotiations settled specific details. Remarkably, the new zeppelin
stamp was available for use at the New York City post office just ten days later.
As printed, the fifty-cent green stamp depicted the *Graf Zeppelin* without the
swastika, the Federal Building at the Chicago fair, and one of the zeppelin hangars
in Friedrichshafen, Germany.[28] The United States Post Office Department would
receive 15 percent of the fifty-cent rate. The remaining forty-two and a half cents
would be paid to the German Postal Administration to help offset the expenses
of the Zeppelin Company for operating the *Graf Zeppelin* at a cost of about $300
an hour.[29] The Zeppelin Company expected to realize $10,000 from the United
States stamp sales, but it actually realized several times that amount. Over 100,000
American stamps on souvenir envelopes were flown in addition to mail carried
from Germany, Brazil, and more than sixty other countries.

In addition to the zeppelin's proposed visit to A Century of Progress, German
Americans viewed the fair as an opportunity to showcase German music, art, and

culture as well as the contributions of Germans and German Americans to the development of the United States.[30] Chicago's German Americans represented Germany in special events and with a "German American" building in the exhibition fairgrounds.[31] Fair authorities, in cooperation with the Department of State, had courted German businessmen and government officials for official German government participation, but they had been unsuccessful due to the economic crisis and the changing politics in Germany.[32] The Robert Koch Institute of Berlin and the Deutsches Hygiene Museum of Dresden sent scientific and medical exhibits, including the popular life-size Transparent Man.[33]

Changing politics in the mother country stirred contention among Chicago's German Americans. Conflict brewed when political supporters of National Socialism, including German government representatives and postwar immigrants, demanded that the swastika flag be flown at the German American building at the fair. Other members of the German American community objected. Under the new German government in 1933, Germany officially had two flags: one of three equal horizontal stripes of black, red, and yellow from top to bottom; and the other, a field of red with a round white center containing a black swastika.[34] The advisory committee of the German national group refused to fly the swastika despite the plea from Consul General Hugo Simon. The members of the committee who objected to the flag thought that it might be regarded as a Nazi Party flag or even as an anti-Semitic symbol rather than as a German Reich flag.[35] The debate intensified when during one of the dedication speeches in August 1933, leaders of the Friends of the New Germany (Bund der Freunde des Neuen Deutschland) removed the traditional German flag and daringly replaced it with the swastika. Fritz Gissibl, leader of this newly organized Midwest Bund, and more recent German immigrants ardently supported Hitler and the Nazi Party.[36] After heated words over what symbols should represent German and German Americans in Chicago at an international venue, the German Group of the World's Fair threatened to call the police if the swastika was not lowered. The dedication ceremony resumed without the swastika flag on display.

Adding to August's conflict, swastikas drawn in chalk appeared on downtown Chicago newsstands and on the front of buildings.[37] While some younger German Americans and recent German immigrants thought that the rise of the New Germany coincided with the rebirth of German culture in America, older German Americans as well as second- and third-generation German Americans denied that the National Socialist government represented their vision of German character. They feared a revival of the anti-German sentiments that still haunted their memories from a decade earlier, and they warned German Americans against consolidating under the auspices of organizations originating in Berlin.[38]

Chicago's Jewish population expressed concerns over the intensifying conflict. Women's Aid, a Jewish women's organization, requested assurance that the swastika would not fly at the fair and threatened to withdraw participation on

Women's Day if it did. Marie Becker, president of the German American Hostess Society, assured the presidents of seventy-five women's organizations that not only had the German Group of the World's Fair prohibited the use of the anti-Semitic flag but that the exhibit that had been shipped after the opening of the fair by the German government also would not be exhibited at the fair.[39] On German Day, the committee again refused to allow the swastika to be displayed in the parade. As a result, the local Friends of the New Germany announced that its members would not participate in the German Day celebration.[40]

Meanwhile, preparations for the *Graf Zeppelin*'s flight continued. Meister traveled to Chicago in August to investigate potential zeppelin landing sites and to make necessary arrangements.[41] There he informed the fair president that the *Graf Zeppelin*, operating under the auspices of the German government, would fly the flags of the German government, including the swastika. He then posed the issue of possible protests by Jewish citizens in response to Nazi harassment of German Jews and laws that stripped them of German citizenship. Rufus Dawes replied that the fair would seek the advice of the Department of State and abide by its recommendations.[42] Dawes wanted to be prepared for a possible demonstration against the swastika emblem or the arrival of the pro-Nazi German ambassador, Hans Luther.[43] He held a conference with the army and navy representatives in Chicago and delegated Ulysses Grant Smith, an American diplomat, to communicate with the Department of State.[44]

Dawes had reason to take the situation seriously. Earlier that year, in May, fifty thousand Chicago Jews had gathered in Grant Park to protest the Nazi burning of books written by Jewish authors and to urge fair officials to refuse to receive Dr. Paul Joseph Goebbels as the German representative to A Century of Progress. Goebbels, the Nazi minister of propaganda, sent a staff member to study the organization and advertising methods of the world's fair a week later. He was met by a thousand protesters at the Brooklyn dock. Tensions heightened when on September 28, protesters blocked traffic and swung clubs as Ambassador Luther arrived at a luncheon in Milwaukee.[45] Throughout the summer, Jewish leaders had promoted a national anti-German boycott movement to fight Hitlerism and its anti-Semitic policies. By the time of the *Graf Zeppelin* visit, the American Federation of Labor supported the boycott.[46]

This political unrest led to security worries for the airship, crew, guests, and hosts. The Post Office Department made special arrangements to examine all mail and parcels intended for delivery to the zeppelin. Farley also requested that local authorities cooperate to assure proper protection for passengers and the crew.[47] Chicago contacts warned Eckener that a potentially disagreeable reception was brewing and that, at the very least, a tense atmosphere awaited the arrival of the *Graf Zeppelin* in Chicago.[48]

A navy serviceman informed Meister, who was in Akron awaiting the *Graf Zeppelin*'s arrival from Miami, of menacing letters and a bomb threat in Chicago.

A tense discussion followed. Should the airship fly to Chicago? If so, should it land? Dawes informed Meister that he could not unqualifiedly advise Eckener on whether to make the trip and land in Chicago. Meister phoned the Cook County sheriff, William D. Meyering, to report that he was sorry, but, due to the bomb threat, he worried that security was inadequate for a landing in Chicago. Meyering replied, "Bring that zepp to Chicago and no one will get near it without your and my authorization."[49]

Eckener adhered to his flight plans with some changes. He decided to fly to Chicago and make a short landing in a closed field. The day before the *Graf Zeppelin*'s arrival in Chicago, the press announced that the great airship would arrive about nine o'clock the next morning. In fact, the *Graf Zeppelin* arrived three and a half hours earlier. Eckener cancelled plans to fly to Milwaukee and return to the fair in the late afternoon. Because of the disinformation provided to the press and the sheriff's order to close the airport to those without passes, only a few hundred spectators were on hand at the landing field besides the landing crew, press, and welcoming officials.

Exceptionally tight security sheltered the zeppelin crew. As Meister and others stepped down from the control car at Curtiss-Wright-Reynolds Field, they found men in large cowboy hats, holsters, and boots surrounding them. At first the German crew thought that the reception committee had dressed up western style for their arrival. Then Meyering stepped up and asked, "Are you Mr. von Meister? Are you satisfied that we can provide security?" The hats and holsters were uniforms worn by Meyering's three hundred deputies.[50] They were accompanied by one hundred Chicago policemen and two companies of soldiers.[51] An assistant navigator on board noted that, although inexperienced, the soldiers had the necessary obedience, discipline, and willingness to serve as a landing crew. On this flight and on others in Spain, Brazil, and the United States, unemployed men and other volunteers had also acted as landing crews and performed perfect landings.[52]

Chicagoans distinguished between Eckener and Luther, and they expressed their opinions at a reception held at the fairgrounds. Eckener and Meister held a joint press conference at the Bismarck Hotel with Ambassador Luther before meeting with Mayor Kelly and receiving the key to the City of Chicago. The press paid little attention to Ambassador Luther's Nazi propaganda, but Eckener sensed a dampened enthusiasm in comparison with his previous visits. He felt that Chicagoans' enthusiasm and esteem for Germany had diminished. At the fairgrounds later that day, the crowds waved and cheered as Luther and Eckener emerged from the Administration Building. Luther moved forward and responded while Eckener hesitated, a few paces behind. Pleased and gratified, Eckener soon realized that the crowd's delayed and enthusiastic reaction was for him. He then understood that, although the public identified Ambassador Luther with the New Germany, it saw Eckener as a separate kind ambassador—one of international goodwill.[53]

Though received with great enthusiasm at the fairgrounds, Eckener encountered a storm of dissension raging among the anti-Hitler and pro-Hitler groups of the city's 600,000 German Americans. Only six of the city's five hundred German American societies gave their support to the evening event.[54] Two days earlier, the Friedrichshafen newspaper *Seeblatt* had announced that a dinner and reception at the Union League Club would display both German flags. Speeches by representatives of the Friends of New Germany aimed to tie Germans in America to the current government in Berlin, and Ambassador Luther planned to broadcast a speech in English about Germany's foreign policy.[55]

Eckener spoke briefly at the Union League Club dinner and made no political references. Rather, he reminisced about his previous visits to Chicago and spoke of his goal for commercial airships. He offered a final wish that science and technology would continue to thrive in Chicago for the benefit and prosperity of the city and the world. On the other hand, Luther spoke for one hour before the six hundred guests. According to the *Chicago Tribune,* he followed the Nazi formula of leaving no doubt as to where Herr Hitler stood.[56] The *Abendpost* described the room's atmosphere as one of antagonistic emotion and noted that Luther had seized the opportunity of the visit of the *Graf Zeppelin* to shed light on events in Germany.[57] Eckener was embarrassed by Luther's didactic tone. When Luther finished, there was an icy silence. Rufus Dawes leaned and whispered to Eckener, "If you were not here, they would have booed the speaker."[58]

Unlike the 1928 reception at Soldier Field which the German Group and Committee on Nationalities had planned as an ethnic celebration to honor Eckener, the acting German consul general with local National Socialists now organized a politically focused celebration. They held the event at the Medinah Temple on October 26, 1933. The event promoted the swastika and National Socialism. A reception to honor Luther and Eckener on what was called Zeppelin Day immediately followed the meal. The supporting German organizations were veterans, military groups, and Friends of New Germany. Gissibl, the Midwest Bund leader, organized this collective group. Thousands of enthusiastic German Americans filled the hall at the Medinah Temple, many wearing the Zeppelin Tag lapel pin that was sold at the door for fifty cents. The program included patriotic German music with speeches by the mayor, representatives of the some of the German community, Eckener, and Luther.[59] Both Postmaster Ernest J. Kruetgen, president of the German Group of the World's Fair, and First Vice President Schmidt refused to attend the Nazi reception.[60]

Theodore Light, a twenty-year-old stamp collector, went with a friend to Medinah Temple that evening, hoping to get Eckener's autograph on some letters he had mailed to himself via the *Graf Zeppelin* using the special zeppelin stamp. Arriving home from work he had found that his mail delivery included envelopes transported by airship from Miami and Akron to Chicago. Meanwhile at Medinah Temple, limousines were dropping off local politicians and members of the diplomatic corps. The young men were delighted to discover that the public was permitted to enter. Once inside, however, Light "found ushers all in storm trooper uniforms and across the stage was the biggest flag I have ever seen and it was the swastika." He looked at his friend, thinking that this was the wrong place for young Jewish men to be at that moment, and said, "Let's forget about autographs and get out of here."[61]

When Eckener and Luther entered the hall, about 150 young people stood erectly, right arms extended, and gave the Hitler salute. Luther returned the greeting as he strode to his seat. Eckener did not respond, content to present a friendly, nonpolitical appearance. He observed that very few others in the festive crowd joined those who ceremoniously welcomed him and Luther with the Nazi salute, which led him to question further the harmony within the German American community. Eckener then spoke briefly about the airship as a technical feat of German achievement. Luther's pro-Nazi speech followed Eckener's, and the evening ended with a rousing rendition of *Deutschland, Deutschland über Alles.*

The *Graf Zeppelin* left Chicago later that day, flying to Akron, Ohio, where it moored for two days. From Akron, it headed east to Washington, D.C., where it flew low over the White House to pay its respects to the president. Roosevelt stood in the middle of a walk, shielded his eyes from the sun, and waved with a white handkerchief. After arrival in Friedrichshafen, Germany, Eckener and the officers of the *Graf Zeppelin* received a letter of appreciation from Air Minister Hermann Göring expressing his anticipation that the crew and airship would continue to promote Hitler's Germany and National Socialism. Eckener, however, learned later that the Chicago National Socialists had denounced his behavior in Chicago as not patriotic enough and had reported him to the Gestapo in Germany.[62] By 1936, Propaganda Minister Goebbels had banned the publication of Eckener's name and picture.[63]

As noted, many individuals and groups had promoted the visit of the *Graf Zeppelin* to Chicago and had used the visit of the airship and Eckener to further their own interests. The Chicago fair officials used the flight to draw more fairgoers and to generate more publicity. Luther and the National Socialists used the visit of Eckener and the *Graf Zeppelin* to promote their Nazi propaganda in direct opposition to Eckener's goals of international cooperation and benevolence. Chicago's German American community hoped to promote its cultural heritage and the success of the community for local, national, and international recognition. The flight highlighted a season of activities that were expected to reunite and showcase the German American community.

The German Group of the World's Fair had tied its nationalism to the proud display of German accomplishments, both cultural and technological. It had fought the display of the swastika at all fair events because it represented a political party and anti-Semitism. When the *Graf Zeppelin* arrived with swastikas on its fins, there was no way to prevent the consul general in Chicago, the Friends of the New Germany, and the German ambassador from displacing the German Group of the

World's Fair as the welcoming leadership of the community. German Americans in Chicago were forced to make choices, not only of their political alliance, but also of their identity as Germans or Americans. When the fair closed that November, division in the German societies in Chicago over Nazi policy and the Jewish question replaced the anticipated unity among Americans of German origin and recent German immigrants.

The press interviews at the Bismarck Hotel, the public reception at the exposition, the German Americans' failure to salute at the reception, and the absence of Jewish demonstrations evidenced that Americans were able to distinguish the differences between the symbols of the *Graf Zeppelin* and the swastika.[64] Americans could keep the two symbols separate despite the swastikas painted on the zeppelin's fins. Eckener's personal popularity and his goal of an international airship line had been well established in Chicago's business community.[65] Chicago's German immigrants and descendants did distinguish between their ethnic ties to a nation and their loyalty to a state. German Jews in America and German Christians in America would, however, find themselves no longer unified as German Americans.

Ethnic pride ran deep among Chicago's immigrants. They looked with fondness and pride to their homelands, treasuring the mother tongue and tradition. In most cases, this pride did not conflict with their new lives in the ethnically plural United States. The events during the 1933 Chicago exposition, however, challenged immigrants and their descendants to scrutinize their identity and allegiance. The swastika experiences at the exposition forced German Americans, Chicago's largest ethnic group, to face difficult choices of national allegiance even before the outbreak of the Second World War, to reassess their identity, and to act on their convictions.

American Technology in the Stratosphere

The gripping personal and community agony with which German Americans grappled during the early 1930s occurred alongside many other dramas, including one in which renowned scientists and American industrialists planned a daring balloon flight to the earth's stratosphere. One dominant image running through fair organizers' visions for the exposition had been the joint venture exhibit—educational projects produced through cooperation of scientists and industrialists.[66] One such venture—in fact the most innovative and visionary aviation event at the exposition—featured a balloon gondola named for the fair: *A Century of Progress.*[67] A Swiss physicist, Auguste Piccard, the first ever to ascend into the stratosphere, designed the gondola. He then turned oversight of the project to his brother, Jean Piccard, a chemist who had taught at the University of Chicago.[68] In cooperation, engineers at Dow Chemical Company built and donated the air- and watertight gondola using their lightweight alloy Dowmetal.[69] The Goodyear-Zeppelin Corporation constructed the rubberized cotton envelope while Union Carbide and Carbon Corporation produced the hydrogen lifting gas and the liquid oxygen for the gondola's interior atmosphere. Two Nobel Prize–winning physicists, Arthur H. Compton at the University of Chicago and Robert A. Millikan at the California Institute of Technology, among others, supplied measurement apparatus to study the cosmic rays and ozone. Compton hoped that his analysis would contribute to a better understanding of the rays and the origins of the universe.

Thousands of spectators arrived at Soldier Field soon after midnight on August 5, 1933, thrilled to watch the army's crew inflating the amazing balloon, which took place against a backdrop of military maneuvers, music, speeches, and the christening of the gondola.[70] A few minutes after 3 A.M., Thomas "Tex" Settle, a lieutenant commander in the U.S. Navy, gave the command "Hands off" to the ground crew of naval reservists. With that he began his solo flight into the stratosphere.[71] Army spotlights illuminated the awe-inspiring liftoff. Moments later, stunned spectators watched the balloon's rapid descent as it collapsed in the rail yards in the heart of Chicago's industrial district just a mile from the stadium.[72] A valve rope had been caught in the pleats of the fabric, and Settle was helpless to avert the mishap.[73]

Undeterred, Settle tried again on November 20, this time from Akron, Ohio. With him was his marine copilot, Major Chester Fordney, who had supervised the salvage operations of the first flight. After Dow corrected the design flaw and refurbished the gondola, with little public fanfare the pilots set their sights on a new challenge. Since the Chicago crash, three Russians had flown into the stratosphere and had surpassed Piccard's record. Determined to beat the Russians, Settle and Fordney soared to a record height, which was recognized by the Bureau of Standards. Their balloon then descended into a swamp.[74] A year later, in October 1934, the couple who owned *A Century of Progress* gondola and balloon attempted another scientific expedition. Chemists and collaborators, Jean Piccard and Jeanette Ridlon Piccard, entered the stratosphere with Jeanette piloting the craft to 57,579 feet.[75]

The successes and failures of the stratosphere balloon *A Century of Progress* brought worldwide attention to the fair and gave a stadium full of spectators the opportunity to witness aviation history in the making. Press coverage of the following two flights continued to point to the fair and to Chicago as an innovative and scientific center of the country. While not in use, the gondola commanded a prominent location in the main hall of the exposition's Hall of Science, near exhibits prepared by the fair officials to explain cosmic ray research. In addition to initiating the race for space with the Russians, the flights pioneered life support systems for space crews, exposed living organisms to the upper atmosphere, and gave cosmic ray scientists new data on the rays and the effects of high-altitude radiation on human subjects.[76] Further, Jeanette Ridlon Piccard became the first woman to enter the stratosphere. Amid the controversy over a woman undertaking such a dangerous role, conservative Dow Chemical, after learning that a mother of three would be on board, requested the removal of its logo from the gondola.

The exposition's stratosphere balloon project demonstrated that private business corporations and engineers could work successfully with university scientists and the military to achieve goals deemed crucial for national and scientific prestige in the economically crippled international community. Rather than focus on the international cooperation of the gondola designer Auguste Piccard, however, fair officials promoted the flight of *A Century of Progress* stratosphere balloon as made by an American pilot with a gondola made by an American manufacturer out of a material developed by an American manufacturer and with a balloon designed and constructed by an American company.[77]

For the German and Italian governments, the exposition had demonstrated to the world their political power and military might at a time when America's aeronautical expertise was focused on commercial aircraft and domestic route expansion. In this atmosphere of international competition for respect, expansion, and global markets, fair officials led American scientists and corporate leaders not only to showcase aeronautics but also to set new goals by entering the stratosphere and leading the international race into space. By promoting cooperation within industry and by coordinating private and public institutions to make the balloon ascensions possible, fair organizers established this exposition as one of the forerunners of collaborative undertakings between military engineers, industrial leaders, and academics for large-scale civil engineering projects, an idea later identified as the military-industrial-university complex.

Epilogue

What an army of psychoanalysts, psychologists and sociologists
would be required to project the Fair of the Future!
—Rufus C. Dawes to Frank B. Jewett

The turnstiles clicked more than six hundred times per minute on
October 31, 1934, as Chicagoans jammed the fairgrounds for their last chance
to absorb the jubilation of their city's second world's fair.[1] Buglers broadcast
a call for assembly from the elevated train platforms. Schools and public offices closed for the day. Military units, high school bands, ethnic groups in
native dress, and people in Halloween costumes contributed to the carnival
atmosphere. The throngs included the mayor and governor and R. E. Wedg-
wood, a seventy-eight-year-old man who had attended more than any other
fairgoer—314 times in two years. Each wanted to experience the fair's optimism and promise one last time.[2]

Fairgoers again toured the ultramodern House of Tomorrow, observed
premature babies in their infant incubators, filled the cafés to capacity, and
anticipated an evening of revelry stretching to the closing hour, 3 A.M. To
sustain their exuberance and memories, they searched the souvenir stands for
special keepsakes. Postcards and guidebooks were most popular, and an array
of knickknacks could be found throughout the fairgrounds: pins and jewelry,
posters, playing cards, token medals, bookends, ashtrays, canes, stereoscope
viewers, purses and compacts, decorative plates and beer steins, salt and pep-
per shakers, and "the World's Smallest Bible." Children asked their parents
for an elongated penny or toy Radio Flyer wagon, a cast-iron Greyhound bus,
or a Fort Dearborn construction kit. A few took home special treasures such
as a world's fair Brownie box camera or a Sears radio in a wooden case.

The fair's closing ceremony drew hundreds of thousands. A glittering panorama enchanted fairgoers gliding over the lagoon on the Sky Ride. Many alighted in the Court of States, planning to enjoy the closing ceremony there. The ceremony's final speaker, Rufus Dawes, the fair president and now city hero, thanked everyone from officials to individuals to the public for making A Century of Progress an extraordinary success. He concluded with a message of praise and optimism that spoke to a world in distress: "Were we to live a thousand years, we would never forget it, for it lifted up our spirits, restored our souls, and brought us hope."[3]

Exactly at midnight, Dawes checked his pocket watch and pushed a switch. The night sky burst into a brilliant spectacle of color as over two thousand fireworks illuminated the awe-struck crowd. The fair had opened with energy drawn from the star Arcturus and on this night Chicago lit the sky with its own energy and exuberance. In a dramatic but somber finale that gripped all who had enjoyed the fair's dazzle, the bugler played taps into the loudspeakers. Tears flowed, and many visitors slowly began their trek home, tired but exhilarated after a long day of merrymaking.

Then, as most weary fairgoers faded into the city's dark streets, some young, probably intoxicated revelers ignited a frenzied celebration by setting off false fire alarms and breaking glass windows in the Streets of Paris, the Hall of Science, and other exhibits buildings. They tore Sally Rand's posters from the walls of the Italian Village. When the fighting began, women visitors hid in the restaurant kitchens. The vandals destroyed banners, unscrewed tube light bulbs, and tried to break away pieces of buildings. They uprooted mushroom lights and signposts from the ground and took everything they could detach, including booth fixtures, plumbing fixtures, park benches, and shrubs, wrecking everything in their path and breaking into exhibits. The farewell party had started out as good-natured fun but descended into utter turmoil. Firemen, police, and guards finally turned fire hoses on the vandals to quash the uproar. Then the ambulances and maintenance crews began the cleanup. The world's fair had started and ended as a sensation.

The fair's achievements made organizers justifiably proud. Not only did it set attendance records but it also made money by opening a second year—all during the peak of the Great Depression. After combining turnstile cash admissions with souvenir ticket sales, regardless of whether the ticket was used or not, and free admissions for employees and others, organizers claimed that the fair had nearly fifty million visitors. They had a surplus of funds to repay all stakeholders and to cover costs of demolition and all liabilities. As a team the fair organizers had created the magic to draw crowds, but most important, Charles Dawes knew how to raise the funds and Rufus Dawes knew how to spend them.

Today only the ancient Roman column donated to Chicago by Mussolini remains on the fairgrounds as evidence of the 1933–34 Chicago world's fair. It stands between Northerly Island and Soldier Field, along Chicago's lakefront bike path. Removal or demolition of everything else began immediately after the close of the fair. Industrial displays and equipment returned to sponsors and corporate plants and headquarters or went to public spaces. Concessions relocated to various sites, with some continuing on the circuit of fairs and carnivals. Public artworks dispersed throughout Chicagoland. Finally, a sealed bidding process allowed individuals, contractors, businesses, organizations, and schools to obtain equipment while recapturing some funds for the fair.

Armour and Company moved its exhibit to its packing plant at the Chicago stockyards for display. Ford re-erected its Rotunda opposite the Ford Administration Building in Dearborn, Michigan, where visitors could view the exhibits from the world's fair.[4] Many of the science and medical exhibits became permanent displays at Chicago's Museum of Science and Industry, including the gondola from the Piccards' *A Century of Progress* stratosphere balloon and Dr. Helen Button's exhibit, the "Formation of the Human Embryo." The *Pioneer Zephyr* is now part of an exhibit entitled "All Aboard the Silver Streak" in which museum visitors experience a recreation of the streamliner's famous run from Denver to A Century of Progress.

Frank Buck packed up his Midway jungle camp and sent his five hundred monkeys and the pygmy elephant to a new site on Long Island, New York. A replica of Lincoln's cabin and the sink fixtures from Sally Rand's dressing room moved to an estate in suburban Lake Forest, Illinois. After an unsuccessful campaign for the Chicago Park District to operate the Du Sable replica cabin as a permanent memorial, it reappeared as an exhibit at the 1940 American Negro Exposition.[5]

The General Motors assembly line murals now hang in Chicago's Lane Technical High School.[6] Louise Lenz Woodruff donated her sculpture based on the themes of progress and "Science Advancing Mankind" to her alma mater, Central High School in Joliet, Illinois. With the sculpture removed from the fountain, the robot and figures were brought down from their pedestal. Following a school contest, the robot's name changed from Science to Steelman to reflect the city's prominent industry and the school's sports teams.[7] In 1935, a real estate developer transported by barge some of the model homes from the Home and Industrial Group across the ice of Lake Michigan to Indiana. Today, visitors can drive by the House of Tomorrow, Wiebolt-Rostone House, Florida Tropical House, Cypress Log Cabin, and Armco-Ferro House in Beverly Shores, Indiana, where they are part of the Indiana Dunes National Lakeshore Park.

Evanston High School bought flags and ticket boxes, a convent bought chairs, and the Chicago Park District obtained benches. The Boy Scouts bid on a typewriter; Janet Ayer Fairbank bid on a Chevrolet panel truck; and Lenox Lohr submitted bids for a phonograph, rug, and lights from the Japanese Pavilion. Materials from the Hall of Religion to the Streets of Paris found their way into the construction of a new Presbyterian church in suburban Cicero. And one man, Silas Fung, scavenged the demolition site regularly, taking home enough to fill his home and start a private world's fair museum.

Chicagoans and fair participants wanted souvenirs to fill their homes and offices, but more than possessing trinkets, they desired something special to rekindle the glorious memories of the good times, the wondrous vistas, the thought-provoking educational exhibits, and the hope of a brighter future. Many fairgoers clipped newspaper articles and pasted them into scrapbooks with postcards and souvenir handouts from the fair. Some people even added their impressions, including expenses. For instance, a woman named Geneva, of Akron, Ohio, arrived with three friends. She bought placemat souvenirs and took the paper beer-stein table centerpiece from the dinner she shared with "George" on August 6, 1934, at the Old Heidelberg Inn. She noted in her scrapbook that ham, cole slaw, rye bread, and beer cost them $1.65—much less than the $2.50 per person cover charge at the French Casino bar and restaurant. A fairgoer from suburban Wilmette wrote in his memory book that the pearl carving of the *Last Supper* interested him most and entrance to the exhibit cost him ten cents. The Otis elevator ride up sixty-four stories to the observation deck of the Sky Ride thrilled him.[8] An estimated 100,000 who felt the same made their way to the lakefront on August 31, 1935, to watch the final demolition and spectacle of the Sky Ride's second column's collapse.

Without question, the fair remained a delightful memory for years to come. Equally if not more important, the fair also served as a positive force for the city of Chicago, a life preserver during the most trying financial times for the bankrupt municipality. Although it did not end gang murders or municipal corruption, it did offer good press, jobs, full hotel rooms and restaurants, infrastructure improvements, and a cooperative entrepreneurship that resurrected the "I Will" spirit that followed the 1871 Chicago Fire and that created the 1893 World's Columbian Exposition. The city rightly saw itself as the front line in a national economic battle. To honor the 1933–34 fair, its leadership, and the citizens who supported it, Chicago city officials added a fourth star to the city flag. The other stars represent the city's ability to overcome adversity after the Fort Dearborn "massacre" and the 1871 fire and the spirit to stage the 1893 world's fair. McCormick Place, a premier convention facility, currently occupies the site of the 1933–34 fair, a fitting use for a locale that brought industries together to promote their products and images.

The legacy of A Century of Progress for the 1930s included the city's citizens pulling together to overcome unprecedented obstacles. The fair organizers had adopted a successful financial plan with immunity from political back-seat driving, had created a new vision for world's fairs, had reconceptualized architecture and display techniques, and had built a fair organization to complete the project. The fair became an antidote to despair for the city and for the nation. And although little evidence of the fair remains along the Chicago lakefront, the fair had lasting effects in Americans' everyday lives, from the development and use of new building materials to the imaginative rethinking of corporate advertising to new educational methodology.

Following the fair, Charles Gates Dawes served as chair of the Reconstruction Finance Corporation, a governmental agency striving to safeguard economic policies in banking and other sectors. Rufus Dawes became president of Chicago's Museum of Science and Industry in 1934. After Dawes's death in 1940, Lenox Lohr succeeded him as president of the museum. Between the time fair operations closed down and 1940, Lohr served as president and chief managing executive of the National Broadcasting Company (NBC). He wrote several books, including one on management of the 1933–34 fair and one on television broadcasting. He also organized the 1948 and 1949 Chicago Railroad Fairs. As his final contribution to preserving the history of the 1933 fair, he donated its organizational papers to the University of Illinois at Chicago. Several of the military men recruited for the fair's organizational team also joined the Museum of Science and Industry leadership, including Col. F. C. Boggs and Col. C. W. Fitch.

Exceptional women of the fair saw their progress from an individual standpoint rather than as part of the larger women's rights movement. Martha McGrew followed Lenox Lohr and remained his assistant throughout his career, promoting public entertainments and education. She oversaw several projects at the Museum of Science and Industry and also continued to work as an editor and manager for the *Military Engineer.* After Lohr's death in 1968 and her own retirement, she maintained an active correspondence with many of the fair staff. She returned to her native Tennessee, where she died in 1990. Helen Dawes lived seven years after the fair's closing, dying in 1941. Following her funeral in Evanston, Illinois, the prominent socialite was buried in the Dawes family plot in Marietta, Ohio. Dorthea Goodrich disappeared from public view. Following her death, her personal scrapbooks appeared in an upstate New York tag sale.

The African American clubwomen of the National De Saible Memorial Society, pioneer public historians in their own right and part of a continuum in the struggle for progress and equality in their community, achieved their mission. Today Du Sable is recognized as the first citizen of Chicago and as a business entrepreneur. In addition to his name on a high school, a park, a harbor, and an African American Museum, a first-class postage stamp features Du Sable's portrait and cabin, bringing national prominence to his legacy. The clubwomen took what many considered obscure, irrelevant history and presented it to the public in a bold way. Each year the Chicago DuSable League, a group of African American clubwomen with ties to the 1930s National De Saible Memorial Society, holds a memorial ceremony in August at the plaque that designates the Jean Baptiste Point Du Sable Homesite as a National Historic Landmark.[9]

Chicago remains a port of entry for migrants. Continuing the shifts in demographics following World War I, more African Americans and Latinos arrived, and their neighborhoods enlarged. Today Latinos are the fastest-growing segment of the city population with increasing numbers of European ethnics and their descendants settling in the suburban surroundings. The old Italian and German neighborhoods continue to feature a few ethnic restaurants and shops, but the population living around these enclaves is diverse. For many of the immigrants and ethnic populations who participated at the fair, their vision of progress, tied to the American dream, found realization in upward mobility to the middle class: home ownership, education, and increasing financial success for them and their children. Germans and Italians addressed their loyalty, divided between their ancestral homelands and America, when the United States declared war on Germany and Italy in World War II, forcing their assimilation and Americanization to immediate realization.

The golden years of the airship age ended when the German zeppelin *Hindenburg* burst into flames on May 6, 1937, at Lakehurst, New Jersey. The National Socialists and their agenda crushed Hugo Eckener's dream of global commerce. As airplane technology improved, regular transatlantic air service developed and, following World War II, the race for space defined the cold war between the Soviet Union and the United States. Should aviation technological progress be measured only by the reduction of time and space, then the twentieth century was without doubt a century of progress. Though Woodruff's sculpture promoted the idea of autonomous technological progress, fairgoers understood the element of human choice in shaping the world's future. They embraced scientific advancement and the comforts it brought to everyday life, but they still retained the belief that humanity itself shapes progress.

The fair offered Chicagoans and Americans of different races and ethnicities, religions, regions, classes, and genders an opportunity to meet, interact, and face the challenges of their times. Most chose to embrace the optimism offered by the colorful spectacle. The fair remained a fond memory for fairgoers and their children, who listened to the memories of this bright moment. Many of them attended the futuristic 1939–40 New York World's Fair and subsequent fairs that displayed ideas of progress while also building upon many of the innovations initiated in Chicago. Today the great-grandchildren of the Chicago fairgoers experience their version of a fair visit at Walt Disney World, a permanent destination for entertainment and education with world cultures on display at its Epcot Center. This experience of entertainment evolution is part of the legacy of A Century of Progress.

In the end, Sally Rand became far more than she ever expected. The showgirl, who would dance the fan dance on stage and film until seventy years of age, became both a metaphor for the American culture of consumption based on spectacle and an icon for the 1933 Chicago world's fair. Fair organizers had determined to illustrate the ideas of progress and optimism through cooperative exhibits based on science and technology, but it was the rags-to-riches girl from the mountains of Missouri who really brought the message home with her freedom, buoyancy, and confidence that things always get better. Many fairgoers carried her spirit and message home with them in the little Tru-Vue souvenir film strip that captured images of her bubble dance. The next day, the next week, and through all the dark days of the Depression, any time they picked up the little plastic viewer, Sally Rand reminded them on the opening frame of the strip: "The bubble dance as created by Sally Rand is a poetic interpretation of life. Just as the bubble silently, gracefully rises, falls, and floats away and returns . . . so too our hopes, dreams, and ambitions move before us."[10] While Sally Rand might have soared to international fame—or notoriety—simply on the swell of her sensationalism, she would not have realized the mythical distinction of icon had A Century of Progress not been staged during the Great Depression.

NOTES

Introduction

1. In 1829 when the Canal Board first surveyed the land, there were only fifty people on three-quarters of a square mile of land. In 1833 Chicago was incorporated as a village and in 1837 as city. Otto Schmidt, President of the Chicago Historical Society, in Ways and Means Committee Minutes, A Century of Progress Papers, Special Collections, University of Illinois at Chicago (UIC).

2. The ten largest cities documented in the world in 1932 were London, New York, Tokyo, Chicago, Berlin, Paris, Moscow, Shanghai, Osaka, and Leningrad. Chicago's population was 4,609,240. *The Chicago Daily News Almanac and Year Book for 1933* (Chicago: Chicago Daily News, 1932), 152.

3. William Edward Leuchtenburg, *Franklin D. Roosevelt and the New Deal, 1932–1940* (New York: Harper and Row, 1963), 8.

4. Ruth Oldenziel, *Making Technology Masculine: Men, Women and Modern Machines in America, 1870–1945* (Amsterdam: Amsterdam University Press, 1999), 24–26, 46–50.

5. John M. Staudenmeier, "Perils of Progress Talk" in *Science, Technology, and Social Progress: Research in Technology Studies*, vol. 2, ed. Steven L. Goodman (Bethlehem: Lehigh University Press, 1989), 268–93; and Lowell Tozer, "A Century of Progress, 1833–1933: Technology's Triumph over Man," *American Quarterly* 4 (Spring 1952): 78–81.

6. *The Inter Ocean* newspaper sponsored a contest in 1892 for an idea of a figure typical of the Chicago spirit, similar to the national expression in Uncle Sam. The World's Columbian Exposition was under construction and it was an energetic time in the city's history. From about three hundred entries, the jury selected a drawing by a local artist, Charles Holloway. He personified the city's dignity, strength, purpose, and energy though a proud and steadfast woman wearing a winged helmet and "I Will" inscribed on her armor breastplate. The "I Will" figure adorned advertising, picture postcards, and cartoons for decades. Artists modernized the image for 1933 fair promotional materials, which effectively used her to promote support and to represent Chicago's determination for the second world's fair. *Chicago Commerce* (April 30, 1915), "I Will" file, Chicago History Museum (CHM).

7. Terry S. Reynolds, ed., "The Engineer in 20th Century America," *The Engineer in America: A Historical Anthology from Technology and Culture* (Chicago: University of Chicago Press, 1991), 169–90.

8. Edwin T. Layton Jr., *The Revolt of the Engineers: Social Responsibility and the American Engineering Profession* (Baltimore: Johns Hopkins University Press, 1986), 57.

Chapter 1: Sally Rand and the Midway

1. The epigraph for this chapter is from Donald Richie with Arturo Silva, *The Donald Richie Reader: 50 Years of Writing on Japan* (Berkeley: Stone Bridge Press, 2001), 14–15.

2. Ibid.

3. "The Dressmaker from Paris," *New York Times*, March 13, 1925, 22.

4. John S. Van Gilder, "Outline for a Quick Two or Three Day Visit to the Cream of A Century of Progress Exposition 1934," Small Collections, CHM.

5. Ibid.

6. "Sally Rand Holds Dance a Business," *New York Times*, February 12, 1935, 23.

7. Ibid.

8. Holly Knox, *Sally Rand: From Film to Fans* (Bend, Ore.: Maverick, 1988), 24.

9. See, for example, Knox, *Sally Rand*, 30–32; Nathaniel Alexander Owings, *The Spaces in Between: An Architect's Journey* (Boston: Houghton Mifflin, 1973), 53; Rachel Shteir, *Striptease: The Untold Story of the Girlie Show* (New York: Oxford University Press, 2004), 146–55; Studs Terkel, *Hard Times: An Oral History of the Great Depression* (New York: Pantheon, 1970), 168–74; and Sally Rand, interview by Studs Terkel, 1971, "Studs Terkel: Conversations with America," terkel-a0a0n7-b.rm, CHM.

10. "Society at the Fair," *Chicago Daily News*, May 29, 1933, 5; and "So This Is Paris! Society Makes Gayety at Fair," *Chicago Tribune*, May 28, 1933, 5, 9. Seymour Blair wrote that the Opening Gala Charity Ball would be held at the Rendezvous de Paris club and in the Streets of Paris. Five-dollar tickets benefited the Illinois Children's Home and Aid Society. Franklin D. Roosevelt, Papers as President, Official File 275, Franklin D. Roosevelt Library and Museum, Hyde Park, New York.

11. Knox, *Sally Rand*, 23–33; Shteir, *Striptease*, 149; Terkel, *Hard Times*, 169. Rand had previously crashed another socialite party in Chicago at the Congress Hotel. For that night, she credited County Commissioner Charlie Weber as her collaborator. The architect Nathaniel Alexander Owings claimed that John Root paid her twenty-five dollars to portray Lady Godiva. Owings, *Spaces in Between*, 53.

12. "Mr. Rogers Notes Revival of the Old Chicago Spirit," *New York Times*, November 2, 1934, 25.

13. Terkel, *Hard Times*, 171.

14. Shteir, *Striptease*, 150.

15. Mary Margaret, "Our Trip to A Century of Progress," Agnes Nestor papers, CHM.

16. "Seen and Heard at the Fair," *Hobbies, the Magazine of Collectors* 38 (November 1933): 11.

17. Kathleen McLaughlin, "Little Egypt of '93 Gets a Shock Today," *Chicago Tribune*, July 30, 1933, A Century of Progress scrapbooks box 41, A Century of Progress records, UIC.

18. Charles Dawes to Rufus Dawes, May 13, 1930, Dawes Collection, Special Collections Department, Charles Deering Library, Northwestern University, Evanston (hereafter, Dawes Collection, NWU).

19. Lenox R. Lohr, *Fair Management: A Guide for Future Fairs, The Story of a Century of Progress Exposition* (Chicago: Cuneo Press, 1952), 116.

20. Rufus Dawes to Charles Dawes, October 30, 1930, Dawes Collection, NWU.

21. See John F. Kasson, *Amusing the Million: Coney Island at the Turn of the Century* (New York: Hill and Wang, 1978), and Kathy Peiss, *Cheap Amusements: Working Women and Leisure in Turn-of-the-Century New York* (Philadelphia: Temple University Press, 1986).

22. Jeanne Madeline Weimann, *The Fair Women* (Chicago: Academy Chicago, 1981), 258.

23. Robert C. Allen, *Horrible Prettiness: Burlesque and American Culture* (Chapel Hill: University of North Carolina Press, 1991), 231. See also Robert M. Lewis, ed., *From Traveling Show to Vaudeville: Theatrical Spectacle in America, 1830–1910* (Baltimore: Johns Hopkins University Press, 2003); and Bernard Sobel, *A Pictorial History of Burlesque* (New York: Putnam, 1956).

24. Burlesque, a nineteenth-century import to America, offered literary or dramatic works

that ridiculed important people and events. Only later in the early twentieth century did the "striptease" dance, so often identified with burlesque, became popular. As burlesque waned in popularity, entertainers moved on to work in carnival girl shows and night clubs. Strip clubs flourished in the 1950s, 60s, and 70s. These evolved into the nude dance clubs of today. During these changes dancers lost much of their individual opportunity for creativity as the business became bureaucratized. See Marilyn Suriani Futterman, *Dancing Naked in the Material World* (New York: Prometheus Books, 1992).

25. In the area where the Harold Washington Public Library stands today on State Street and just south of it were the Rialto Burlesque, 336 S.; Gem Theater, 450 S.; Wonderland, 462 S.; Folly Theater, 526 S.; State Harrison Burlesque, 546 S.; Fashion Burlesque Theater, 557 S.; National Theater Live Burlesque, 610 S.; and Chicago Theater, 614 S. The Star and Garter Theater operated at 815 W. Madison. Box 6, folder 89, Juvenile Protective Association Papers, UIC.

26. *General Summary* (Chicago: Juvenile Protective Association of Chicago, July 7, 1934), box 6, folder 89, Juvenile Protective Association Papers, UIC.

27. The higher-class burlesque house costs would be in line with the fifty cents admission to the fairgrounds plus the additional cost of attending floor shows or entertainment concessions.

28. Jessie L. Binford, *Burlesque Shows in Chicago during the Summer of 1934* (Chicago: Juvenile Protective Association of Chicago, September 8, 1934), box 6, folder 89, Juvenile Protective Association Papers, UIC.

29. The educational exhibits and official entertainment ended at 10 P.M. Initially concessions were open until 3 A.M., but in July 1933 the fair officials began closing the gates at 11:30 P.M. and required concessions to be closed by 1:30 A.M. despite the protest of the concessionaires. One reason given for the earlier closing was that unescorted, drunken girls were creating a nuisance. "Fair Nudes 'Out'; Blame the Ladies," (Chicago) *Daily Times*, July 1933, A Century of Progress scrapbooks box 41, A Century of Progress records, Special Collections Department, University Library, University of Illinois at Chicago (UIC). Admission data was based on sold admissions, not actual turnstyle clicks.

30. Timothy J. Gilfoyle, *City of Eros: New York City, Prostitution, and the Commercialization of Sex, 1790–1920* (New York: W. W. Norton, 1992), 20.

31. One fair visitor, Wanda Bridgeforth, watched Sally Rand's dance and reminisced that "we girls, we went home and we did a little fan dance on our own." *Chicago Stories: A Break in the Clouds, Chicago's 1933 World's Fair*, WTTW PBS Television, Chicago, 2000.

32. Jimmy Corcoran, "Nude Is Nude!" *Chicago American*, July 19, 1933; and "Beauty and Thrills O.K., Vulgarity and Indecency Are Not," *Chicago American*, August 3, 1933, A Century of Progress scrapbooks boxes 41, 43, A Century of Progress records, UIC.

33. Repeal of prohibition also revived café and club life in Chicago where nightlife thrived in hotels, B-girl emporiums, and neighborhood taverns. Lewis A. Erenberg, "From New York to Middletown: Repeal and the Legitimization of Nightlife in the Great Depression," *American Quarterly* 38 (Winter 1986): 765.

34. "Fair, Beer Kept Tourist Money in U.S. Last Year," *Chicago Tribune*, April 9, 1934, 18.

35. *General Conditions* (Chicago: Juvenile Protective Association of Chicago, June 12, September 9, and December 31, 1934), folder 89, Juvenile Protective Association Papers, UIC; and "Final Report of Committee on Protective Services during A Century of Progress," folder 1-7, Welfare Public Relations Forum, CHM.

36. Knox, *Sally Rand*, 10.

37. The Western Association of Motion Picture Advertisers selected Hollywood actresses most likely to succeed and named them Wampas Baby Stars during the 1920s–30s.

38. Knox, *Sally Rand*, 18.

39. This is the version based on oral interviews with Rand, family, and friends in Knox, *Sally*

Rand, 18–22. Rand told another version of her first fan dance to Studs Terkel. She was given a job at a club because a friend of hers had an uncle who delivered illegal alcohol to the club. She saw a pair of fans at a costume shop and ordered a pair C.O.D. from New York. A friend hocked his rings so that she could obtain the fans and then she went to the club where she was announced without notice. Her gown was still at home, so she went on nude, but no one seemed to notice. Terkel, *Hard Times,* 170–71. Another fan dancer, Faith Bacon, told yet a third version of the origins of the fan dance. She claimed to have performed the dance in New York while assuming a "statuary" pose in order to meet the New York law that "statuary" was art. She claimed that Sally Rand served as one of the showgirls on stage who handed Faith her fans before Bacon's arrest for an indecent performance. Kate Susman, "New Deal in Nudity," *Chicago Daily Times,* August 13, 1933, 10–11, A Century of Progress scrapbooks box 43, A Century of Progress records, UIC.

40. Knox, *Sally Rand,* 34–37; and Terkel, *Hard Times,* 172.

41. Interview with Johnny Carson, *Tonight Show,* Armed Forces Radio (November 1967), LPA 55487, Motion Picture, Broadcasting and Recorded Sound Division, Library of Congress, Washington, D.C.

42. Sally Rand's fan dance, both stage and studio versions, have been captured on film. The film shot at the café in the Streets of Paris shows men and women in the audience, all clapping enthusiastically at the finale. See *A Century of Progress Exposition: Sally Rand,* Burton Holmes Films, Inc., 1933; *Fan Dance,* Official Films, Greentree Productions, 1988; and *Chicago Stories.* The 1930s Paramount studios film *Bolero,* starring George Raft and Carole Lombard, features Rand doing her fan dance. A recreation of her dance can be seen in the 1983 Ladd Production film *The Right Stuff.*

43. Van Gilder, "Outline for a Quick Two or Three Day Visit."

44. John Hyde to Sally Rand, April 16, 1934, Sally Rand Papers, CHM.

45. Sally Rand to Annette Beck, August 3, November 1, 5, 1934, Sally Rand Papers, CHM.

46. In the 1942 short film *Artist Model,* Sally Rand first dresses in an oriental-style dress to model for a painter. After the two leave the studio, a plaster statue—also Rand—comes to life. Draped in a gauze bodice, she dances barefoot with a scarf in a style reminiscent of that of Isadora Duncan. *Artist Model,* Official Films, 1942, Greentree Productions, 1988.

47. Christine Stansell, *American Moderns: Bohemian New York and the Creation of a New Century* (New York: Metropolitan Books, 2000), 4, 232–33.

48. Andrea Stuart, *Showgirls* (London: Jonathan Cape, 1996), 2, identifies showgirls as "the most instantly recognizable icons of modern times. . . . Glamour and pleasure, sexuality and fantasy, beauty and desirability, consumerism and power, anonymity and stardom, these are the conceptual threads that pull the showgirl's story together."

49. Mark Franco, *The Work of Dance: Labor, Movement, and Identity in the 1930s* (Middletown, Conn.: Wesleyan University Press, 2002), 17, argues that during the formative period of dance in the 1930s, chorus dance aligned with capitalism while modern dance aligned with communism. Miguel Covarrubias, "Impossible Interview: Sally Rand vs. Martha Graham," *Vanity Fair,* December 1934, 40, parodied the similarities and differences between Rand and Graham's ideas of dance performance.

50. Sally Rand to John Hyde, August 19, 1934, Sally Rand Papers, CHM.

51. "Sally Dances in Loop; Arrest Her Four Times," *Chicago Tribune,* August 5, 1933, 1.

52. Terkel, *Hard Times,* 173.

53. "Sally Listens to Judges, Then Wraps Herself in Coat of Paint," *Chicago Tribune,* August 6, 1933, 3.

54. Ibid.

55. "Sally Dances in Loop," 1.

56. Photograph, *New York Times,* October 24, 1926, p. RPA1.

57. "Sally Listens to Judges," 3.

58. "Sally Rand Has Day in Court with the Cops," *Chicago Tribune,* August 9, 1933, 3.

59. Twenty-five dollars in 1933 was the equivalent to more than $375 in 2007 dollars.

60. "Sally Listens to Judges," 3.

61. "Miss Rand and Mr. Druggan Won't Stay in Them," *Chicago Tribune,* August 9, 1933, 10; and "Tactful Nude, Expert's View of Sally Rand," *Chicago Tribune,* August 7, 1933, 17.

62. Sally Rand to Ted Gonzales, April 6, 1935, Sally Rand Papers, CHM. Seventy-nine thousand dollars in 1933 was equal to more than a million dollars in 2007.

63. A thousand dollars in 1933 was equal to more than $15,000 in 2007 dollars.

64. "'Paris Streets' Big Money Maker of World's Fair," *Chicago Tribune,* July 27, 1933, A Century of Progress scrapbooks box 41, A Century of Progress records, UIC.

65. Susman, "New Deal in Nudity," 11. Faith Bacon's interpretation of the fan dance created a strong emotional atmosphere with athletic movements. See *A Lady with Fans,* Official Films, 1942, Greentree Productions, 1988; and *A Century of Progress Exposition: Faith Bacon the Fan Dancer of Hollywood,* Burton Holmes Films, Inc., 1933.

66. Large numbers responded to ads to work in the Streets of Paris. For many young women, aged eighteen to twenty-five, the dress or lack of dress required was similar to what was being worn at the beaches at that time. *Chicago Tribune,* August 3, 1933, A Century of Progress scrapbooks box 43, A Century of Progress records, UIC. In 1933, $20 a week was more than a sales clerk for cosmetics earned at $15 a week, but less than a schoolteacher at $25 a week.

67. B. L. Grove to Lenox R. Lohr, November 14, 1933, folder 7-41, A Century of Progress records, UIC.

68. Robert Dubard, "What a French Visitor to the Fair Thinks about the 'Streets of Paris,'" *Milwaukee Journal,* October 10, 1933, folder 1-3322, A Century of Progress records, UIC.

69. *General Summary* (July 7, 1934), box 6, folder 89, Juvenile Protective Association Papers, UIC.

70. Robert Isham Randolph to Jessie F. Binford, June 20, 1934, box 1, Juvenile Protective Association Papers, UIC.

71. Jessie F. Binford to Charles H. Weber, Cook County Commissioner, May 27, 1933, and Jessie F. Binford to Rufus C. Dawes, June 8, 1933, box 1, Juvenile Protective Association Papers, UIC.

72. Robert Isham Randolph, Director of Operations, to Jessie F. Binford, June 10, 1933, box 1, Juvenile Protective Association Papers, UIC.

73. F. R. Moulten to Lenox R. Lohr, June 6, 1933, folder 1-12726, A Century of Progress records, UIC.

74. Hazel Macdonald, "Woman Boss Rules over the Fair," *Chicago American,* July 1933, A Century of Progress scrapbooks box 41, A Century of Progress records, UIC.

75. "Fair without Pants," *Time,* July 31, 1933, 20.

76. *People of the State of Illinois, ex rel Mary Belle Spencer vs Honorable Rufus C. Dawes, Century of Progress International Exhibition, a corporation, Streets of Paris (June 1933),* 7, folder 7-16, A Century of Progress records, UIC.

77. Spencer argued that the lease between A Century of Progress and the concessionaires should be cancelled because concessions were used for the "purpose of lewdness, assignation, or prostitution." Ibid., 11–18 (quote, 17), and *Illinois Revised Statutes, 1933* (Springfield: State of Illinois, 1933), 1005–6, 1050. The Indecent Exposure code stated that "if any person shall appear in a public place in a state of nudity . . . or be guilty of any lewd or indecent act . . . he or she would be subject to a fine." Ibid., 19, and *Revised Chicago Code of 1931, Passed by the City Council of Chicago, May 27, 1931* (Chicago: City of Chicago, 1931), 1514.

78. *People of the State of Illinois*, 17.

79. "Let the Boobs Look, Judge's Idea on Nudes," *Chicago Tribune*, July 19, 1933, 1.

80. Compiled from news clippings of the *Chicago American*, (Chicago) *Daily Times*, *Chicago Herald and Examiner*, *Chicago Daily News*, and *Chicago Tribune*, July 18–19, 1933, A Century of Progress scrapbooks box 41, A Century of Progress records, UIC.

81. Julian Jackson, *For Our Friends, About Our Friends, From Your Friends, Merry Christmas and Happy New Year*, Chicago, c. 1980, folder 40, Special Collections, CHM.

82. Thomas H. Slusser to Lenox R. Lohr, July 21, 1933, folder 7-15, A Century of Progress records, UIC. The criminal code does not define obscene, nor does it mention nudity. It states that anyone involved at any level in the presentation is subject to fine or imprisonment. *Illinois Revised Statutes, 1933*.

83. *Chicago Daily News and Chicago American*, July 20, 1933, A Century of Progress scrapbooks box 41, A Century of Progress records, UIC.

84. "Fair Nudes 'Out'; Blame the Ladies," *Chicago Daily Times*, July 1933, A Century of Progress scrapbooks box 41, A Century of Progress records, UIC.

85. *Annual Report on the Century of Progress* (Chicago: Juvenile Protective Association of Chicago, 1934), box 5, folder 89, Juvenile Protective Association Papers, UIC.

86. Compiled from news clippings of the *Chicago American*, (Chicago) *Daily Times*, *Chicago Daily News*, and *Chicago Tribune*, August 1–3, 1933, A Century of Progress scrapbooks box 43, A Century of Progress records, UIC.

87. "Lohr Inspects Fair; O.K.'s Shows as Moral," *Chicago Daily News*, July 1933, A Century of Progress scrapbooks box 41, A Century of Progress records, UIC.

88. Compiled from unattributed clippings, A Century of Progress scrapbooks box 41, A Century of Progress records; and box 6, folders 89–91, Juvenile Protective Association Papers, UIC.

89. Compiled from news clippings of the *Chicago American*, (Chicago) *Daily Times*, *Chicago Herald and Examiner*, *Chicago Daily News*, and *Chicago Tribune*, August 2–7, 1933, A Century of Progress scrapbooks box 43, A Century of Progress records, UIC.

90. *Report on Century of Progress—1934* (Chicago: Juvenile Protective Association of Chicago, 1934), box 6, folder 89, Juvenile Protective Association Papers, UIC.

91. *Annual Report on the Century of Progress* (1934) UIC.

92. Edouard Manet's *Olympia* hangs in the Musée d'Orsay in Paris. In 1863 critics had found this painting of a reclining nude girl staring at the viewer (or artist) to be indecent. Nicholas Wadley, *Manet* (London: Paul Hamlyn, 1967), 34.

93. *Cati Mount vs. A Century of Progress*, Superior Court of Cook County, folder 7-10; Opinion of Judge McGoorty in Case of *Cati Mount vs. A Century of Progress*, folder 7-60; and, Thomas H. Slusser to Lenox R. Lohr, June 6, 1934, folder 7-12, all in A Century of Progress records, UIC.

94. *Annual Report on the Century of Progress*, (1934), 1; Order 585916, Superior Court of Cook County, *Cati Mount vs. Century of Progress, et al.*, folder 7-14, A Century of Progress records, UIC.

95. Lohr, *Fair Management*, 170.

96. Martha McGrew to Rufus C. Dawes, July 29, 1938, folder 1-10065, A Century of Progress records, UIC.

97. Claude O. Pike, ed., *Chicago Daily News Almanac and Year Book for 1933* (Chicago: Chicago Daily News, 1932), 71.

98. Thomas Doherty, *Pre-Code Hollywood: Sex, Immorality, and Insurrection in American Cinema, 1930–1934* (New York: Columbia University Press, 1999), 112.

99. Ibid., 331. A Century of Progress represented the peak of Sally Rand's career and stardom. She continued to fan dance at international expositions, appeared in small parts in a few films, and toured America with her act until 1979.

100. Joanne J. Meyerowitz, *Women Adrift: Independent Wage Earners in Chicago, 1880–1930* (Chicago: University of Chicago Press, 1988), 116.

Chapter 2: Chicago Boosters Set the Stage

1. The epigraph for this chapter comes from a remark made by Rufus C. Dawes, Hotel LaSalle, Chicago, February 19, 1930, folder 4-47, A Century of Progress records, UIC.

2. For a biography of Rufus Dawes, see *Rufus C. Dawes, Commemorating the Excellent and Unselfish Service* (Chicago: J. W. Allen, 1933). Charles S. Peterson headed several printing companies in Chicago including Peterson Linotyping Company. His public service included Chicago's boards of education and county commissioners. Born in Sweden, Peterson held positions as trustee and vice president of the American Scandinavian Foundation.

3. Conference re Worlds Fair, Stenographic Report, December 13, 1927, folder 1-12017, A Century of Progress records, UIC.

4. Ibid.

5. For American world's fairs and expositions before Chicago's second world's fair, in 1933, see John E. Findling, ed., *Historical Dictionary of World's Fairs and Expositions, 1851–1988* (New York: Greenwood, 1990).

6. Robert D. Parmet and Francis L. Lederer, "Competition for the World's Columbian Exposition: The New York Campaign and the Chicago Campaign," *Journal of the Illinois State Historical Society* 65 (Winter 1972): 364–94.

7. Memorandum to Floyd L. Bateman, folder 1-1392, A Century of Progress records, UIC; *Chicago Tribune*, November 18, 1919, 13. For instance, J. Scott Matthews of the recorder's office proposed a permanent trade fair in 1919.

8. Examples of Chicago world's fair promotional literature that countered skepticism and predicted a better city include S. J. Duncan Clark, *Beauty of Balance: The Prophetic in Mass and Line at A Century of Progress Exposition* (Chicago: A Century of Progress, 1932); Franklyn Hobbs, *The World's Fair of 1893 Made Chicago* (Chicago: Chicago World's Fair Centennial Celebration 1933, 1929); Charles S. Peterson, *The Chicago World's Fair: Why? Where? When? How Much?* (Chicago: Chicago World's Fair Centennial Celebration, 1928); and *Chicago and You: A Loyal Partnership* (Chicago World's Fair Centennial Celebration 1933, 1929).

9. See Daniel H. Burnham and Edward H. Bennett, *Plan of Chicago* (reprint; New York: Princeton Architectural Press, 1993).

10. Harry de Joannis to Otto L. Schmidt, April 21, 1926, folder 6-11, Otto L. Schmidt Papers, CHM.

11. Between 1910 and 1920 the African American population in Chicago increased 148 percent, with the population concentrated in one ghetto on the South Side. By 1920 African Americans comprised 6 percent of the Chicago adult population. William M. Tuttle Jr., *Race Riot: Chicago in the Red Summer of 1919* (New York: Athenaeum, 1978), 75–76, 192.

12. David E. Ruth identifies Al Capone as a self-sufficient businessman who used contemporary efficiency methods of the business world. Linking crime and aggressive capitalism together, the media presented Chicago as the perfect environment for Capone's entrepreneurial spirit. See David E. Ruth, *Inventing the Public Enemy: The Gangster in American Culture, 1918–1934* (Chicago: University of Chicago Press, 1996).

13. Controversial reports brought additional negative national attention to Chicago's crime. Mayor Dever wrote to Congressman A. J. Sabath on January 27, 1925, that "the Crime Commission report . . . is substantially untrue." He felt that the commission had ulterior motives. William E. Dever Papers, CHM. Dever had been a judge and the Chicago Crime Commission had

placed observers in the courts. "The orientation of the commission was punitive, and its major goal was to make 'justice' more certain, swift, and severe," writes Mark H. Haller, in "Urban Crime and Criminal Justice: The Chicago Case," *Journal of American History* 57 (December 1970): 632. John H. Wigmore, ed., *The Illinois Crime Survey* (Chicago: Illinois Association for Criminal Justice, 1929), has a section on organized crime in Chicago by John Landesco.

14. Address of Rufus C. Dawes, Association of Commerce, Hotel LaSalle, February 19, 1930, folder 4-47, A Century of Progress records, UIC.

15. Lisa Krissoff Boehm, *Popular Culture and the Enduring Myth of Chicago, 1871–1968* (New York: Routledge, 2004), addresses this question in her chapter "'All the World Is Waiting for the Sunrise': A Century of Progress and the National Image of Chicago," 105–25.

16. "'Clean' Chicago Promised for Its World Fair," *Washington Herald*, February 14, 1930, A Century of Progress scrapbooks box 29, A Century of Progress records, UIC. See also James D. Nowlan, *Glory, Darkness, Light: A History of the Union League Club of Chicago* (Evanston, Ill.: Northwestern University Press, 2004), 93–95.

17. Campaign ads, Dever Papers, CHM.

18. In 1913 women in Illinois could vote for local offices and president. The Nineteenth Amendment in 1920 extended their suffrage to governor and state and federal representatives.

19. Dever Papers, CHM.

20. Interview in *Denver Express*, July 31, 1926, clipping, ibid.

21. *Chicago Herald and Examiner*, August 6, 1925, clipping, ibid. The *San Francisco Bulletin*, June 28, 1924, noted that in 1924 Chicago had 295 automobile deaths, 157 persons were shot to death, and 113 died of moonshine poisoning. Ibid.

22. Wigmore, *Illinois Crime Survey*, 1095.

23. After Thompson's return to office in 1927, "the city's leading businessmen no longer concerned themselves greatly with local politics. . . . The Independent Republicans for Dever Committee constituted a last stand for the business vision of good government in Chicago." Douglas Bukowski, "Big Bill Thompson: The "Model" Politician," in *The Mayors: The Chicago Political Tradition*, rev. ed., ed. Paul M. Green and Melvin G. Holli (Carbondale: Southern Illinois University Press, 1995), 76.

24. William E. Clow, vice president of James B. Clow and Sons, manufactured plumbing and heating supplies, folder 1-3537, A Century of Progress records, UIC.

25. *Chicago Daily News*, May 27, 1933, clipping, A Century of Progress scrapbooks box 36, A Century of Progress records, UIC.

26. Adams and Sprague had contact through the Public Service Association. Sprague was a wholesale grocer and political appointee of Dever. Sprague's background included serving as chair, Sprague Warner and Company; director, Chicago and Northwestern Railway and the Continental Illinois Bank and Trust Company; vice chair, Chicago Plan Commission; and commissioner of public works. He later served as a member of the board of trustees of A Century of Progress; folder 1-13911, A Century of Progress records, UIC. Adams died in 1930, unable to see his idea realized. Myron E. Adams, folders 1-56, 15-19, A Century of Progress records, UIC.

27. Plan for the Celebration of the Centennial of Chicago as Submitted to Mayor William E. Dever on August 17, 1923, by Myron E. Adams, A Century of Progress Papers, Special Collections, University of Illinois at Chicago.

28. Ibid. Although this recreated village was not realized, a replica of Fort Dearborn was a popular attraction during the fair years.

29. Journal of the Proceedings of the City Council of the City of Chicago, Illinois, regular meetings, Thursday, March 13, 1926, from the History of the Centennial, folder 15-19, A Century of Progress records, UIC. The size of the committee, originally envisioned as one hundred people, increased to one hundred fifty and later to more than two hundred members. Dever

wanted a diverse representation and requested Francis X. Busch, corporation council for the City of Chicago, to draft a list of groups to be represented, including nationalistic (and racial), business, commercial, and professional organizations, as well as city chairmen and civic club leaders. Busch recommended that an additional "fifty citizens at large, (preferably 25 men and 25 women)" be appointed. Francis X. Busch to William E. Dever, March 13, 1926, Dever Papers, CHM.

30. William E. Dever to John Fitzpatrick, April 1, 1926, Dever Papers, CHM.

31. Although the Ways and Means Committee was not to exceed twenty-five, the mayor appointed thirty-seven members. Edward N. Hurley Report, folder 15-19, A Century of Progress records, UIC.

32. Dever later served as a legal council to A Century of Progress.

33. *Chicago Tribune*, April 18, 1928, clipping, Dever Papers, CHM.

34. *Journal*, April 1, 1927, Dever Papers, CHM.

35. Edward Nash Hurley originated and developed the pneumatic tool industry in the United States and Europe. He served as president of several pneumatic tool companies and a bank in addition to serving on many utility and corporate boards. Gen. John J. Pershing awarded him the Distinguished Service Medal for his services shipping troops and supplies during the world war.

36. Edward N. Hurley to William E. Dever, April 8, 1926, folder 1-7755, A Century of Progress records, UIC.

37. Resume of the History of the Chicago Centennial, folder 15-19, A Century of Progress records, UIC.

38. The *Chicago Daily News* published many of the suggested names on September 13, 1926, and delivered all letters with suggestions to Hurley. Examples varied from "Father Dearborn World's fair" to "The World's Twentieth Century Progress exposition." Frequently used terms were Chicago, Centennial, Century, Exposition, Fair, "I Will," Progress, and World's. Folder 1-7755, A Century of Progress records, UIC.

39. William E. Dever to Edward N. Hurley, February 7, 1927, folder 1-7755, A Century of Progress records, UIC.

40. Today the stadium is known as Soldier Field, the Fine Arts Building is the Art Institute of Chicago, the aquarium is the Shedd Aquarium, and the Rosenwald Industrial Museum is the Museum of Science and Industry.

41. William H. Thompson to Edward N. Hurley, September 16, 1926, folder 1-7755, A Century of Progress records, UIC.

42. *The Post*, n.p., April 25, 1927, Century of Progress Planning file, CHM.

43. "Cancel 1933 World's Fair," *Chicago Tribune*, August 2, 1927, 1, clipping, Century of Progress Planning File, CHM. Getz was chair of the board for Globe Coal Company and Eureka Coal and Dock Company.

44. *Chicago Daily News*, September 13, 1927, clipping, Century of Progress Planning file, CHM.

45. Dennis F. Kelly was president of the Fair department store and Chicago Athletic Association and a director of the Continental Illinois Bank and Trust Company. Albert D. Lasker, a leader in advertising, had chaired the U.S. Shipping Board and was active in Jewish organizations. Victor A. Olander, a trades union official, had been a member of the National War Labor Board. Melvin A. Traylor, was an officer of several banks and corporate boards, including president of First National Bank. Harry A. Wheeler, president of Union Trust Company, was an officer in the Chicago Association of Commerce.

46. "Conference re Worlds Fair, Stenographic Report," December 13, 1927, folder 1-12017, A Century of Progress records, UIC.

47. Rufus Dawes to Edward N. Hurley, October 23, 1926, folder 1-7755, A Century of Progress records, UIC. The group included Samuel Insull, Bernard E. Sunny, James E. Gorman, Floyd L. Bateman, Chauncey McCormick, Dennis F. Kelly, and Edward Hurley.

48. Minutes of the Organization Committee, December 20, 1927, folder 15-19, A Century of Progress records, UIC.

49. It had been necessary to amend the constitution of the State of Illinois for the World's Columbian Exposition and therefore it was assumed that it would be necessary for the 1933 fair.

50. Daniel H. Burnham, secretary of the Chicago world's fair, was the son of Daniel H. Burnham Sr., chairman of the Architectural Commission and Director of Works of the 1893 World's Columbian Exposition.

51. Charles Dawes to Rufus Dawes, October 31, 1929, folder 4-38, A Century of Progress records, UIC.

52. Henry F. Pringle, "Dawes Brothers," *American Magazine* (May 1932): 20–21, 116–20.

53. Charles Dawes to Rufus Dawes, October 20, 1930, Dawes Collection, NWU.

54. Milton S. Mayer, *Reflections on "It Can't Be Done,"* Special Collections, Chicago Public Library, Chicago (CPL).

55. "Rufus Cutler Dawes," *Time*, May 22, 1933, cover, 14–16.

56. Charles Dawes to Rufus Dawes, October 20, 1930, and Rufus Dawes to Charles Dawes, October 30, 1930, Dawes Collection, NWU.

57. Bascom M. Timmons, *Portrait of an American: Charles G. Dawes* (New York: Henry Holt, 1953), 153.

58. He resigned in 1900 as comptroller of the currency and ran an unsuccessful bid for the United States Senate from Illinois on an anti–machine politics platform.

59. Their "opposition undoubtedly caused the withdrawal of William Hale Thompson as a candidate for reelection as mayor in 1923." Timmons, *Portrait of an American*, 215. In 1928, Loesch, the chairman of the Chicago Crime Commission, asked Dawes to coordinate approximately seven hundred local associations devoted to constructive civic progress, but Dawes was unable to assume this task while serving as vice president.

60. Keith Spade to General Abel Davis, Chairman of the Committee on Founder Members, February 4, 1929, A Century of Progress records, UIC. Skeptical businessmen who voiced concerns following a meeting on how to meet the Chicago schools payroll included George Getz, William Wrigley Jr., W. R. Abbott, Thomas E. Wilson, James Simpson, John Hertz, George M. Reynolds, Silas Strawn, and Elmer Stevens. Getz, Wrigley, Abbott, Hertz, Strawn, and Stevens were members of the Thompson committee that opposed the fair during the previous year. Simpson and Strawn were in the group of skeptics called into Charles Dawes's office in late May. Getz, Wrigley, Reynolds, and Stevens were later listed in publicity as sponsors for the fair. Wrigley was president of the Wrigley chewing gum company; Abbott was president of Illinois Bell; Wilson edited *Power*; Simpson was president of Marshall Field and Company; Hertz founded Yellow Cab; Reynolds was chair of the board of Continental and Commercial National Bank; Strawn chaired the board of Montgomery Ward; and Stevens was the treasurer of B. F. Goodrich tire manufacturers.

61. Lenox R. Lohr, "How Dawes Financed the World's Fair," *Finance* (August 25, 1945): 35, 49.

62. Stuyvesant Peabody, president of Peabody Coal Company and Consumers Company, secured $5 each from 142,000 Chicagoans. Since admission was 50¢, the ten complimentary tickets served as an advance payment for entry to the fair. Other campaigns sought higher donations. For example, founding members were requested to donate $1,000 each. In 1928, $5 equaled approximately $50 in 2008's exchange.

63. Charles Dawes to Rufus Dawes, May 13, 1930, Dawes Collection, NWU.

64. Charles Dawes to Rufus Dawes, September 17, 1930, Dawes Collection, NWU.

65. Charles Dawes to Rufus Dawes, May 13, 1930, Dawes Collection, NWU.

66. Public Resolution—No. 82—70th Congress, H. J. Res. 365, A Century of Progress records, UIC.

67. Rufus Dawes to Charles Dawes, December 6, 1928, and Charles Dawes to Rufus Dawes, December 8, 1928, Dawes Collection, NWU.

68. When interviewed for his biography, Charles felt that in addition to the success of his bank, the outcome of A Century of Progress had given him great pleasure. He had piloted a resolution through Congress, raised the necessary private funds, seen that no state or municipal taxes were required to support the fair, and had paid back subscribers with interest. See Timmons, *Portrait of an American.*

69. By the 1920s, engineers led General Motors, Singer Sewing Machine, General Electric, Dupont, and Goodyear. David F. Noble, *America by Design: Science, Technology, and the Rise of Corporate Capitalism* (New York: Knopf, 1977), 310–12. In addition, a short-lived technocracy movement in the early 1930s promoted the idea that engineers in government leadership roles could solve problems of unemployment resulting from increasing mechanization in the workplace. The established engineering community, however, rejected the agenda of the technocracy promoters. Oldenziel, *Making Technology Masculine,* 46–47.

70. For some of Lohr's ideas, see Lenox R. Lohr, *Magazine Publishing* (Baltimore: Williams and Wilkins, 1932); idem, "The Teaching Mission," *Military Engineer* 19 (January 1927): 39; idem, "The Engineer as a Public Servant," *Military Engineer* 20 (September 1928): 405; idem, "Effective Organization," *Military Engineer* 19 (March 1927): 131.

71. Lenox R. Lohr, "To Quit Is the Easier Way," *Military Engineer* 17 (January 1925): 32.

72. Quoted in James G. Mann, "Engineer of Mass Education: Lenox R. Lohr and the Celebration of American Science and Industry" (Ph.D. diss., Rutgers University, 1988), 46.

73. Lenox R. Lohr to Rufus C. Dawes, May 13, 1929, folder 4-38, A Century of Progress records, UIC.

74. See Press of the Engineering School, *Functions and Staff Relations of the Engineer Service* (Washington, D.C.: Washington Barracks, 1918).

75. Figure 1 has been redrawn from the sketch prepared by Business Research Corporation and sent to General Abel Davis, October 17, 1929, folder 1-2417, A Century of Progress records, UIC. Figure 2 has been prepared by the author based on information in Stanley P. Farwell to Lenox R. Lohr, March 3, 1920, folder 1-2417, A Century of Progress records, UIC.

76. On February 12, 1930, Business Research Corporation prepared a "Chart of Proposed Organization," which included ten departments. Lenox R. Lohr to Rufus C. Dawes, May 8, 1930, folder 1-2417, A Century of Progress records, UIC. Later the Comptroller Department centralized all financial operations, including those from the Treasury Department and the Admissions Department. General Services evolved into Operations and Maintenance. Special Features shifted to other committees and departments.

77. Martha McGrew diary, September 23, 1930, 2, and October 22, 1930, 5, folder 371, Lenox R. Lohr Papers, UIC.

78. The group included eight men: Britton I. Budd, railroads and utilities; Francis X. Busch, law and academia; Abel Davis, banking and law; Paul H. Davis, finance; D. F. Kelly, retail; Amos C. Miller, law; F. R. Moulton, astronomy and academia; and William Allen Pusey, medicine. Janet Ayer Fairbank, the lone woman member, was a novelist who had raised funds for World War I while serving on the Woman's National Liberty Loan Committee.

79. George D. Bushnell, "Chicago's Leading Men's Clubs," *Chicago History* 11 (Summer 1982): 78–88.

80. As chief of staff of the War Department, J. Franklin Bell had coordinated the preparations for the *Engineer Field Manual* (Washington, D.C.: Government Printing Office, 1918). After the war he served as the District of Columbia engineer commissioner.

81. T. H. Jackson, "The Basic Principles of Organization," *The Military Engineer* 16 (March 1924): 95–99; Layton, *Revolt of the Engineers,* 8.

82. Lenox R. Lohr to Martha McGrew, October 12, 1930, folder 352, Lenox R. Lohr Papers, UIC.

83. For illustrated, detailed descriptions of the Administration Building, see E. H. Bennett, H. Burnham, J. A. Holabird, and Louis Skidmore, "The Administration Building," *Architectural Forum* 55 (August 1931): 133–42, 213–16; and Robert Bruegmann, *Holabird and Roche, Holabird and Root: An Illustrated Catalog of Works,* 3 vols. (New York: Garland, 1991), 3:145–50. For fair architecture, see Lisa D. Schrenk, *Building A Century of Progress: The Architecture of Chicago's 1933–34 World's Fair* (Minneapolis: University of Minnesota Press, 2007).

84. Chicago World's Fair Centennial Celebration press release, May 29, 1929, folder 14-1, A Century of Progress records, UIC.

Chapter 3: A New Vision for a World's Fair

1. This point was addressed in the remark that forms the epigraph for this chapter, which is drawn from Harvey Wiley Corbett, "The Significance of the Exposition," *Architectural Forum* 59 (July 1933): 29.

2. Col. R. McCormick was editor of the *Chicago Tribune* and Walter A. Strong was publisher of the *Daily News.* James Simpson was president of Marshall Field Company and a director of the Federal Reserve Bank, Seventh Federal Reserve District, and of Commonwealth Edison. Silas H. Strawn, an attorney, was a director of the First National Bank and chairman of the board of Montgomery Ward and Company. Melvin A. Traylor was president of First National Bank of Chicago and later an early member of the Executive Committee of A Century of Progress; and John W. O'Leary, a banker and manufacturer, was president of Arthur J. O'Leary and Son Company and first vice president of Chicago Trust Company.

3. Charles G. Dawes, *A Journal of the Great War,* 2 vols. (Boston: Houghton Mifflin, 1921), 1:241.

4. Fifteen or twenty board members protested the name change at a subsequent meeting, but the leadership easily pacified them, and in the end the vote in favor of the name change was unanimous. The local newspapers, however, continued to refer to the event as the "World's Fair."

5. See John B. Bury, *The Idea of Progress: An Inquiry into Its Origins and Growth* (London: MacMillan, 1921).

6. Charles A. Beard, ed., *A Century of Progress* (New York: Harper, 1932).

7. Charles A. Beard, "The Idea of Progress" in his *A Century of Progress,* 4; J. B. Bury, *The Idea of Progress: An Inquiry into Its Origin and Growth,* with an introduction by Charles A. Beard (New York: Dover, 1955), ix–xl.

8. Beard, "Idea of Progress," 11.

9. Charles A. Beard to Rudolph A. Clemen, December 14, 1931, folder 1-1449, A Century of Progress records, UIC.

10. For information on the Crystal Palace, see Jeffrey A. Auerbach, *The Great Exhibition of 1851: A Nation on Display* (New Haven: Yale University Press, 1999); Tobin Andrews Sparling, *The Great Exhibition: A Question of Taste* (New Haven: Yale Center for British Art, 1982); Marilyn Symmes, *Fountains, Splash, and Spectacle: Water and Design from the Renaissance to the Present* (New York: Rizzoli, 1998); and John Tallis, *Tallis's History and Description of the Crystal Palace, and the Exhibition of the World's Industry in 1851* (London: John Tallis, 1852).

11. Horace Greeley, *Art and Industry as Represented in the Exhibition at the Crystal Palace,*

New York 1853–4 Showing the Progress and State of the Various Useful and Esthetic Pursuits (New York: Redfield, 1853), 55; Ivan D. Steen, "America's First World's Fair: The Exhibition of the Industry of All Nations at New York's Crystal Palace, 1853–1854," *New-York Historical Society Quarterly* 47 (July 1963): 257–87.

12. Staudenmeier, "Perils of Progress Talk," 271.

13. On MacMonnies's work, see Halsey C. Ives, *The Dream City: A Portfolio of Photographic Views of the World's Columbian Exposition* (St. Louis: N. D. Thompson, 1893); and E. Adina Gordon, *A Flight with Fame: The Life and Art of Frederick MacMonnies, 1863–1937* (Madison, Conn.: Sound View Press, 1996).

14. Louise Lentz Woodruff had studied at Columbia University and at the School of the Art Institute of Chicago. Her artistic mentors included Lorado Taft, who taught many aspiring women artists in Chicago, and Emile Antoine Bourdelle of Paris. Bourdelle urged his students to seek essential truths and free themselves from superfluous ornamentation. Taft, whose Chicago studio produced many works for the 1893 World's Columbian Exposition, was dedicated to the sculptural beautification of Chicago. He believed that public sculptures captured the essence of the cultural ideas and ideals of those who collaborated to erect them. These views influenced Woodruff's own artistic vision and more modernist style.

15. Woodward's sculpture, removed from its pedestal, is currently located in a Chicagoland high school lobby. See Archives Committee, *The Steelman Tradition* (Joliet: Joliet Township High Schools, Central Campus, 1988) and Dorothy Crombie, "Louise Lentz Woodruff Collection," Joliet Public Library, Joliet, Illinois.

16. "Fountain of Science," folder 1-15902, A Century of Progress records, UIC. For a discussion on the scientific educational role of the fair, see National Research Council, *National Research Council Science Advisory Committee to A Century of Progress, Chicago World's Fair, Centennial Celebration 1933* (New York: National Research Council, 1929); "Adult Education," *Engineering News-Record* 111 (June 1, 1933): 720–21; and Robert W. Rydell, *World of Fairs: The Century-of-Progress Expositions* (Chicago: University of Chicago Press, 1993).

17. F. B. Jewett, "Dedication of the Hall of Science of the Century of Progress Exposition: The Social Effects of Modern Science," *Science* 76 (July 1932): 23–26.

18. The opening of Tutankhamen's tomb in 1922 had ignited the popular imagination. American newspapers and magazines regularly ran photo essays portraying this ancient culture. Jewelry, furniture, architecture, advertising, and films fueled Egyptomania, material culture adapting Egyptian designs to fit the context of modern times. For Americans, Egypt symbolized immortality and represented achievement in the fields of art, science, and learning. See National Gallery of Canada, *Egyptomania: Egypt in Western Art, 1730–1930* (Ottawa: National Gallery of Canada, 1994); and Shelly Jayne Foote, "Egypt in America: The Popularization of Ancient Egypt and Its Influence on American Jewelry, 1869–1925" (M.A. thesis, George Washington University, 1985).

19. A Century of Progress, *Official Guide: Book of the Fair 1933* (Chicago: A Century of Progress, 1933), 11; and Carroll Pursell, *The Machine in America: A Social History of Technology* (Baltimore: Johns Hopkins University Press, 1995), 267–68.

20. See Staudenmeier, "Perils of Progress Talk," 268–93; and Tozer, "A Century of Progress, 1833–1933," 78–81.

21. Rufus C. Dawes, Address to Association of Commerce, February 19, 1930, folder 4-47, A Century of Progress records, UIC.

22. Charles Dawes to Rufus Dawes, May 13, 1930, Dawes Collection, NWU.

23. John Stephen Sewell to Lenox R. Lohr, March 18, 1931, folder 11-13, A Century of Progress records, UIC.

24. John Stephen Sewell to Lenox R. Lohr, December 24, 1931, folder 1-14990, A Century of Progress records, UIC.

25. Rufus C. Dawes to Frank B. Jewett, March 14, 1936, Dawes Collection, NWU.

26. John W. Phillips, "A Century of Progress" (Ph.D. diss. Wharton School of Finance and Commerce, Philadelphia, 1934), 47–48. Later Daniel H. Burnham of Chicago became Director of Works and Ferruccio Vitale of New York joined the team. Norman Bel Geddes served for a time as an adviser and Joseph Urban developed the color scheme and advised on the illumination.

27. Forrest Crissey, "Why the Century of Progress Architecture? An Interview with Allen D. Albert, Secretary of the Architectural Commission," *Saturday Evening Post,* June 10, 1933, 16–17, folder 16-270, A Century of Progress records, UIC.

28. Edwin F. Clably, "A Century of Progress," *Greater Chicago Magazine* 4 (July 1929).

29. Susan M. Matthias, "Paris 1925: Exposition Internationale des Arts Decoratifs et Industriels Modernes," in Findling, *Historical Dictionary of World's Fairs,* 239–43; and Martin Greif, *Depression Modern: The Thirties Style in America* (New York: Universe, 1975), 16–17. "Modernism" referred to something new and different in the 1920s and 1930s. Since 1966, many historians have used the term "Art Deco" when referring to "Modern" designs. The "Modern" type of architecture at the 1933 Chicago world's fair is also called "Classic-Modern." Patricia Bayer, *Art Deco Architecture: Design, Decoration, and Detail from the Twenties and Thirties* (New York: Thames and Hudson, 1999), 42.

30. Corbett, "The Significance of the Exposition," 29–31; Schrenk, *Building A Century of Progress,* 68–69.

31. Crissey, "Why the Century of Progress Architecture?" 18.

32. For architecture at the fair, see Bruegmann, *Holabird and Roche, Holabird and Root,* all three vols.; C. W. Farrier, "Exposition Buildings Unique in Form and Structure," *Engineering News-Record* 110 (March 2, 1933): 278–82; Owings, *Spaces in Between,* 44–60; Schrenk, *Building A Century of Progress; Architectural Forum,* 1928–34; and Nathaniel A. Owings, "Temple of Science for World's Fair," *Chicago Commerce* 28 (August 1931): 25, 92. For designs that were never executed, see Martha Thorne, *Unbuilt Chicago* (Chicago: Art Institute of Chicago, 2004).

33. The carillon could play musical programs via a keyboard and it could sound Westminster chimes every fifteen minutes. "Build Chimes for Hall of Science," *Progress* 2 (January 13, 1932): 4; and "Chicagoland's Music Festival to Use Chimes," *Progress* 2 (August 17, 1932): 1.

34. Henry Crew to Paul Philippe Cret, August 2, 1933, Paul Philippe Cret Papers, Special Collection Department, Van Pelt Library, University of Pennsylvania, Philadelphia.

35. On Cret, see Elizabeth Greenwell Grossman, *The Civic Architecture of Paul Cret* (Cambridge: Cambridge University Press, 1996); and Theo B. White, ed., *Paul Philippe Cret: Architect and Teacher* (Philadelphia: Art Alliance Press, 1973).

36. Cret Collection, Athenaeum of Philadelphia, Philadelphia; and Paul Philippe Cret Architectural Records, 1823–1945, Architectural Archives, University of Pennsylvania, Philadelphia.

37. Paul P. Cret, "Exposition Buildings, Particularly of the Century of Progress 1933," n.d., 3, Paul Philippe Cret Papers, Annenberg Rare Book and Manuscript Library, Van Pelt–Dietrich Library, University of Pennsylvania, Philadelphia.

38. For Cret's ideas on the evolution of architects and engineers working on projects together, see Paul Philippe Cret, "The Architect as Collaborator with the Engineer," *Architectural Forum* 49 (July 1928): 97–104.

39. Sources vary concerning the exact number of colors with some citing twenty-six used in 1933.

40. Cret, "Exposition Buildings, Particularly of the Century of Progress 1933," 2.

41. For Joseph Urban's influence on consumerism, see William Leach, *Land of Desire: Merchants, Power, and the Rise of a New American Culture* (New York: Vintage, 1993).

42. "Urban," July 10, 1933, 2, folder 1-14990, A Century of Progress records, UIC. For a defense of the art of color at the fair, see Shepard Vogelgesang, "Some New Thoughts on Color," *Chicago Commerce* 28 (August 1931): 36, 93.

43. Lee Lawrie believed that sculpture should accent or characterize buildings, not decorate them. For his perspective on mural sculpture, see Lee Lawrie, *Modern Mural Sculpture* (Pasadena, Calif.: Esto Publishing, 1934).

44. John A. Holabird to Harvey W. Corbett, January 18, 1932, and A Century of Progress to Joseph Urban, October 29, 1932, both in folder 1-14990; and Joseph Urban to Shepard Vogelgesang, March 3, 1932, folder 1-14990, all in A Century of Progress records, UIC.

45. Daniel H. Burnham to Joseph Urban, July 23, 1932, folder 1-14990, A Century of Progress records, UIC.

46. The American Asphalt Paint Company received the contract to supply aluminum, oil, and casein paints and the labor to apply them during the two months preceding the May 1933 opening.

47. Lenox R. Lohr to Joseph Urban, December 17, 1931, folder 1-14990, A Century of Progress records, UIC; and John Hogan, *A Spirit Capable: The Story of Commonwealth Edison* (Chicago: Mobium Press, 1986), 180–85. For the history of exposition illumination, see John A. Jakle, *City Lights: Illuminating the American Night* (Baltimore: Johns Hopkins University Press, 2001), 143–68; David E. Nye, *Narratives and Spaces: Technology and the Construction of American Culture* (New York: Columbia University Press, 1997); and idem, "Electrifying Expositions: 1880–1939," in *Fair Representations: World's Fairs and the Modern World*, ed. Robert W. Rydell and Nancy E. Gwinn (Amsterdam: VU University Press, 1994), 140–56.

48. Teegan sought Urban's advice on Westinghouse's path lighting designs. Further, fair officials sought Urban's reaction to such various decorative features as banners, kiosks, benches, and umbrellas.

49. Otto Teegen to Joseph Urban, October 20, 1932, folder 1-14990, A Century of Progress records, UIC.

50. Charles Borland, "Glass Pipe Magic," *Chicago Commerce* 30 (December 1933): 23–25, 32; Charles J. Stahl, "The Rainbow of Light that Came to the Fair," *Chicago Commerce* 30 (January 1934): 53–63; Louis Skidmore, "The Hall of Science, A Century of Progress Exposition: Details of Structure and Equipment," *Architectural Forum* 57 (October 1932): 361–66; and "The Story of Neon Light and Its Brothers," *Official World's Fair Weekly* 1 (June 24, 1933): 16–17.

51. "Urban," July 10, 1933, folder 1-14990, A Century of Progress records, UIC.

52. Wade Ware Bennett, "A Color Palette for Your Mood," *Chicago Commerce* 31 (June 1934): 44, 46.

53. Louis Skidmore, "Science Dictates the Building Mode for 1933," *Chicago Commerce* 26 (February 21, 1931): 18–19, 28. Skidmore's duties included sales promotional work, contact with the Architectural Commission, consultation on proposed exhibits, consideration of designs and exhibits submitted by exhibitors, and supervision of the construction of several buildings, including Firestone, Chrysler, and General Motors.

54. Daniel H. Burnham, "Turning Architecture to Modern Life," *Chicago Commerce* 29 (May 1932): 28.

55. John Stephen Sewell to Lenox R. Lohr, October 22, 1930, folder 11-11, A Century of Progress records, UIC.

56. National Research Council, *National Research Council Science Advisory Committee to A Century of Progress; National Research Council, Preliminary Report of the Science Advisory*

Committee to the Trustees of A Century of Progress (April 1930), folder 5-269, A Century of Progress records, UIC; and National Research Council, *Consolidated Report upon the Activities of the National Research Council, 1919 to 1932* (Washington, D.C.: National Research Council, 1932).

57. A. W. Shaw, "Book Series for Century of Progress," *Chicago Commerce* 28 (January 1932): 17, 71.

58. Frank B. Jewett to Harvey Wiley Corbett, March 3, 1936, Dawes Collection, NWU.

59. Mary Lackritz Gray, *A Guide to Chicago's Murals* (Chicago: University of Chicago Press, 2001), 362.

60. A. Frederick Collins, *The New World of Science* (Philadelphia: J. B. Lippincott, 1934); and Paul Paddock, "New Scientific Marvels of the World's Fair," *Modern Mechanix and Inventions* 12 (July 1934): 34–36, 143.

61. For the Hall of Science exhibits, see A Century of Progress, *Official Catalog of Exhibits in the Division of the Basic Sciences, Hall of Science* (Chicago: A Century of Progress International Exhibition, 1933); A Century of Progress, *Official Handbook of Exhibits in the Division of the Basic Sciences, Hall of Science* (Chicago: A Century of Progress, 1934); Kenneth S. Davis, *FDR: The New Deal Years, 1933–1937: A History* (New York: Random House, 1986), 225; Jeffrey L. Meikle, *American Plastic: A Cultural History* (New Brunswick, N.J.: Rutgers University Press, 1997), 84–85; and Eben J. Carey, *Medical Science Exhibits: A Century of Progress* (Chicago: A Century of Progress, 1936).

62. William Allen Pusey, "Man's Conquest of Nature Is Theme of the Exposition," *Chicago Commerce* 26 (October 1930): 9–11.

Chapter 4: The Vision on Display

1. The statement by William Randolph Hearst that forms the epigraph for this chapter comes from Alfred P. Sloan Jr., ed., *Previews of Industrial Progress in the Next Century: A Dinner Conference at the Hall of Progress, General Motors Building, Century of Progress Exposition Grounds, Chicago, May 25, 1934* (New York: General Motors Corporation, 1934), 23.

2. General Electric and Westinghouse Electric files, folder 16-263-65, A Century of Progress records, UIC; "670 Million Miles an Hour by Arcturus—the Fair Star," *Official World's Fair Weekly* 1 (June 3, 1933): 10–11; and "Arcturus, Giant of Skies, Cast for Lead Role," *Progress* 1 (August 19, 1931): 1.

3. Roland Marchand studied corporate imagery as giant corporations in the early twentieth century aspired to become institutions with a social and moral legitimacy. Although he identified the shift at world's fairs in 1933 to individual corporate exhibits and pavilions, he failed to explain how and why cooperative exhibits failed, a story crucial to understanding how the change took place. Roland Marchand, *Creating the Corporate Soul: The Rise of Public Relations and Corporate Imagery in American Big Business* (Berkeley: University of California Press, 1998), 2–4, 249–66.

4. John Stephen Sewell, "Using Showmanship to Sell Science at World's Fair," *Chicago Commerce* 28 (September 1931): 30, 42.

5. Charles M. Fitch to Files, September 24, 1930, folder 11-37, A Century of Progress records, UIC.

6. "Trigg Luncheon, January 5, 1928," and "Minutes of Meeting Held at Luncheon at the Mid Day Club," both in folder 1-14723, A Century of Progress records, UIC.

7. Ernest T. Trigg, "The Value of World's Fairs," 7, folder 1-14723, A Century of Progress records, UIC.

8. See Allen D. Albert, *Planning Real Estate Activities in Preparation for the World's Fair, 1933* (Chicago: Chicago Regional Planning Association, 1929); Rufus C. Dawes, *A New Thought on World's Fairs* (Chicago: Chicago World's Fair Centennial Celebration, c. 1929); and idem, *A Century of Progress, Report of the President to the Board of Trustees* (Chicago: A Century of Progress, 1936), 27.

9. Robert Piper Boyce, "George Fred Keck, 1895–1980: Midwest Architect" (Ph.D. diss., University of Wisconsin–Madison, 1986); Joseph C. Folsom, "The House of Tomorrow," *Official World's Fair Weekly* 1 (September 30, 1933): 34; Brian Horrigan, "The Home of Tomorrow, 1927–1945," in *Imagining Tomorrow: History, Technology, and the American Future*, ed. Joseph J. Corn (Cambridge, Mass.: MIT Press, 1986), 137–63; Dorothy Raley, ed., *A Century of Progress Homes and Furnishings* (Chicago: M. A. Ring Company, 1934); and "The Modern Homes of the Century of Progress Exposition," *Architectural Forum* 59 (July 1933): 51–62.

10. R. P. Shaw to Frank R. Lillie, May 7, 1930, folder 11-6, A Century of Progress records, UIC.

11. "Tentative Analysis of Exhibits, August 1930," and "Conference on Exhibits, November 10, 1930," both in folder 11-56, A Century of Progress records, UIC.

12. Research Committee on Social Trends, *Recent Social Trends in the United States: Report of the President's Research Committee on Social Trends* (New York: McGraw-Hill, 1933); S. C. Gilfillan, "Inventions and Discoveries," *American Journal of Sociology* 38 (May 1933): 835–44; idem, *The Sociology of Invention* (Chicago: Follett, 1935); S. Colum Gilfillan to Donald Slesinger, November 17, 1932, folder 1-6311, A Century of Progress records, UIC; S. Colum Gilfillan collection, 461; Melvin Kranzberg Papers, 266, National Museum of American History Archives Center, Washington D.C.; and Rudi Volti, "Classics Revisited: William F. Ogburn, Social Change with Respect to Culture and Original Nature," *Technology and Culture* 45 (April 2004): 396–405. For the Ogburn and Gilfillan reports to the world's fair see folders 11-215–18, A Century of Progress records, UIC.

13. "A Successful World's Fair Means a Successful Business Year for Chicago," *Chicago Commerce* 31 (March 1934): 7; and M. M. Tveter, "The Fair in Figures," *Chicago Commerce* 30 (January 1934): 42–45.

14. The $20,000,000 in 1933 included $3,000,000 for rental of exhibit space, $3,500,000 for special exhibit buildings, about $10,000,000 for the preparation and installation of exhibits, and about $3,500,000 for maintenance, operations, and payroll. The Sesqui-centennial in Philadelphia in 1926 was the only previous exposition to charge rent for exhibit space. J. Franklin Bell, "Selling a World's Fair," *Chicago Commerce* 31 (December 1934): 24.

15. Oscar Holbert to J. Franklin Bell, January 10, 1933, folder 1-4926, A Century of Progress records, UIC.

16. A West Point graduate, John Stephen Sewell was serving as commanding officer of the Seventeenth Railway Engineers regiment when Charles Gates Dawes joined the regiment in World War I. After the war, he worked on government construction projects, including the printing office, the war college, and the department of agriculture. Although originally hired away from his presidency of the Alabama Marble Company to handle all foreign participation for the exposition, he soon took on the role of overseeing all exhibits. Dawes, *Journal of the Great War*, 1:3–5; and "Acquiring Expert Staff Men," *Chicago Commerce* 26 (August 1930): 20.

17. "Industrial Leaders See Exposition as Symbol of Reviving Prosperity," *Progress* 1 (September 23, 1931): 1; and Edward H. Sniffin, "The World Needs a World's Fair Now," *Chicago Commerce* 29 (May 1932): 31.

18. Charles G. Dawes, "The End of the Depression," *Chicago Commerce* 31 (January 1935): 13–15, 42–43.

19. Charles W. Fitch, "Big Business Plans 1933 Fair on Prosperity Basis," *Chicago Commerce* 28 (October 1931): 26.

20. Bell, "Selling a World's Fair," 23–24, 40–41.

21. John Stephen Sewell, "An Unparalleled Opportunity for Science, Industry and Invested Capital to Tell Their Story of Service to the Public," folder 11-13, A Century of Progress records, UIC; and idem, "Paying Civilization's Debt to Industry, Science and Capital," *Chicago Commerce* 28 (August 1931): 37, 90.

22. Beard, "Introduction," in Bury, *The Idea of Progress*, xxiii.

23. Timothy Palmer, "Barcelona 1929–1930: Exposición Internacional de Barcelona"; idem, "Seville 1929–1930: Exposición Ibero-Americana"; Paul Greenhalgh, "Antwerp 1930 and Liège 1930: Exposition Internationale, Colonial, Maritime, et d'Art Flemmand Exposition Internationale de la Grande Industrie, Science et Application Art Walloon"; Marc Lagana, "Paris 1931: Exposition Coloniale Internationale," all in Findling, *Historical Dictionary of World's Fairs*, 252–65.

24. John M. MacKenzie, "Wembley 1924–1925: British Empire Exhibition," in Findling, *Historical Dictionary of World's Fairs*, 235–38.

25. Lenox R. Lohr to John Stephen Sewell, October 18, 1930, folder 11-11; Charles W. Fitch to Albert Halstead, April 4, 1931, folder 11-51; Edward J. Ashenden to Director of Exhibits, April 17, 1933, folder 11-44; and Edward J. Ashenden, "A New Showmanship to Charm for the World's Fair," folder 11-49, all in A Century of Progress records, UIC. Although Dwight Franklin had made dioramas while working at the American Museum of Natural History in New York from 1906 to 1914, and later he and others had made some museum models, the fair organizers of A Century of Progress demonstrated the possibilities of this medium for display both commercially and in museums. Irene Fletcher Cypher, "The Development of the Diorama in the Museums of the United States" (Ph.D. diss., New York University, 1942), 70–77, 146–49.

26. The first building to open on the fairgrounds was a replica of Fort Dearborn. Open to the public for five months in 1931, it demonstrated early on the drawing power of the fair when 115,000 visitors arrived from other states and more than twenty countries. Morris S. Daniels Jr., "A Harbinger for the 1933 Fair," *Chicago Commerce* 28 (November 1931): 26, 54; and "Fort Dearborn Public Opening May 16," *Progress* 3 (May 13, 1933): 1.

27. "Ship Dioramas to Paris Exposition," *Progress* 1 (April 29, 1931): 2.

28. Edward J. Ashenden to Director of Exhibits, January 27, 1933, folder 11-44; Edward J. Ashenden to Mr. Bowe, June 8, 1932, folder 11-42; and "Exhibits," May 21, 1933, folder 11-3, all in A Century of Progress records, UIC. Most official guidebooks from the fair illustrate exteriors of buildings rather than interiors and exhibits. The exception is James Weber Linn, introduction in *The Official Pictures of A Century of Progress Exposition Chicago 1933* (Chicago: Reuben H. Donnelley, 1933), which includes a photograph of the diorama "Electricity at Work" on page 58.

29. Edward J. Ashenden to Rufus Dawes, March 12, 1932, folder 11-43, A Century of Progress records, UIC; and Leon Morgan, *The World a Million Years Ago* (Chicago: Magill-Weinsheimer, 1933).

30. "Millions See Weird Sinclair Dinosaurs," *Big News* 1 (New York: Sinclair Refining Company, 1933).

31. "Otis Century of Progress Literature" and "The End of the Sky Ride," both in folder 16-247, A Century of Progress records, UIC; *Sky-Ride: See the Fair from the Air* (Chicago: Participating Contractors, 1933); "Something New under the Sun," *Chicago Commerce* 29 (August 1932): 26; and "Thrill and View Promised in Sky Ride Rocket Car," *Progress* 2 (July 6, 1932): 1–2.

32. Great Lakes Dredge and Dock Company laid the foundations, Inland Steel Company furnished the steel for the towers, and the Mississippi Valley Structural Steel Company fabricated and erected them. The steel cables came from John A. Roebling's Sons Company.

33. F. C. Boggs to Lenox R. Lohr, January 29, 1931, folder 9-113, A Century of Progress records, UIC.

34. Marchand, *Creating the Corporate Soul*, 266; idem, "Corporate Imagery and Popular Education: World's Fairs and Expositions in the United States, 1893–1940," in *Consumption and American Culture*, ed. David E. Nye and Carl Pedersen (Amsterdam: VU University Press, 1991), 18–33; and Roland Marchand and Michael L. Smith, "Corporate Science on Display," in *Scientific Authority and Twentieth-Century America*, ed. Ronald G. Walters (Baltimore: Johns Hopkins University Press, 1997), 148–82.

35. H. E. Van Norman, *Dairy Products Build Superior People* (Chicago: Century Dairy Exhibit, 1933), 1 (quote); Lohr, *Fair Management*, 131; "Dairy Industry Development Will Be Shown in Fair Exhibit," *Progress* 2 (March 23, 1932): 1; and "Leaders of Dairy Industry Christen Fair's Building," *Progress* 2 (November 9, 1932): 3–4.

36. Colonel Sewell to Major Lohr, June 11, 1931, folder 11-18, A Century of Progress records, UIC.

37. "What a Night," folder 16-264, A Century of Progress records, UIC.

38. Collins, *New World of Science*, 117–18. Later in his career, Lenox R. Lohr would become president of the National Broadcasting Company and be a leader in the television industry. See Lenox R. Lohr, *Television Broadcasting: Production, Economics, Technique* (New York: McGraw-Hill, 1940).

39. "General Electric Company Signs for Space," *Progress* 1 (August 26, 1931): 1; "Mammoth Diorama to Show Modern Uses of Electrical Energy at Exposition," *Progress* 3 (February 1, 1933): 2.

40. Lenox R. Lohr to Charles Gates Dawes, May 6, 1930, folder 1-12506; and Frank B. Jewett to Lenox R. Lohr, June 27, 1930, folder 1-674, A Century of Progress records, UIC.

41. James G. Harbord to Lenox R. Lohr, August 21, 1931, folder 1-12505, A Century of Progress records, UIC. Because only RCA and the Stewart Warner Corporation had paid for space in the Radio Building, the plans for financing a separate building failed.

42. American Telephone and Telegraph Company, *The Bell System: Its Organization and Service as Exhibited at a Century of Progress Exposition* (n.p.: American Telephone and Telegraph Company, 1933), 19.

43. Stanley R. Edwards, "World's Fair; Psychology, Human Nature," *Telephony: The American Telephone Journal* 105 (November 18, 1933): 10–14.

44. "Exhibiting Telephone Progress at the World's Fair," *Bell Telephone Quarterly* 13 (January 1934): 21. See also "A Visit to Bell System's Exhibit at the World's Fair," *Bell Telephone News* 23 (June 1933): 1–4; "Mr. Dawes Greets Mr. Farley from Bell System's Exhibit," *Bell Telephone News* 23 (June 1933): 5; "Filling the Communications Needs of a World's Fair," *Bell Telephone News* 23 (June 1933): 6–7; "The Bell System Exhibit at 'A Century of Progress,'" typescript, Ameritech Corporation Collection, SBC Archives, folder 2-5, Archives and History Center, San Antonio, Texas; John Mills, "The Bell System Exhibit at the 'Century of Progress' Exposition," *Bell Telephone Quarterly* 12 (January 1933): 42–54, folder 1-674, and John Stephen Sewell to Walter S. Gifford, January 11, 1932, folder 1-673, A Century of Progress records, UIC; and "Telephones and What Makes Them Click," *Official World's Fair Weekly* 1 (June 10, 1933): 58–59.

45. For AT&T visitor analysis, see "Memorandum on Results at the Bell System Exhibit," folder 1-670, and "Data on Long Distance Calls Made at the Bell System Exhibit," 1-669, A Century of Progress records, UIC.

46. Edwards, "World's Fair; Psychology, Human Nature," 14. Bell Telephone Laboratories estimates placed numbers at 90 percent of visitors, but this was likely exaggerated.

47. F. O. Clements to J. Parker Van Zandt, February 24, 1931, folder 1-6216, A Century of Progress records, UIC.

48. J. Parker Van Zandt to Chief of Division and Director of Exhibits, April 20, 1931, folder 1-6216, A Century of Progress records, UIC.

49. Knudsen remark reported in J. Parker Van Zandt to Director of Exhibits and General Manager, July 3, 1931, folder 1-6216, A Century of Progress records, UIC.

50. Assistant Secretary to J. Parker Van Zandt, January 12, 1932, folder 1-6215, and Director of Exhibits to Division Chiefs, September 9, 1931, folder 11-2, A Century of Progress records, UIC. As a result of the GM arrangement, fair officials developed an exclusive rights policy for use with other corporations. Firestone Tire and Rubber Company, for example, had exclusive rights to show the manufacturing process of tires.

51. "Two Big Buildings to Be Erected," *Progress* 1 (July 22, 1931): 1.

52. "Of News to Us at the World's Fair Concerning General Motors Trucks, Fisher Guild, Designers and Artists" *General Motors Magazine* 1 (March 1933): 6.

53. *General Motors at the World's Fair* (Detroit: General Motors, 1933).

54. "Of News to Us at the World's Fair," 5.

55. Miklos Gaspar, Axel Linus, and T. C. Wick painted the murals. Gray, *Guide to Chicago's Murals*, 248–49, and Palmer, "We Make a Car," *Official World's Fair Weekly* 1 (June 10, 1933): 12–15.

56. "What We Saw in the General Motors Exhibit Building," "The General Motors Exhibit," and "General Motors Hall of Progress" are examples GM handout brochures from 1933–34. For a listing of corporate handouts, see J. K. Wilcox, *Checklist of the Official Publications of the Century of Progress International Exposition and Its Exhibitors, 1933* (Chicago: John Crerar Library, 1933), and idem, *Checklist of the Official Publications of the Century of Progress International Exposition and Its Exhibitors 1933*, 2 supplements (Chicago: John Crerar Library, 1934, 1935).

57. *Words of Wisdom: Ancient and Modern* (General Motors, 1933), 2.

58. See *Things You Don't Want to Forget about Chrysler at the Century of Progress Exposition* (Detroit: Chrysler Motors, 1933); *Thrilling Movie Shots of Dodge in Action* (Detroit: Chrysler Motors, 1933); *Chrysler Motors at A Century of Progress Presents the Drop Forge Hammer* (Detroit: Chrysler Motors, 1933); and *Whiting Auto-parking Tower Built for Nash Moving Auto Display at The Century of Progress* (Chicago: Whiting Corporation, 1933).

59. See Jeffrey L. Meikle, *Twentieth-Century Limited: Industrial Design in America, 1925–1939* (Philadelphia: Temple University Press, 1979); Walter Dorwin Teague, "1893: World's Fair: 1933" (n.p., 1933), 13–14; idem, *Design This Day: The Technique of Order in the Machine Age* (New York: Harcourt, Brace, 1940), 92–94, 170–73; idem, "Designing Ford's Exhibit at A Century of Progress," 450–52, Henry Ford Papers, Henry Ford Museum and Greenfield Village Research Center, Dearborn, Michigan; and Claire Winslow, "Modern Decor Scores Another Success at Fair," *Chicago Tribune*, August 12, 1934, C4. For film footage of the Ford exhibits, see *Century of Progress Exposition* (Detroit: Ford Motor Company, 1934); and *Ford and A Century of Progress*, (Detroit: Ford Educational Library, 1934).

60. Roland Marchand, "The Designers Go to the Fair, I: Walter Dorwin Teague and the Professionalization of Corporate Industrial Exhibits, 1933–40," in *Design History: An Anthology*, ed. Dennis P. Doordan (Cambridge, Mass.: MIT Press, 1995),folder 89–102; idem, "The Designers Go to the Fair, II: Norman Bel Geddes, the General Motors 'Futurama,' and the Visit-to-the-Factory Transformed," in Doordan, *Design History*, 103–23.

61. Walter Dorwin Teague, "Exhibition Technique," *American Architect and Architecture* (September 1937): 31.

62. Marchand, *Creating the Corporate Soul*, 268–76; idem, *Advertising the American Dream: Making Way for Modernity, 1920–1940* (Berkeley: University of California Press, 1985), 320–24; "Ford Contracts for 11 Acres for Huge Exhibit in 1934 Exposition," *Progress* 4 (March 1, 1934): 1; and Albert Kahn, Inc., Architects, "Ford Exposition Building: Century of Progress," *Architectural*

Forum 61 (July 1934): 2–10. Ford brochures distributed at the fair included James Sweinhard, *The Industrialized American Barn: A Glimpse of the Farm of the Future* (Detroit: Ford Motor Company, 1934); *Roads of the World: Ford Exposition "A Century of Progress"* (Detroit: Ford Motor Company, 1934); *Henry Ford: Welcome to the Ford Exposition* (Detroit: Ford Motor Company, 1934); *How to See the Ford Exposition* (Detroit: Ford Motor Company, 1934); and *Why Women Prefer the Ford V-8* (Detroit: Ford Motor Company, 1934).

63. David Farber, *Sloan Rules: Alfred P. Sloan and the Triumph of General Motors* (Chicago: University of Chicago Press, 2002), 173.

64. Alfred P. Sloan Jr. to Lenox R. Lohr, May 1934, folder 1-6212, A Century of Progress records, UIC.

65. Albert Shaw, "Chicago Presents an Object Lesson," *Review of Reviews* 90 (July 1934): 47–48.

66. Farber, *Sloan Rules*, 178.

67. Sloan, *Previews of Industrial Progress in the Next Century*, 18.

68. Lohr, *Fair Management*, 128.

Chapter 5: Women's Spaces at the Fair

1. The epigraph for this chapter is from Helen M. Bennett, "A Woman Looks at The Century of Progress," *Woman's World: The Magazine of the Town and Country* 50 (June 1934): 18.

2. Mary R. Beard, "The Social Role of Women in History," 10, Mrs. Harlan Ward Cooley Collection of Women in the Century of Progress, Special Collections Department, CPL.

3. Henry Adams, *The Education of Henry Adams* (1918; New York: Modern Library, 1999), 384. For "new women," see Anne Firor Scott, "What, Then, Is the American: This New Woman?" *Journal of American History* 65 (December 1978): 679–703, and Susan A. Glenn, *Female Spectacle: The Theatrical Roots of Modern Feminism* (Cambridge, Mass.: Harvard University Press, 2000), 6.

4. Adams, *Education of Henry Adams*, 445.

5. Beard, "Social Role of Women in History," 3.

6. Ibid., 5.

7. David F. Noble, "Command Performance: A Perspective on the Social and Economic Consequences of Military Enterprise," in *Military Enterprise and Technological Change: Perspectives on the American Experience*, ed. Merritt Roe Smith (Cambridge, Mass.: MIT Press, 1985), 329–35, 340–46.

8. For women's representation at international expositions in the United States, see Mary F. Cordato, "Representing the Expansion of Woman's Sphere: Women's Work and Culture at the World's Fairs of 1876, 1893, and 1904" (Ph.D. diss., New York University, 1989); Weimann, *Fair Women*; and the Board of Lady Managers records, CHM. For women's representations at European exhibitions, see Maria Grever and Fia Dieteren, eds., *A Fatherland for Women: The 1898 "Nationale Tentoonstelling van Vrouwenarbeid" in Retrospect* (Amsterdam: VVG/Stichting beheer IISG, 2000). Estelle Freedman, in her study of early twentieth-century feminism, argued that a gradual decline in female separatism in social and political life precluded the emergence of a strong women's political bloc and further gains. Furthermore, an erosion of women's culture was connected to the decline of public feminism. To support this argument she compared the 1893 World Columbian Exposition in Chicago, which had a Board of Lady Managers and a separate Woman's Building, to the 1939 New York World's Fair, which had no separate building. She quoted a fair bulletin from New York that explained a woman "will not sit upon a pedestal, not be segregated, isolated; she will fit into the life of the Exposition as she does into

life itself—never apart, always a part." She noted that this new "part" was in fashion, food, and vanity. Estelle Freedman, "Separatism as Strategy: Female Institution Building and American Feminism, 1870–1930," in *U.S. Women in Struggle: A Feminist Studies Anthology*, ed. Claire Goldberg Moses and Heidi Hartmann (Urbana: University of Illinois Press, 1995), 81.

9. Karen Blair, *The Clubwoman as Feminist: True Womanhood Redefined, 1868–1914* (New York: Holmes and Meier, 1980); and Barbara Welter, "The Cult of True Womanhood," *American Quarterly* 13 (Summer 1966): 151–75.

10. Frances K. Pohl, "Historical Reality or Utopian Ideal? The Woman's Building at the World's Columbian Exposition, Chicago, 1893," *International Journal of Women's Studies* 5 (October 1982): 289–311; and T. J. Boisseau, "White Queens at the Chicago World's Fair," *Gender and History* 12 (2000): 63.

11. Gail Bederman, *Manliness and Civilization: A Cultural History of Gender and Race in the United States, 1880–1917* (Chicago: University of Chicago Press, 1995), 35; Weimann, *Fair Women*; and Susana Torre, ed., "Some Professional Roles," *Women in American Architecture: A Historic and Contemporary Perspective* (New York: Whitney Library of Design, 1977). Sophia Hayden was the first female to complete the four-year program in architecture at the Massachusetts Institute of Technology. Her design for the Woman's Building won a competition offered by the Board of Lady Managers and Daniel H. Burnham, chief of construction.

12. "No Women's Department," *Buffalo Evening News*, January 18, 1901, 1.

13. Louise deKoven Bowen, foreword in *The Woman's World's Fair, Chicago, Souvenir Program, 1925* (Chicago: Woman's World's Fair, 1925), 52, Women's World's Fair records, CHM.

14. *Official Catalogue and Guide Book to the Pan-American Exposition* (Buffalo: Ahrhart, 1901), 26.

15. *Official Guide to the World's Fair* (St. Louis: Louisiana Purchase, 1904), 139.

16. *The Sesqui-Centennial Exhibition: 150 Years of American Independence* (Philadelphia: Sequi-Centennial Exhibition Association, 1926), 19 (quote); *The Sesqui-Centennial Exhibition Guide* (Philadelphia, n.p., 1926), 9; *The Sesquicentennial International Exposition* (Philadelphia: Sesqui-Centennial Exhibition Association, 1926), 28;; and E. L. Austin and Odell Hauser, *The Sesqui-Centennial International Exposition: A Record Based on Official Data and Departmental Reports* (Philadelphia: Current Publications, 1929).

17. John Brisben Walker, "Women's Progress since the World's Fair at Chicago," *The Cosmopolitan* 37 (September 1904): 519–22.

18. "Woman Comes into Her Own," in *The Woman's World's Fair Souvenir Program, 1925*, 52, Women's World's Fair records, CHM.

19. Ellen Bass, foreword in *The Woman's World's Fair Souvenir Program, 1927* (Chicago: Woman's World's Fair, 1927), 5, 44, Women's World's Fair records, CHM.

20. "Woman's Progress, The Advocate, Stamford, Conn., June 4, 1927," *Editorial Comment on the Woman's World's Fair*, folder 1-15865, A Century of Progress records, UIC.

21. Louise De Koven Bowen to Edward N. Hurley, September 8, 1926, folder 1-7755, A Century of Progress records, UIC.

22. *Chicago Tribune*, April 19, 1928, 25; and *Chicago Daily News*, September 13, 1927, clipping, A Century of Progress scrapbooks box 29, A Century of Progress records, UIC.

23. Kristie Miller, "Of the Women, For the Women, and By the Women," *Chicago History* 24 (Summer 1995): 58–72; *The Woman's World Fair Souvenir Program, 1925*, 44, and *Woman's World's Fair Souvenir Program, 1927*, 52, both programs in the Women's World's Fair records, CHM.

24. Jan Ginsberg Flapan, "Blake, Margaret Day," in *Women Building Chicago, 1790–1990: A Biographical Dictionary*, ed. Rima Lunin Schultz and Adele Hast (Bloomington: Indiana University Press, 2001), 88–91; Ida M. Gurwell, "A Century of Progress Art Exhibit, and Entertaining and

Feeding the Multitude in Chicago," *The Modern Review* 57 (March 1935): 317–23; Art Institute of Chicago, *Catalogue of A Century of Progress Exhibition of Paintings and Sculpture: Lent from American Collections* (Chicago: Art Institute of Chicago, 1933); C. J. Bulliet, *Art Masterpieces in a Century of Progress Fine Arts Exhibition at the Art Institute of Chicago*, 2 vols. (Chicago: North-Mariano Press, 1933); and Daniel H. Burnham Jr. diary, February 10, 1932, Daniel H. Burnham Jr. and Hubert Burnham Collection, Ryerson and Burnham Archives, Art Institute of Chicago.

25. Kay Hoyle Nelson, "Fairbank, Janet Ayer," in Schultz and Hast, *Women Building Chicago*, 256–58.

26. Susan E. Hirsch, "Nestor, Agnes," in Schultz and Hast, *Women Building Chicago*, 623–26.

27. "Committee on Social Functions," box 5, Dawes Collection, NWU.

28. Minna Moscherosch Schmidt, *400 Outstanding Women of the World and Costumology of Their Time* (Chicago: Minna Moscherosch Schmidt, 1933), 544–46.

29. Rufus C. Dawes to Charles G. Dawes, March 28, 1930, Dawes Collection, NWU. McCormick opposed Wilsonian internationalism during her 1928 and 1930 Republican campaigns for Congress. Kristie Miller, *Ruth Hanna McCormick: A Life in Politics 1880–1944* (Albuquerque: University of New Mexico Press, 1992), 114.

30. Cathy and Richard Cahan, "The Lost City of the Depression," *Chicago History* 4 (Winter 1976–77): 233–42; and Associated Press report from unidentified press, July 27, 1933, A Century of Progress scrapbooks box 41, A Century of Progress records, UIC.

31. Burnham quoted in Martha McGrew diary, September 14, 1930, 5, folder 371, Lenox R. Lohr Papers, UIC.

32. Barbara Haggard Matteson, "Yesterday's City," *Chicago History* 12 (Fall 1983): 68–70.

33. Martha McGrew diary, September 25, 1930, 1, folder 371, Lenox R. Lohr Papers, UIC.

34. Fay Cooper Cole to Rufus Dawes, August 26, 1933, folder 4-45, A Century of Progress records, UIC.

35. Helene Throckmorton, "Woman's World Fair Marks Epoch," *Women's Viewpoint* (May 1925), Woman's World Fair Scrapbook, CHM; Miller, *Ruth Hanna McCormick*; and "Business Women to Be Honored," *Chicago Tribune*, November 25, 1956, F8. Bennett wrote a children's book to be sold at the Fort Dearborn exhibit: *The White Indian Boy: A Tale of William Wells, Pioneer, Warrior and Border Scout* (Chicago: A Century of Progress, 1933).

36. For the feminist movement after the suffrage movement, see Nancy F. Cott, *The Grounding of Modern Feminism* (New Haven: Yale University Press, 1987); Leila J. Rupp and Verta Taylor, *Survival in the Doldrums: The American Women's Rights Movement, 1945 to the 1960s* (Columbus: Ohio State University Press, 1990); and Susan Ware, *Still Missing: Amelia Earhart and the Search for Modern Feminism* (New York: Norton, 1993).

37. Martha McGrew diary, October 22, 1930, 4, folder 371, Lenox R. Lohr Papers, UIC.

38. Helen P. Dawes to Martha McGrew, March 12, 1934, folder 380, Lenox R. Lohr Papers, Special Collections, UIC.

39. Ibid.

40. Ibid.

41. F. C. Boggs to Lenox R. Lohr, July 3, 1930, folder 9-43, A Century of Progress records, UIC.

42. Dorthea A. Goodrich to Lenox R. Lohr, July 3, 1930, folder 9-43, A Century of Progress records, UIC.

43. Charter of The Temple of Womanhood to the Officers and Members of the Board of Trustees of A Century of Progress, n.d., folder 9-43, A Century of Progress records, UIC.

44. Dorthea A. Goodrich to Lenox R. Lohr, July 3, 1930, folder 9-43, A Century of Progress records, UIC.

45. Ibid.

46. Dorthea A. Goodrich, *The Temple of Womanhood, Inc.* (Chicago: Temple of Womanhood, 1932), 5.

47. Proposal for Temple of Womanhood, folder 9-43, A Century of Progress records, UIC.

48. For feminist writings about architecture's relationship to women's bodies, see Leslie Kanes Weisman, *Discrimination by Design: A Feminist Critique of the Man-Made Environment* (Urbana: University of Illinois Press, 1992); Margrit Kennedy, "Seven Hypotheses on Female and Male Principles in Architecture," *Heresies* 11 (1981): 12–13; and Mimi Lobell, "The Buried Treasure: Women's Ancient Architectural Heritage," in *Architecture: A Place for Women*, ed. Ellen Perry Berkeley (Washington, D.C.: Smithsonian Institution Press, 1989), 139–57.

49. Goodrich, *Temple of Womanhood*, 5.

50. Lenox R. Lohr to Dorthea A. Goodrich, July 12, 1930, folder 9-43, A Century of Progress records, UIC.

51. Both women lived in Evanston and their husbands had railway business backgrounds.

52. After meeting with Goodrich, Burnham noted in that day's diary entry that he lunched with Rufus C. Dawes and spoke to Lenox R. Lohr by phone, Daniel H. Burnham Jr. diary, April 22, 1932, Daniel H. Burnham Jr. and Hubert Burnham Collection, Ryerson and Burnham Archives, Art Institute of Chicago.

53. F. R. Moulton to Dorthea A. Goodrich, May 17, 1932, folder 9-43, A Century of Progress records, UIC.

54. Howard W. Odum to Daniel H. Burnham, March 21, 1931, folder 9-43, A Century of Progress records, UIC.

55. Dorthea A. Goodrich to Dear Madam, June 4, 1932, folder 9-43, A Century of Progress records, UIC.

56. Lenox R. Lohr to Dorthea A. Goodrich, June 7, 1932, folder 9-43, A Century of Progress records, UIC.

57. "Dolly Matters to Renew Fight for Baby Ireane," *Chicago Tribune*, April 15, 1919, 9; "Woman Names Dolly Matters in Annulment Suit," *Chicago Tribune*, February 6, 1920, 9; "Woman, 68, Does 'Leap of Death': Dolly Matters Seized in Ottawa after Kidnapping Is Foiled," *Chicago Tribune*, August 7, 1919, 1; and "Leading Club Women Stand by Dolly Matters: Ignore 'Expose' as Case of Jealousy," *Chicago Tribune*, November 25, 1923, 9.

58. Martha McGrew to Files Division, June 9, 1932, folder 9-43, A Century of Progress records, UIC.

59. Ibid.

60. B. L. Grove to Thomas Slusser, June 7, 1932, folder 7-50, A Century of Progress records, UIC.

61. Martha McGrew to Lenox Lohr, May 23, 1932, folder 9-43, A Century of Progress records, UIC.

62. Martha McGrew to Lenox Lohr, June 8, 1932, folder 9-43, A Century of Progress records, UIC.

63. B. L. Grove to Thomas Slusser, June 7, 1932, folder 7-50, A Century of Progress records, UIC.

64. For the debates and factions of the feminist movement, see Cott, *Grounding of Modern Feminism*.

65. "Women," June 8, 1932, folder 1-10946, A Century of Progress records, UIC.

66. Helen M. Bennett to Rufus Dawes, October 10, 1931, folder 1-10950 (quote); National Council of Women files, folders 1-10946–51, A Century of Progress records, UIC; and National Council of Women, *The National Council of Women of the United States, Inc.: What It Is, What It Does, What It Offers Women* (New York: National Council of Women, 1933).

67. Mrs. Charles J. Reeder to Helen M. Bennett, August 4, 1931, folder 1-10950, A Century of Progress records, UIC.

68. Weimann, *Fair Women*, 492; Mrs. Charles J. Reeder to Helen M. Bennett, August 4, 1931; Helen M. Bennett to Mrs. Charles J. Reeder, August 11, 1931; Howard Odum to Miss Lena Madesin Phillips, September 14, 1931, all in folder 1-10950, A Century of Progress records, UIC.

69. Helen M. Bennett to Mrs. Charles J. Reeder, July 23, 1931, folder 1-10950, A Century of Progress records, UIC.

70. Howard W. Odum to Miss Lena Madesin Phillips, September 14, 1931, folder 1-10950, A Century of Progress records, UIC.

71. Helen M. Bennett to Mrs. Kellogg Fairbank, October 2, 1932, folder 9-39, A Century of Progress records, UIC.

72. The National Council of Women sponsored the publication of Inez Haynes Irwin's *Angels and Amazons: One Hundred Years of American Women* (New York: Doubleday, Doran, 1933). The appendix lists the member organizations of the council.

73. Helen M. Bennett to Lena Madesin Phillips, September 28, 1931, folder 1-10950, A Century of Progress records, UIC.

74. "Women's Century of Progress," *Official World's Fair Weekly* 1 (May 27, 1933): 42–43; and Gray, *Guide to Chicago's Murals*, 364–65.

75. National Council of Women, *Women through the Century: A Souvenir of the National Council of Women Exhibit, A Century of Progress, 1833—Chicago—1933* (New York: National Council of Women, 1933), 1.

76. National Council of Women, *International Congress of Women, Advance Program* (New York: National Council of Women, 1933), 1.

77. Harriet M. Hoig, ed., *Official Register Women's Clubs, City of Chicago, 1913* (Chicago: Linden Brothers and Harry H. De Clerque, 1913), 60–79.

78. The Chicago Woman's Club organized in 1876 for social action through home, education, philanthropy, and reform. Previous women's clubs in Chicago stressed social and cultural activities. Wealthy socialites, reformers, and professionals sought self-improvement and activism. They cooperated with other women's clubs both locally and nationally, and with Hull-House settlement activities. Originally named the Chicago Women's Club, in 1895 the group changed it to Chicago Woman's Club. See Maureen A. Flanagan, *Seeing with Their Hearts: Chicago Women and the Vision of the Good City, 1871–1933* (Princeton: Princeton University Press, 2002); and Lana Ruegamer, "The Paradise of Exceptional Women: Chicago Women Reformers, 1863–1893" (Ph.D. diss., Indiana University, 1982).

79. Weimann, *Fair Women*, 492.

80. "Club Women Will Organize to Boost Fair," *Chicago Tribune*, March 31, 1933, 16.

81. Ibid.

82. "A Possible Contribution of the Chicago Woman's Club to the Century of Progress," n.d., Mrs. Harlan Ward Cooley Collection of Women in the Century of Progress, Special Collections Department, CPL.

83. Ibid.

84. The Chicago Woman's Club's building was not the first effort by women to establish place within the city. Earlier the Woman's Christian Temperance Union owned a Romanesque- and Gothic- inspired structure planned by Daniel H. Burnham and John W. Root to convey both a militant and homelike appearance. Rachel E. Bohlmann, "Our 'House Beautiful': The Woman's Temple and the WCTU Effort to Establish Place and Identity in Downtown Chicago, 1887–1898," *Journal of Women's History* 11 (Summer 1999): 110–34. Jane Addams and Ellen Gates Starr established the Hull-House settlement house in a former mansion, creating space for middle-class women urban reformers. Helen Lefkowitz Horowitz, "Hull-House as Women's Space," *Chicago History*

12 (Winter 1983–84): 40–55; and Kathryn Kish Sklar, "Hull House in the 1890s: A Community of Women Reformers," *Signs: Journal of Women in Culture and Society* 10 (1985): 658–77.

85. Mrs. Payton S. Wild, "Evolution of Women's Clubs: A Pageant in Four Episodes," Chicago Woman's Club Theatre, May 26, 1933, box 32, Chicago Woman's Club records, CHM.

86. See Virginia Woolf, *A Room of One's Own* (New York: Fountain Press, 1929).

87. Perry R. Duis, "'All Else Passes—Art Alone Endures': The Fine Arts Building, 1918 to 1930," *Chicago History* 7 (Spring 1978): 40–51. The building is still standing, and it is owned by Columbia College.

88. Weisman, *Discrimination by Design*, 1.

89. Bruegmann, *Holabird and Roche, Holabird and Root*, 2:394–97.

90. Holabird and Root, "Interior Views of New Women's Club of Chicago," *Architectural Record* 68 (July 1930): 22–28.

91. Henry J. B. Hoskins, "Chicago Woman's Club," n.d., 50, Chicago Woman's Club records, CHM. The modern style and simple design and furnishings of the Chicago Woman's Club Building provided a striking contrast to the Woman's Athletic Club of Chicago's headquarters constructed in the same era at Michigan Avenue and Ontario Street, north of the business district. Celia Hilliard, *The Woman's Athletic Club of Chicago, 1898–1998* (Chicago: Woman's Athletic Club of Chicago, 1998), 66. In addition, architects used strikingly different colors and materials for men's clubs of the era, including Holabird and Roche's 1908 University Club, located at Michigan Avenue and Monroe Street. Bruegmann, *Holabird and Roche, Holabird and Root*, 1:268–77.

92. Bederman, *Manliness and Civilization*.

93. "Annual Report of Progress of Women Committee," Chicago Woman's Club records, folder 32, CHM.

94. Clipping, n.d., Mrs. Harlan Ward Cooley Collection of Women in the Century of Progress, Special Collections Department, CPL.

95. *Woman's Home Companion, The Chicago Woman's Club Bulletin*, n.d., Mrs. Harlan Ward Cooley Collection of Women in the Century of Progress, Special Collections Department, CPL.

96. For a study that emphasizes women's power to shape the city, see Sarah Deutsch, *Women and the City: Gender, Space, and Power in Boston, 1870–1940* (New York: Oxford University Press, 2000).

Chapter 6: African Americans and the Du Sable Legacy

1. The epigraph for this chapter is from "Demand Your Rights," *Chicago Defender*, May 13, 1933, 14.

2. The name Jean Baptiste Point Du Sable appears in the literature with a variety of spellings and variations. I use Jean Baptiste Point Du Sable unless citing a name or title that uses another spelling, such as the National De Saible Memorial Society. The most frequently found variations include the spelling of Point as Pointe or Sable as Saible, and du as de, d', or de', with or without capitalization and with or without spacing before Sable. In 1936, the renaming of New Wendell Phillips High School to Jean Baptiste Point Du Sable High School established the spelling followed today. Raymond L. McCants Sr., January Class of 36, "History of Du Sable High School," n.d., "Du Sable Information" file, Du Sable High School Media Center, Du Sable High School, Chicago; June Provines, "Front Views and Profiles," *Chicago Tribune*, April 23, 1936, 15; and Ann Williams, "The Negro in Illinois," February 10, 1941, 2, folder 2-8, Illinois Writers' Project, Vivian G. Harsh Research Collection of Afro-American History and Literature, CPL. For the African Americans and place, see Earl Lewis, "Connecting Memory, Self, and the Power of Place in African American Urban History," *Journal of Urban History* 21 (March 1995): 347–71.

3. "Southern Style Cooking," *Chicago Daily News*, Special Photogravure section, May 1934, 34.

4. In the demonstration exhibition for Aunt Jemima pancakes, a heavy black woman wore a head rag, checked dress, apron, and large gold earrings while flipping pancakes on a grill in front of a log cabin wall. Her sharp head turns, rolling and blinking of wide-open eyes, exaggerated smiling, and talking with gold teeth showing all reinforced the Mammy stereotype. *A Century of Progress Exposition: Exhibits of the World's Fair*, Burton Holmes Films, Inc., 1933. A free brochure distributed at the fair included a photograph of the demonstration's Aunt Jemima standing in contrast between two young, thin, conventionally attractive white females. *America's Most Famous Recipe* (Chicago: Quaker Oats Company, 1933). Anna Robinson followed Nancy Green in the portrayal of Aunt Jemima and continued with Quaker Oats until 1951. The Aunt Jemima package was redesigned with Robinson's image. Marilyn Kern-Foxworth, *Aunt Jemima, Uncle Ben, and Rastus: Blacks in Advertising, Yesterday, Today, and Tomorrow* (Westport, Conn: Greenwood, 1994), 67–68.

5. "World's Fair Employment Racket Halted," NAACP Midwest Branch reel 3, Library of Congress, Washington, D.C.

6. Carnahan and Slusser Law Officers to Chief of Legal Section of A Century of Progress, March 20, 1934, folder 7-13, A Century of Progress records, UIC.

7. "A Century of Progress," *Chicago Defender*, June 10, 1933, 14, and "Waiting for the New Deal," *Chicago Defender*, March 18, 1933, 1.

8. After leaving the fairgrounds, attendees could visit taverns located around the entrances at Eighteenth, Twenty-third, Thirty-first, and Thirty-fifth streets, negotiate with a female street solicitor, or visit one of the many houses of prostitution located in the Eighteenth street entrance area. *General Conditions*. By 1930, the Chicago vice district had moved into the "Bright Lights" district in the African American "black belt." Kevin J. Mumford, *Interzones: Black/White Sex Districts in Chicago and New York in the Early Twentieth Century* (New York: Columbia University Press, 1997), 25–27. Centered near Thirty-fifth and State Streets, this interracial sex zone served as a gateway to the exposition's southern Thirty-fifth Street entrance gates. "Black belt" refers to a constrictive urban housing zone where African Americans lived in segregated, crowded conditions on Chicago's South Side, especially concentrated in 1934 from Twenty-sixth Street south to Seventy-first Street, east of State Street.

9. L. Cole to Martha McGrew, September 27, 1930, folder 6-135, A Century of Progress records, UIC.

10. Louis G. Gregory, "A Century of Progress," *Chicago Defender*, July 24, 1933, 16. The Dawes Hotel, a lodging house for less fortunate men established in Chicago by Charles G. Dawes, however, rejected blacks and avoided dealing with them by referring them to the Urban League. James R. Grossman, *Land of Hope: Chicago, Black southerners, and the Great Migration* (Chicago: University of Chicago Press, 1989), 134.

11. William P. Fitzgerald to Rufus C. Dawes, June 30, 1932, and Col. Robert Isham Randolph to Rufus C. Dawes, June 21, 1932, both in folder 11-230, A Century of Progress records, UIC.

12. Dr. Jasper Phillips, Dr. Joseph Plummer, and Rev. W. L. Sledge to President F. D. Roosevelt, June 6, 1933, folder 11-210, A Century of Progress records, UIC.

13. For the role of African Americans at the exposition, emphasizing the role of men, see August Meier and Elliott M. Rudwick, "Negro Protest at the Chicago World's Fair, 1933–34," *Journal of the Illinois State Historical Society* 59 (Summer 1966): 161–71; Christopher R. Reed, "In the Shadow of Fort Dearborn: Honoring Du Sable at the Chicago World's Fair of 1933–1934," *Journal of Black Studies* 21 (June 1991): 398–413; and idem, "A Reinterpretation of Black Strategies for Change at the Chicago World's Fair, 1933–1934," *Illinois Historical Journal* 81 (Spring 1988): 2–12.

14. Howard W. Odum to Director of Exhibits, September 21, 1931, folder 11-213, A Century of Progress records, UIC. Odum was the assistant director of the President's Research Committee on Social Trends, president of the American Sociological Society, and a prolific scholar who specialized in social research, public welfare, folk culture, African American songs, southern regionalism, and race relations. Odum resigned from the fair in December 1931 after determining that the obstacles to staging effective social science exhibits were insurmountable: lack of funding, insufficient space, poor cooperation of organizations, and lack of public appeal. John M. Jordan, *Machine-Age Ideology: Social Engineering and American Liberalism, 1911–1939* (Chapel Hill: University of North Carolina Press, 1994), 185–92.

15. Howard W. Odum to Director of Exhibits, September 14, 1931, folder 11-213, A Century of Progress records, UIC.

16. "League Exhibit at World's Fair Wins Approval of Public," *Chicago Defender*, June 10, 1933, 1, 12; and "Attracting Attention at A Century of Progress," *Chicago Defender*, July 1, 1933, 17. Dawson's work was also exhibited at the Illinois Host House at the fair. He had studied at the School of the Art Institute of Chicago and was a founder of the Chicago Art League for black artists. Gary A. Reynolds and Beryl J. Wright, *Against the Odds: African-America Artists and the Harmon Foundation* (New Jersey: Newark Museum, 1989), 172.

17. Diary, Box C397, Records, 1933–34, Century of Progress Exposition, Radcliffe College Archives, Schlesinger Library, Cambridge, Mass.

18. Howard W. Odum to Director of Exhibits, September 9, 1931, folder 11-213, A Century of Progress records, UIC. One hundred African American church and civic leaders protested this idea again just months before the exposition opened. "Plans of African Assn. for Fair Exhibition Hit Snag," *Chicago Defender*, February 18, 1933, 2. The exhibit "Darkest Africa," which drew a large African American audience, featured tribal leaders brought over for the exposition and met with mixed reviews from the African American community. "'Darkest Africa' at A Century of Progress," *Chicago Defender*, July 29, 1933, 16. On the Nigerian royalty and Belgian Congo pygmies who appeared, see "Anthropology in Africa," *Official World's Fair Weekly* 1 (October 14, 1933): 10.

19. A brief clip of the Old Plantation show appears in *Along the Fair Way*, Metropolitan Motion Picture Company. African American men play instruments while dressed in dungarees, women on a balcony wear dresses or long pants, and a few singers and dancers are in blackface.

20. Operations and Management Department to Duke Mills, Old Plantation Show, May 30, 1933 (quote), and Robert Isham Randolph, Director of Operations to Negro Plantation Show, August 2, 1933, both in folder 1-1986, A Century of Progress records, UIC.

21. Commercial radio broadcasting reached the masses during the 1930s with comedy and linguistic slapstick, including blackface skit in which white actors portrayed stereotyped African Americans. See Susan J. Douglas, *Listening In: Radio in the American Imagination, from Amos 'n' Andy and Edward R. Murrow to Wolfman Jack and Howard Stern* (New York: Times Books, 1999), 100–23.

22. Dewey R. Jones, "The Last Day at the Fair," *Chicago Defender*, November 11, 1933, 17.

23. A typical settlement would be for $150. *Bulletin, Chicago Branch—NAACP*, n.d., and *Statement of the Case of Mrs. Bernice McIntosh*, both in Papers of the NAACP, Library of Congress, Washington, D.C.

24. Christopher Robert Reed, *The Chicago NAACP and the Rise of Black Professional Leadership, 1910–1966* (Bloomington: Indiana University Press, 1997), 99.

25. "Demand Your Rights," *Chicago Defender*, May 13, 1933, 14 (quote); "Scores 'Uncle Tom' Attitude of Visitors to World's Fair," *Chicago Defender*, October 28, 1933, 13.

26. "DePriest Not to Take Part in 'Negro Day' Program," *Chicago Defender*, August 5, 1933, 2, and August 12, 1933, 1.

27. Meier and Rudwick, "Negro Protest at the Chicago World's Fair," 165. African American clubwomen helped elect DePriest. Anne Meis Knupfer, *Toward a Tenderer Humanity and a Nobler Womanhood: African American Women's Clubs in Turn-of-the-Century Chicago* (New York: New York University Press, 1996), 7. In turn, when he resigned from Mayor Thompson's Jean Baptiste Point Du Sable committee in 1928, DePriest recommended Annie E. Oliver as his replacement. "A Scrap Book for Women in Public Life," *Chicago Defender*, September 28, 1929, 31.

28. For flyers and details of the planning for the pageant, see folder 1-11707, A Century of Progress records, UIC.

29. "Negro Day at Fair Flops," *Chicago Defender*, August 19, 1933, 2.

30. Dewey R. Jones, "A Day at the Fair," *Chicago Defender*, August 19, 1933, 10.

31. Dennis A. Bethea, "More about 'Negro Day,'" *Chicago Defender*, August 26, 1933, 11.

32. "Rise of Negro Dramatized in Pageant at Fair," *Chicago Tribune*, August 13, 1933, 7; "'Let's Go, Chicago,' Is Slogan of City for the World's Fair," *Chicago Defender*, June 3, 1933, 17.

33. Paula Giddings, *In Search of Sisterhood: Delta Sigma Theta and the Challenge of the Black Sorority Movement* (New York: Morrow, 1988), 146–55. As pointed out by Knupfer in *Toward a Tenderer Humanity and a Nobler Womanhood*, 5, the 222 Delta Sigma Theta women wearing elaborate evening gowns at their 1933 banquet actually helped support African American dressmakers, milliners, and hairdressers in difficult economic times.

34. Elizabeth Lindsay Davis, *Lifting as They Climb* (New York: G. K. Hall, 1996), 7. Sieglinde Lemke, in her introduction to this reprint edition, fails to mention the connection of the original publication by the National Association of Colored Women to the 1933 Chicago world's fair. On page 132, Davis again uses the fair theme to promote the role of the Illinois Association of Colored Women and the organizations' efforts for social uplift and interracial cooperation.

35. Charles Harris Wesley, *The History of the National Association of Colored Women's Clubs: A Legacy of Service* (Washington, D.C.: National Association of Colored Women's Clubs, 1984), 106–9.

36. "'Negro Day' Soldier Field Receipts and Expenditures," folder 7-64, A Century of Progress records, UIC.

37. For information on Woodson, see Jacqueline Goggins, *Carter G. Woodson: A Life in Black History* (Baton Rouge: Louisiana State University Press, 1993), and Lorenzo J. Greene, *Selling Black History for Carter G. Woodson: A Diary, 1930–1933* (Columbia: University of Missouri Press, 1996).

38. "Negro History Week," *Journal of Negro History* 13 (January 1928): 109–15.

39. "Proceedings of the Annual Meeting of the Association for the Study of Negro Life and History Held in St. Louis, Missouri," *Journal of Negro History* 14 (January 1929): 3.

40. M. M. Quaife, "Property of Jean Baptiste Point Sable," *Mississippi Valley Historical Review* 15 (June 1928): 89–92. Quaife expanded his analysis of Du Sable and the significance of his property in *Checcagou: From Indian Wigwam to Modern City, 1673–1835* (Chicago: University of Chicago Press, 1933), 28–46. For a biographical sketch of Quaife, see Perry R. Duis, "Introduction," in Milo Milton Quaife, *Chicago and the Old Northwest, 1673–1835* (Urbana: University of Illinois Press, 2001), vii–xviii. For the Du Sable property site, see Commission on Chicago Historical and Architectural Landmarks, *Site of the Du Sable/Kinzie House* (Chicago: The Commission, 1977). For a recent updated biography of Du Sable, see Christopher Robert Reed, "DuSable," in *3 Acres on the Lake: DuSable Park Proposal Project*, ed. Laurie Palmer (Chicago: WhiteWalls, 2003), 16–17.

41. Quaife, *Checcagou*, 46.

42. Henrietta Lee had been the first landlord for the original publishing site of *Chicago Defender* newspaper. The Quinn Chapel at 2401 S. Wabash was the home of Chicago's oldest African

American congregation. Annie E. Oliver, a life member of the Frederick Douglass Memorial and Historical Association, became active on local, state, and national levels in the Federation of Colored Women's Clubs. She founded the Annie E. Oliver Civic and Charity Club within the Chicago and Northern District Association of Colored Women, Inc. (CNDA). Dolores White, *The Story of Seventy-Five Years of the Chicago and Northern District Association of Club Women, Inc.* (Chicago: CNDA, 1981), 49.

43. Floris Barnett Cash, *African American Women and Social Action: The Clubwomen and Volunteerism from Jim Crow to the New Deal, 1896–1936* (Westport, Conn.: Greenwood, 2001), 4. For discussion of African American organized women, see also Elizabeth Lindsay Davis, *The Story of the Illinois Federation of Colored Women's Clubs,* and Mrs. S. Joe Brown, *The History of the Order of the Eastern Star among Colored People* (New York: G. K. Hall, 1997); Flanagan, *Seeing with Their Hearts;* Darlene Clark Hine, "Black Professionals and Race Consciousness: Origins of the Civil Rights Movement, 1890–1950," *Journal of American History* (March 2003): 1279–94; St. Clair Drake, *Churches and Voluntary Associations in the Chicago Negro Community* (Chicago: Work Projects Administration District 3, 1940); and Paula Giddings, *When and Where I Enter: The Impact of Black Women on Race and Sex in America* (New York: Bantam, 1985).

44. Disillusioned with some of the actions and policies of the National Association of Colored Women regarding this debate, in 1935, Mary McLeod Bethune established her own organization, the National Council of Negro Women.

45. Cash, *African American Women and Social Action,* 133–35.

46. On respectability and African Americans, see James R. Grossman, "African-American Migration to Chicago," in *Ethnic Chicago: A Multicultural Portrait,* 4th ed., ed. Melvin G. Holli and Peter d'A. Jones (Grand Rapids, Mich.: Eerdmans, 1995), 303; Allan H. Spear, *Black Chicago: The Making of a Negro Ghetto, 1890–1920* (Chicago: University of Chicago Press, 1967); and Victoria W. Wolcott, *Remaking Respectability: African American Women in Interwar Detroit* (Chapel Hill: University of North Carolina Press, 2001).

47. "A Scrap Book for Women in Public Life: Annie Oliver Member of Committee," *Chicago Defender,* September 18, 1929, 31; and Irene McCoy Gaines, "Tribute to Annie E. Oliver," folder 5, Irene McCoy Gaines Papers, CHM.

48. The initial committee included Aldermen Jackson, Coughlin, Anderson, Cronson, and Clark plus citizens Robert S. Abbott (editor), Joseph Bibb, Oscar DePriest (politician), and Anthony Overton (beauty product entrepreneur). "A Scrap Book for Women in Public Life," *Chicago Defender,* September 28, 1929, 31.

49. Annie E. Oliver to D. C. Collier, November 21, 1928, folder 1-10957, A Century of Progress records, UIC.

50. C. W. Fitch, Assistant Director of Exhibits to Director of Exhibits, June 9, 1931, folder 1-10957, A Century of Progress records, UIC.

51. Annie E. Oliver to Allen D. Albert, June 11, 1931, folder 1-10957, A Century of Progress records, UIC.

52. Irene M. Gaines to Helen Bennett, May 14, 1932, and Charles S. Duke to Forest Ray Mouton, May 16, 1932, both in folder 1-10957, A Century of Progress records, UIC. Oliver was the Unemployment Committee Chair of the Colored Women's Republican Clubs of Illinois when Gaines was its president.

53. M. P. Kerr to Charles S. Duke, June 3, 1932, folder 1-10957, A Century of Progress records, UIC.

54. Helen M. Bennett to Mary McDowell, July 13, 1932, folder 1-10957, A Century of Progress records, UIC.

55. C. W. Fitch to H. D. Nuber, May 3, 1934, folder 1-10956, A Century of Progress records, UIC.

56. Drawing of Du Sable Cabin location, folder 19-6, A Century of Progress records, UIC.

57. "Chicago's First Citizen," *Official World's Fair Weekly* 1 (August 12, 1933): 27; and Quaife, *Checagou*, 40. *Wau-Bun* was first published in 1856. Juliette M. Kinzie, *Wau-Bun: The "Early Days" in the Northwest* (Menasha, Wisc.: National Society of Colonial Dames in Wisconsin, 1948), 147.

58. List of Du Sable Cabin contents, folder 1-10957, A Century of Progress records, UIC.

59. Dawson also worked as an illustrator for the Poro School of Beauty Culture's line of African American hair products. Annie E. Oliver was a past president of the Chicago Poro Club.

60. Arranged by Blanche V. Shaw and Mrs. Charles S. Duke, a committee appointed by Annie E. Oliver, *Some Historical Facts about Jean Baptiste Point De Saible: Chicago's First Permanent Citizen* (Chicago: National De Saible Memorial Society, 1933), 9.

61. Invitation to the dedicatory services, folder 1-10957, A Century of Progress records, UIC; "Crowd at Dedication of Du Sable Cabin in World's Fair," *Chicago Defender*, June 17, 1933, 1, 12, 17.

62. Mrs. Charles S. Duke, "History in the Making: The De Saible Cabin: A Study in Contrasts," *Chicago Defender*, October 28, 1933, 17.

63. Mrs. Charles S. Duke, "Mrs. Duke Writes about Du Saible Cabin at Fair," *Chicago Defender*, September 16, 1933, 3.

64. Duke, "History in the Making."

65. "Chicago's First Citizen," 27.

66. John L. Tilley, *A Brief History of the Negro in Chicago, 1779–1933: From Jean Baptiste Du Sable to "A Century of Progress"* (Chicago: Tilley, 1933).

67. Duke, "History in the Making."

68. Mary McLeod Bethune, "A Century of Progress of Negro Women" in *Black Women in White America: A Documentary History*, ed. Gerda Lerner (New York: Vintage, 1972), 583.

Chapter 7: Ethnic Identity and Nationalistic Representations of Progress

1. The epigraph for this chapter is from Maj. Felix J. Streyckmans, WGN Radio Address, May 14, 1929, folder 5-185, A Century of Progress records, UIC.

2. After six test flights around Germany in 1928, on October 11, Eckener made a bold statement by flying the new *Graf Zeppelin* across the Atlantic to the United States. This flight marked the first step in transoceanic passenger, mail, and freight service by air because airplanes did not yet have the capacity to make transoceanic commercial flights. Eckener wanted to make a midwestern tour with the *Graf Zeppelin*, including a stop in Chicago, but repairs had delayed the return trip to Germany. He wired friends in Chicago that he had postponed but not abandoned a visit to the city. Eckener flew over Chicago, without landing, on the *Graf Zeppelin*'s Round the World Flight in 1929. The success of that flight resulted in Eckener's portrait on the cover of *Time*, September 16, 1929. "Gut Heil" does not have an exact translation into English.

3. Felix J. Streyckmans specialized in freight rate matters and interstate commerce law. He served in the Spanish American War and was president of the Belgian American National Alliance.

4. "Racial Groups and Chicago in Welcoming Fliers," 1928, folder 5-184, A Century of Progress records, UIC. Israel Zangwill popularized the "Melting Pot" metaphor in his 1908 melodrama of that title; see Holli and Jones, *Ethnic Chicago*, 2.

5. Anton Kvist, ed., *Jubilee and World's Fair Year Book* (Chicago: Danish National Committee, 1933), 13.

6. The 1924 Johnson-Reed Act reduced all European immigration; however, the quota did not apply to Canada and Latin American countries. John Higham, *Strangers in the Land: Patterns of American Nativism, 1860–1925* (New Brunswick, N.J.: Rutgers University Press, 1955, 1994), 300–330.

7. Felix J. Streyckmans to Lenox Lohr, June 18, 1930, folder 5-185, A Century of Progress records, UIC.

8. *Progress: Official Bulletin, Committee on Coordination of Nationalities*, various issues and languages, all in folder 5-187, A Century of Progress records, UIC.

9. Felix J. Streyckmans to Board of Trustees, March 5, 1929, folder 5-179, A Century of Progress records, UIC.

10. *Progress: Official Bulletin, Committee on Coordination of Nationalities* 1 (September 28, 1928): 1, folder 5-187, A Century of Progress records, UIC.

11. Ibid., 2.

12. Stuyvesant Peabody to Felix J. Streyckmans, August 30, 1928, folder 5-179, A Century of Progress records, UIC.

13. "Chicago's Citizens Comprise Many Nationalities," *Chronicle of Chicago* 1 (August 1928): 6.

14. Ibid. (quote); "The First Town Meeting of the Chicago World's Fair Centennial Celebration, 1933," and "Town Meeting, Chicago world's fair, April 19, 1928, 'Americans All,'" 1928 scrapbook of Chicago world's fair printed documents, both page 93, Cheryl R. Ganz Collection, Washington, D.C.

15. *Progress: Official Bulletin, Committee on Coordination of Nationalities* 1 (August 21, 1928), folder 5-187, A Century of Progress records, UIC.

16. "Mr. Dawes, of Chicago, Speaks to New York about World's Fairs," ibid., 1. New York merchants had considered planning a New York world's fair for 1932 to commemorate the two-hundredth anniversary of George Washington's birth.

17. Felix J. Streyckmans to my dear Compatriot, October 22, 1928, folder 5-175, A Century of Progress records, UIC.

18. Committee on the Coordination of Nationalities, folder 5-175, A Century of Progress records, UIC.

19. Manuscript, November 28, 1928, folder 5-185, A Century of Progress records, UIC.

20. These self-published handbooks, often bilingual, featured stories of each ethnic group's contributions to Chicago and the nation with photographs of its local events committee and advertisements from its local businesses. For examples, see Czechoslovak Group (Czechs and Slovaks), *World's Fair Memorial of the Czechoslovak Group (Czechs and Slovaks), International Exposition, Chicago, 1933* (Chicago: Czechoslovak Group, 1933); Oscar A. Stoffels, ed., *Year Book of the German Club of Chicago: Twentieth Anniversary of Its Organization* (Chicago: German Club of Chicago, 1933); and, Polish Day Association, *Poles in America: Their Contribution to A Century of Progress* (Chicago: Polish Day Association, 1933).

21. Walter Roth, "Jewish Day Shook Chicago," *Chicago Jewish History* 15 (Spring 1992): 1.

22. Rabbi S. Felix Mendelsohn, "Topics of the Week," (Chicago) *Sentinel: A Weekly Newspaper Devoted to Jewish Interests*, July 13, 1933, 5.

23. (Chicago) *Sentinel*, June 29, 1933.

24. David E. Hirsch, ed., *The Romance of a People: A Pageant-Drama in Observance of Jewish Day at A Century of Progress* (Chicago: Jewish Day Committee, 1933). For a description of the Jewish exhibit in the Hall of Religion, see Louis L. Mann and Gerson B. Levi, *Glimpses of the Jewish Exhibit* (Chicago: Regensteiner Corp., 1933–34).

25. Memoradum for the Information of Organized Groups of Citizens of Foreign Origin or Descent in the City of Chicago, 1931, folder 5-178, A Century of Progress records, UIC.

26. "Notes taken during meeting of Committee on Nationalities which was held in the Administration Building of the fair on January 19, 1931," folder 5-180, A Century of Progress records, UIC; Allen D. Albert, "Learning from Other World's Fairs," *Chicago Commerce* 26 (November 22, 1930): 13–14; and Barbara A. Rogers, "Mellowed Europe Comes to Chicago in 1933," *Chicago Commerce* 26 (February 1931), 12–13.

27. Documentary films depicting the fair villages include *Along the Fair Way*, Metropolitan Motion Picture Company, Allan Forrest, director, General Motors Corporation, c. 1935; *A Century of Progress Exposition: Belgian Village*, Burton Holmes Films, Inc., 1933; *A Century of Progress Exposition: Indian Village*, Burton Holmes Films, Inc., 1933; *A Century of Progress Exposition: Streets of Paris*, Burton Holmes Films, Inc., 1933; *Villages of the World's Fair*, Burton Holmes Films, Inc., released by Kaufmann and Fabry, 1934; and *The World's Fair Black Forest*, Burton Holmes Films, Inc., released by Kaufmann and Fabry, 1934.

28. Lt. Comdr. E. D. Langworthy, USN, Ret'd., to Rufus Dawes, August 17, 1932, folder 1-9101, A Century of Progress records, UIC.

29. For country exhibits that emphasized the arts, see Berthold Laufer, *The Gold Treasure of the Emperor Chien Lung of China* (Chicago: A Century of Progress, 1934); Bengt Lundberg, *Arts and Crafts at the Swedish Chicago Exposition 1933* (Stockholm: Centraltryckeriet, 1933); and *The Archipenko Exposition of Sculpture and Painting in Ukrainian Pavilion at A Century of Progress Chicago, 1933* (Chicago: Siege Printing, 1933). For the Chinese Lama Temple, replicated in China and sponsored by an American idustrialist to contain religious artifacts, see Sven Hedlin and Gösta Montell, *The Chinese Lama Temple, Potala of Jehol: Exhibition of Historical and Ethnographical Collections* (Chicago: Lakeside Press, 1932). For architecture of ethnic pavilions, see Lisa D. Schrenk, "From Historic Village to Modern Pavilion: The Evolution of Foreign Architectural Representation at International Expositions in the 1930s," *National Identities* 1, no. 3 (1999): 287–311.

30. Ethnic villages in 1933 included the Belgian Village, Chinese Village, Old Mexico, Moroccan Village, Oriental Village, and Streets of Paris. Other types of villages included the American Indian Village and Midget Village. In 1934, the Belgian Village and Streets of Paris continued operation with new villages added, including the Black Forest Village, Dutch Village, English Village, Hawaiian Village, Irish Village, Italian Village, Mexican Village, Oasis (South Mediterranean), Spanish Village, Streets of Shanghai, Swiss Village, and Tunisian Village. The Colonial Village and Bowery offered American cultural settings in the second year.

31. For discussion of Mexico's cultural history and cultural exchanges with the United States, see Brenda Jo Bright and Liza Bakewell, eds., *Looking High and Low: Art and Cultural Identity* (Tucson: University of Arizona Press, 1995); Helen Delpar, *The Enormous Vogue of Things Mexican: Cultural Relations between the United States and Mexico, 1920–1935* (Tuscaloosa: University of Alabama Press, 1992); and James Oles, *South of the Border: Mexico in the American Imagination, 1914–1947* (Washington, D.C.: Smithsonian Institution Press, 1993).

32. See Stuart Chase, *Mexico: A Study of Two Americas* (New York: Macmillan, 1931).

33. "Way Down South in Mexico," *Official World's Fair Weekly* 1 (July 22, 1933): 10–11; and A Century of Progress, *Official Guide Book of the Fair* (Chicago: Cuneo Press, 1934).

34. "Noted Mexican Here to Choose Exposition Site," *Progress* 1 (November 4, 1931): 3.

35. A Century of Progress, *Official Guide Book of the World's Fair of 1934* (Chicago: Cuneo Press, 1934), 138.

36. *Chicago World's Fair Rodeo Official Daily Program* (Chicago, 1933). For correspondence regarding Mexican exhibits at the fair, see Mexican Village, folders 1-10237 and 13-663, 708;

Mexico Correspondence, folders 2-1139–47; Social Work Exhibits, folder 10-1071; Mexican Pavilion, folder 10-1673; and Photographs, folders 17-40–44, A Century of Progress records, UIC.

37. *Chicago Herald and Examiner,* August 30, 1933, 7.

38. "Way Down South in Mexico," 11.

39. Carnahan and Slusser to the General Manager, August 14, 1933, folder 7-15, A Century of Progress records, UIC; and "Way Down South in Mexico," 11.

40. A Century of Progress, *Official Guide Book of the World's Fair of 1934,* 138.

41. *The Monte Alban Treasure* (Chicago: A Century of Progress, 1933).

42. "Mexico Day," July 19 and July 21, 1934, folder 2-1143, and "Mexican Government Exhibit," September 4, 1934, folder 14-1, A Century of Progress records, UIC.

43. In the 1920s, choreographers created modern renditions of Mexican popular dances, such as the *jarabe tapatío,* in their search for a distinctively Mexican aesthetic. Rick A. López, "Forging a Mexican National Identity in Chicago: Mexican Migrants and Hull-House," in *Pots of Promise: Mexicans and Pottery at Hull-House, 1920–40,* ed. Cheryl R. Ganz and Margaret Strobel (Urbana: University of Illinois Press, 2004), 95.

44. See appendices "Directory of Mexican Organizations" and "Mexican Commercial Establishments" in Anita Jones, *Conditions Surrounding Mexicans in Chicago* (San Francisco: A and E Research Associates, 1971), 164–73. On Mexicans in Chicago, see also Juan R. Garcia, *Mexicans in the Midwest, 1900–1932* (Tucson: University of Arizona Press, 1996); Rita Arias Jirasek and Carlos Tortolero, *Images of America: Mexican Chicago* (Chicago: Arcadia, 2001); Anita Edgar Jones, "Mexican Colonies in Chicago," *Social Service Review* (December 1928): 579–97; Dennis Nodín Valdés, *Al Norte: Agricultural Workers in the Great Lakes Region, 1917–1970* (Austin: University of Texas Press, 1991); and Dionicio Nodín Valdés, *Barrios Norteños: St. Paul and Midwestern Mexican Communities in the Twentieth Century* (Austin: University of Texas Press, 2000).

45. In the previous century, many European immigrants also had to shift their identity from regional to national as they created their American cultural space. For Mexicans in America and the issue of ethnicity and identity, see Gabriela F. Arredondo, *Mexican Chicago: Race, Identity, and Nation, 1916–39* (Urbana: University of Illinois Press, 2008); López, "Forging a Mexican National Identity in Chicago"; Richard Rodriguez, *Brown: The Last Discovery of America* (New York: Penguin, 2001); and George J. Sánchez, *Becoming Mexican American: Ethnicity, Culture, and Identity in Chicano Los Angeles, 1900–1945* (New York: Oxford University Press, 1993).

46. Italy Report from London, folder 2-1196, A Century of Progress records, UIC.

47. This Columbus statue stands in Grant Park at Columbus Drive and Roosevelt Road in Chicago.

48. Italo Balbo, *My Air Armada* (London: Hurst and Blackett, 1934), 195.

49. Claudio G. Segré, *Italo Balbo: A Fascist Life* (Berkeley: University of California Press, 1987), 231.

50. Mario de Renzi and Adalberto Libera, "Italian Pavilion, Century of Progress," *Architectural Forum* 58 (June 1933): 495.

51. Italian Pavilion photographs, folder 17-20, A Century of Progress records, UIC; see also photo of exhibit in Dennis P. Doordan, "Exhibiting Progress: Italy's Contribution to the Century of Progress Exposition," in *Chicago Architecture and Design, 1923–1993: Reconfiguration of an American Metropolis,* ed. John Zukowsky (Chicago: Art Institute of Chicago, 1993), 219–32.

52. Ibid. For more examples of Italy's progress represented in exhibits, see Italian Tourist Information Office, *Ten Years of Italian Progress* (Milan: Italian State Tourist Department, 1933); Italian State Tourist Department, *Do You Know Italy?* (Rome: ENIT, 1934); and *The Italian Pavilion: A Century of Progress, 1933* (Chicago: Cuneo Press, 1933).

53. Segré, *Italo Balbo,* 250.

54. Italians in Chicago Oral History Project, UIC.

55. According to Eric Hobsbawm, in his "Introduction: Inventing Traditions," in *The Invention of Tradition*, ed. Eric Hobsbawm and Terence Ranger (New York: Cambridge University Press, 1992), "'invented tradition' is taken to mean a set of practices, normally governed by overtly or tacitly accepted rules and of a ritual or symbolic nature, which seek to inculcate certain values and norms of behavior by repetition, which automatically implies continuity with the past" (1).

56. Humbert S. Nelli, *Italians in Chicago, 1880–1930: A Study in Ethnic Mobility* (New York: Oxford University Press, 1970), 242, and John P. Diggins, *Mussolini and Fascism: The View from America* (Princeton: Princeton University Press, 1972), 81. For Italians in Chicago, see also Dominic Candeloro, *Italians in Chicago* (Chicago: Arcadia, 1999); Thomas A. Guglielmo, *White on Arrival: Italians, Race, Color, and Power in Chicago, 1890–1945* (New York: Oxford University Press, 2003); and Giovanni E. Schiavo, *The Italians in Chicago: A Study of Americanization* (Chicago: Italian American Publishing, 1928).

57. "Shoot Straighter," *Chicago Tribune*, August 5, 1933, 1.

58. Alan Dawley, *Struggles for Justice: Social Responsibility and the Liberal State* (Cambridge, Mass.: Belknap Press of Harvard University Press, 1991), 133.

Chapter 8: Aviation, Nationalism, and Progress

1. The epigraph for this chapter is from a cablegram from the foreign commissar of the Soviet Union sent via the Soviet Embassy to the U.S. Navy stratosphere balloon pilot Lt. Cmdr. Thomas "Tex" Settle to congratulate him on his successful flight into the stratosphere. Quoted in J. Gordon Vaeth, "When the Race for Space Began," *U.S. Naval Institute Proceedings* 89 (August 1963): 78.

2. This special triangular flight to Chicago was an extension of the ninth and final 1933 transatlantic crossing of the *Graf Zeppelin*. After flying from Germany to Brazil, the *Graf Zeppelin* made stops in Miami, Akron, Chicago, and Akron again before returning to Friedrichshafen, Germany, by way of Seville, Spain. Some of this chapter appeared in Cheryl R. Ganz, "The *Graf Zeppelin* and the Swastika: Conflicting Symbols at the 1933 Chicago World's Fair," *1998 National Aerospace Conference Proceedings* (Dayton: Wright State University, 1999), 56–66.

3. "Hoheitszeichen der Luftschiffe," *Reichsgesetzblatt* 77 (July 8, 1933): 457, *Graf Zeppelin* files, Dieter Leder collection, Meersburg, Germany.

4. *Chicago Tribune*, October 26, 1933, 4; LZA 016/385-6 Fahrtberichte LZ127 [logbook], 1933, Archiv der Luftschiffbau Zeppelin G.m.b.H., Friedrichshafen; Wilhelm von Meister, interview with author, Peapack, N.J., July 1976. As a result of the arrival time, the choice of the flight path, and the press's selections of which photographs to publish to represent this flight, the local population saw more images of the *Graf Zeppelin* with the swastika than without it. In flying a route that brought the airship toward Chicago from the east at daybreak, the *Graf Zeppelin* became a silhouette against the sunrise. Photographers could take photographs either of the shadow side of the airship over the lake or, as it made its circle over the fairgrounds and central business district, of the sunlit side, with the less photogenic elements of the city in the background. In order to photograph the *Graf Zeppelin* with the fairgrounds in the same image, one newspaper photographer flew in an airplane. He was able to capture the sunlit side of the *Graf Zeppelin* over the Chicago world's fair and as a result, his photograph showcased the swastika. The *Chicago Daily News* and the *New York Times* published these images, reaching yet a larger audience than the eyewitnesses. *Chicago Daily News*, October 26, 1933, 4–5; "Mid-Week Pictorial," *New York Times*, November 4, 1933, 7.

5. Edward Hungerford, *The Catalogue of the Centenary Exhibition of the Baltimore and Ohio*

Railroad, 1827–1927 (Baltimore: Centenary Exhibition of the Baltimore and Ohio Railroad, 1927); idem, *The Story of the Baltimore and Ohio Railroad, 1827–1927* (New York: Putnam, 1928); and idem, "T and T: The Iron Horse Plays at Showmanship," *Chicago Commerce* 26 (November 22, 1930): 8, 24–25. The pageant program *Wings of a Century: The Romance of Transportation* (Chicago: Neely Printing, 1933) identified Hungerford as the author and Helen Tieken for staging and direction. "Wings of a Century" script, folder 16-253, A Century of Progress records, UIC. For motion picture film of the pageant, see *A Century of Progress Exposition: Wings of a Century*, Burton Holmes Films, Inc., 1933. Hungerford later wrote *Railroads on Parade: A Pageant Drama of Transport* (New York: World's Fair Committee, 1939) for the 1939 New York World's Fair. For "Wings of a Century" folder 3-25 and scrapbook, see Helen Tieken Geraghty Theater Collection, UIC.

6. *Burlington Zephyr: The West Wind* (Chicago: Chicago, Burlington and Quincy Railroad, 1934); "Zephyr," July 12, 1934, folder 1-3062, A Century of Progress records, UIC; "Chicago to Greet Own Rail Masterpiece," *Chicago Commerce* 31 (May 1934): 18, 49; and Richard C. Overton, "The Zephyrs: Evolutionary or Revolutionary?" *Perkins/Budd: Railway Statesmen of the Burlington* (Westport, Conn: Greenwood, 1982). For film footage, see *Silver Streak*, Radio Pictures, 1934. The Chicago architects Holabird and Root consulted on the train's styling and the Hall of Science architect Paul Cret consulted on the interior treatment. For streamlining designs at the fair, see Barbara Hauss-Fitton, "Streamlining at the World's Fair: Chicago 1933/34—New York 1939/40," in *Streamlined: A Metaphor for Progress, the Esthetics of Minimized Drag*, ed. Franz Engler and Claude Lichtenstein (Baden, Switz.: Lars Müller, 1995), 68–77.

7. After World War II, Chicago renamed Municipal as Midway Airport. "Heavier-than-air" refers to aircraft technology that does not acquire lift from gases such as helium or hydrogen, known as "lighter-than-air."

8. Carl Mitman to Mr. Ravenel and Mr. Graf, May 15, 1931, Smithsonian Institution Archive, Washington, D.C.

9. At that time, United Airlines advertised eleven trips daily to New York City, lasting less than five hours, for $47.95 per ticket. *Chicago Daily News*, October 26, 1933, 4. See also Robert Van der Linden, *The Boeing 247: The First Modern Airliner* (Seattle: University of Washington Press, 1991).

10. Rufus Dawes to Smithsonian Institute, February 25, 1933, Smithsonian Institution Archive, Washington, D.C.

11. Frank M. Kennedy, "The Gordon-Bennett Balloon Race" and "Speed and Thrills at Chicago," *National Aeronautic Magazine* 11 (September 1933): 9–11; Fred Wallace, "The Air Race Controversy," *Popular Aviation* 13 (1933): 365–66.

12. Joseph J. Corn, *The Winged Gospel: America's Romance with Aviation* (Baltimore: Johns Hopkins University Press, 1983, 2001), x.

13. Ibid., 17–27.

14. For discussion about zeppelins, see Peter Fritsche, *A Nation of Fliers: German Aviation and the Popular Imagination* (Cambridge, Mass.: Harvard University Press, 1992); Henry Cord Meyer, *Airshipmen, Businessmen and Politics, 1890–1940* (Washington: Smithsonian Institution Press, 1991); and Guillaume de Syon, *Zeppelin! Germany and the Airship, 1900–1939* (Baltimore: John Hopkins University Press, 2002). For "airmindedness" see Corn, *The Winged Gospel*, 12. For studies of aviation and nationalism, see Michael Paris, *From the Wright Brothers to Top Gun: Aviation, Nationalism, and Popular Cinema* (Manchester, Eng.: Manchester University Press, 1995); and Edward M. Young, *Aerial Nationalism: A History of Aviation in Thailand* (Washington, D.C.: Smithsonian Institution Press, 1995).

15. Although the *Graf Zeppelin* was the 127th design of the Zeppelin Company, it was its 117th airship constructed.

16. "King of Wind and Wave," *Chicago Daily Times*, October 26, 1933, 5.

17. "Chicago, with its large German and very much larger foreign population, and with its comparative territorial remoteness from Europe, saw perhaps the strongest manifestation of this spirit" of German Americanism. John A. Hawgood, *The Tragedy of German-America: The Germans in the United States of America during the Nineteenth Century—and After* (New York: Putnam, 1940), 292.

18. Melvin G. Holli, "Teuton vs Slav: The Great War Sinks Chicago's German Kultur," *Ethnicity* 8 (1981): 431.

19. Melvin G. Holli, "German American Ethnic and Cultural Identity from 1890 Onward," in Holli and Jones, *Ethnic Chicago*, 93–109; Leslie V. Tischauser, *The Burden of Ethnicity: The German Question in Chicago, 1914–1941* (New York: Garland, 1990), 169.

20. See John Duggan and Jim Graue, *Commercial Zeppelin Flights to South America* (Valleyford, Wash.: J. L. Diversified, 1995).

21. See Hugo Eckener, *Informe Técnico y Económico de la Sociedad Constructora de Dirigibles "Zeppelin"* (Friedrichshafen, 1922). Seeking an East Coast base, Eckener negotiated to use the naval air station at Lakehurst, New Jersey, for the transatlantic service of the LZ129 *Hindenburg* in 1936–37.

22. *Chicago Daily News*, October 26 1933, 1.

23. U.S. Post Office—Commemorative Stamps file, B. F. Grove to Rufus C. Dawes, July 29, 1933, A Century of Progress records, UIC; Stamp Design File, National Postal Museum Library, Smithsonian Institution Libraries, Washington, D.C.

24. F. W. von Meister to F. M. Harpham, Vice President, Goodyear-Zeppelin Corporation, July 28, 1933, and F. W. von Meister to Paul W. Litchfield, President, Goodyear-Zeppelin Corporation, July 29, 1933, University Archives, University of Akron, Akron, Ohio; Meister interview.

25. Meister interview.

26. Memorandum of conversation between Secretary Hull and the German Chargé, Herr Rudolf Leitner, September 14, 1933, and Acting Postmaster General to Cordell Hull, September 18, 1933, National Archives, College Park, Maryland.

27. *Deutsche Bodensee-Zeitung* (Constance), October 6, 1933, 3.

28. The artists at the Bureau of Engraving and Printing used a 1929 photograph of the *Graf Zeppelin* from its landing at Mines Field in Los Angeles on the world flight. At that time the zeppelin carried no government flag on its fins. Stamp Design File, National Postal Museum Library, Smithsonian Institution Libraries, Washington D.C.; *Graf Zeppelin* postage stamp files, Bureau of Engraving and Printing, Washington, D.C.

29. *Chicago Daily News*, October 26, 1933, 1. In 1934, Eckener stated that the cost of operating the *Graf Zeppelin* was approximately $3.50 per mile. Hugo Eckener, "Speech to Federal Aviation Commission," 16, University Archives, University of Akron, Akron. See also, Cheryl Ganz, "United States Zeppelin Mail Rates," in *Via Airmail: An Aerophilatelic Survey of Events, Routes, and Rates*, ed. Simine Short with Cheryl Ganz (Chicago: American Air Mail Society, 1992), 69. On March 26, 1931, the Reichspost and Luftschiffbau Zeppelin agreed to the Zeppelin Company's share of the postal revenue: five-sixths of the total fees paid for mail carried by the airship. John Duggan, "Income from Carrying the Zeppelin Mail," *Zeppelin* 12 (February 1997): 12. For arrangements of the United States fees for this flight, see E. R. White to F. W. von Meister, Stamp Design File, National Postal Museum Library, Smithsonian Institution Libraries, Washington, D.C.

30. Otto L. Schmidt Papers, 15-1, CHM.

31. The German Americans sponsored and staffed the German American building only in 1933. The next year that same building instead housed the Brewery Exhibits. Nineteen thirty-four's fair also included a Black Forest Village concession, recreating a winter village setting and featuring strolling musicians in German mountaineer costumes and the carving of cuckoo clocks.

32. The German government cited economic distress as its reason for declining participation. James Clement Dunn, Chief, Division of International Conferences, Department of State, to Major Lenox R. Lohr, April 29, 1932, folder 2-764, A Century of Progress records, UIC. Because many members of the German government had expressed their desire to participate, as late as two weeks before the opening of the exposition fair officials were still trying to obtain Germany's official participation. Dr. H. F. Simon, German Consul General, to E. Ross Bartley, Director, Department of Promotion, May 18, 1933, folder 2-1036, A Century of Progress records, UIC.

33. The Mayo Foundation of Rochester, Minnesota, purchased the Transparent Man so that after the close of the fair it could be displayed in its museum. Carey, *Medical Science Exhibits*, 38–42, 50.

34. Jefferson Patterson, Assistant Chief, Division of Protocol and Conferences, Department of State, to J. V. Houghtaling, Supervisor of Nationalities Groups, May 29, 1934, folder 2-764, A Century of Progress records, UIC.

35. (Chicago) *Abendpost*, July 20, 1933, 1–4.

36. Sander A. Diamond, *The Nazi Movement in the United States, 1924–1941* (Ithaca, N.Y.: Cornell University Press, 1974), 115. In one of the Bund's Jew-baiting efforts, Charles G. Dawes was called Charles Davidson; ibid., 238.

37. (Chicago) *Sentinel*, August 3, 1933, 12.

38. Tischauser, *Burden of Ethnicity*, 192; Rudolf A. Hofmeister, *The Germans of Chicago* (Champaign, Ill.: Stipes, 1976), 80.

39. A Century of Progress scrapbooks box 43, A Century of Progress records, UIC.

40. (Chicago) *Abendpost*, August 12, 1933, 3.

41. Potential landing sites included the Municipal Airport (now Midway Airport), Forty-seventh and Lake Michigan, Washington Park, and Curtiss-Wright-Reynolds Field, a civilian airbase in Glenview.

42. Fair letter to James Clement Dunn, Chief of Protocol and Foreign Conferences, Department of State, September 1, 1933, folder 2-764, A Century of Progress records, UIC.

43. Hans Luther was a minister of finance, the German chancellor in 1925, and president of the Reichsbank before being appointed ambassador to the United States in March 1933.

44. U. Grant Smith to fair officials, October 6, 1933, folder 2-764, and Rufus Dawes, *Report of the President*, 79.

45. For details of German American conflicts in Milwaukee, see Dieter Berninger, "Milwaukee's German American Community and the Nazi Challenge of the 1930s," *Wisconsin Magazine of History* 71 (Winter 1987–88): 118–42.

46. *New York Times*, May 11, May 18, September 28, 1933, 7, 5, 2, respectively; and (Chicago) *Sentinel*, October 6, 26, 1933, 10.

47. James Farley, Postmaster General, to Cordell Hull, Secretary of State, October 23, 1933, National Archives, College Park, Maryland.

48. Hugo Eckener, *Im Zeppelin Über Länder und Meere: Erlebnisse und Erinnerungen* (Flensburg, Ger.: Verlagshaus Christian Wolff, 1949), 470.

49. Meister interview (quote); telegrams between Rufus C. Dawes and F. W. von Meister, October 24, 1933, folder 1-4943, A Century of Progress records, UIC; Eckener, *Im Zeppelin*, 470; and J. Gordon Vaeth, *Graf Zeppelin: The Adventures of an Aerial Globetrotter* (New York: Harper, 1958), 161–62.

50. Meister interview. Miami hosts likely reinforced the image of Americans dressed up in Wild West attire. A few days earlier they took the crew by omnibus to see an authentic western cabin. Georg Holl, "Tagebuch von Herrn Georg Holl" (Friedrichshafen, 1933), 5, Manfred Bauer Collection, Immenstaad, Germany.

51. General Frank Parker informed Rufus Dawes that even though he preferred not to have his

men assist in the landing, he would hold his men ready to perform the service if desired. Rufus C. Dawes to Ross Bartley, September 8, 1933, folder 2-764, A Century of Progress records, UIC.

52. J. E. Van Tijen, *Appendix I, Memorandum Regarding the Development of International Airship Traffic,* July 1934, University Archives, University of Akron, Akron, Ohio; and (Miami) *Herald,* October 22, 1933, 10.

53. Eckener, *Im Zeppelin,* 471–73.

54. *New York Times,* October 27, 1933, 7. In 1935 the (Chicago) *Abendpost* published a roster of 452 active German clubs in the Chicago area; Hofmeister, *Germans of Chicago,* 113.

55. *Seeblatt* (Friedrichshafen), October 24, 1933.

56. *Chicago Tribune,* October 27, 1933, 3.

57. (Chicago) *Abendpost,* October 27, 1933, 1.

58. Eckener, *Im Zeppelin,* 473.

59. Invitation and *Zeppelin Tag Fest Programm,* Cheryl R. Ganz Collection, Washington, D.C.

60. (Chicago) *Sentinel,* November 9, 1933, 13.

61. Theodore Light, interview with author, tape recording, Morton Grove, Ill., October 25, 1993.

62. *New York Times,* October 30–31, 1933; (Akron) *Times-Press,* October 30–November 1, 1933; Ernst A. Lehmann, *Zeppelin: The Story of Lighter-than-air Craft* (London: Longmans, Green, 1937), 306–8; Hermann Göring to Hans von Schiller, November 2, 1933, Archiv der Luftschiffbau Zeppelin G.m.b.H., Friedrichshafen; Hermann Göring to Obersteward H. Kubis, November 2, 1933, Cheryl R. Ganz Collection, Washington, D.C.; *Seeblatt* (Friedrichshafen), November 2, 1933; *Kreuz-Zeitung* (Berlin), November 3, 1933; Eckener, *Im Zeppelin,* 475.

63. Vaeth, *Graf Zeppelin,* 181.

64. For discussion of how National Socialists paradoxically rejected the Enlightenment and embraced technology at the same time—the crux of the conflict between the competing nationalisms of Hitler and Eckener—see Jeffrey Herf, *Reactionary Modernism: Technology, Culture, and Politics in Weimar and the Third Reich* (Cambridge: Cambridge University Press, 1984), 3, 13, 16. For discussion of ethnics and nationalism see Benedict Anderson, *Imagined Communities: Reflections on the Origin and Spread of Nationalism,* rev. ed. (New York: Verso, 1991); Walker Conner, *Ethnonationalism: The Quest for Understanding* (Princeton: Princeton University Press, 1994); Ernest Gellner, *Nations and Nationalism* (Ithaca, N.Y.: Cornell University Press, 1983); E. J. Hobsbawm, *Nations and Nationalism since 1780: Programme, Myth, Reality* (Cambridge: Cambridge University Press, 1995); and Anthony D. Smith, *Nationalism and Modernism: A Critical Survey of Recent Theories of Nations and Nationalism* (New York: Routledge, 1998).

65. "Association Gives Banquet for Dr. Eckener and *Graf Zeppelin* Crew," *Chicago Commerce* 24 (October 27, 1928): 16; "*Graf Zeppelin* a Welcome Sight to Chicagoans," *Chicago Commerce* 25 (August 31, 1929): 8.

66. In addition to backing the exposition, the *Chicago Daily News* and National Broadcasting Company sponsored the event. The latter provided radio equipment for the gondola.

67. Jean Piccard had suggested the name *Charles* after Jacques Charles, the first person to fly in a hydrogen-filled free balloon one hundred fifty years earlier. Jean Piccard, manuscript draft, "A Century and a Half of Ballooning, 1783–1933," 1933, folder 1-71, Piccard Family Papers, Library of Congress, Washington, D.C.

68. Auguste Piccard, *Auf 16,000 Meter: Meine Fahrten in die Stratosphäre* (Zürich: Schweizer Aero-Revue, 1933). Forest Ray Mouton, a former University of Chicago astronomy professor and director of concessions for the exposition, invited Auguste Piccard to design the balloon while he was on a lecture tour in the United States. Piccard drew his gondola designs on stationery at the Palmer House Hotel in Chicago. Part of the negotiations required that Piccard would not

attempt another flight himself until after the Chicago flight. Folders 1-62, 71, 73, Piccard Family Papers, Library of Congress, Washington, D.C.

69. Dow Chemical Company, folder 1-4762, A Century of Progress records, UIC.

70. Souvenir program, *The Piccard-Compton Stratosphere Ascension* (Chicago: A Century of Progress, 1933), Cheryl R. Ganz Collection, Washington, D.C.

71. Tex Settle served as the navy's chief inspector at Goodyear-Zeppelin during the construction of the airships *Akron* and *Macon*. He held licenses to pilot most types of aircraft and had won the international Gordon Bennett balloon race in Europe the previous year.

72. David E. McMillan Jr., "A Ringside View of the Compton-Piccard Fiasco," *Popular Aviation* 13 (October 1933): 223–24, 266–67.

73. Jean Piccard, "Our Stratosphere Flight," n.d., 1-62, 71, 73, Piccard Family Papers, Library of Congress, Washington, D.C.; and 1-73, Piccard Family Papers, Library of Congress, Washington, D.C.

74. The Soviet Union was not a member of the Fédération Aeronautique Internationale, which certified world flying records. Vaeth, "When the Race for Space Began," 77.

75. The gondola *A Century of Progress* is on display at the Museum of Science and Industry in Chicago.

76. Vaeth, "When the Race for Space Began," 68–78.

77. Irving E. Muskat, Chemistry Section, A Century of Progress, to Willard H. Dow, President, Dow Chemical Company, folder 1-4762, A Century of Progress records, UIC.

Epilogue

1. The epigraph for this epilogue comes from Rufus C. Dawes to Frank B. Jewett, March 14, 1936, Dawes Collection, NWU.

2. See *Chicago Daily News* and *Chicago Tribune*, November 1, 1934.

3. *Chicago Tribune*, November 1, 1934, 1.

4. Thomas Burke, *The History of the Ford Rotunda: 1934–1962, Dearborn's Pride of the Past* (Hicksville, N.Y.: Exposition Press, 1977), 15.

5. Annie E. Oliver to Rufus C. Dawes, January 26, 1935, and Rufus C. Dawes to Annie E. Oliver, February 2, 1935, folder 1-10956, A Century of Progress records, UIC; and "Du Sable Society to Show Cabin at Negro Fair," *Chicago Tribune*, August 18, 1940, S5.

6. Gray, *Guide to Chicago's Murals*, 248–49.

7. Archives Committee, *The Steelman Tradition* (Joliet: Joliet Township High Schools, Central Campus, 1988), and Dorothy Crombie, "Louise Lentz Woodruff Collection," Joliet Public Library, Joliet, Illinois.

8. World's Fair Scrapbooks, 1933–34, Cheryl R. Ganz Collection, Washington D.C.

9. The plaque is located on Pioneer Court between the Tribune Tower and the Chicago River just east of Michigan Avenue.

10. *Sally Rand Bubble Dance*, Rock Island, Ill., Tru-Vue, 1934, film strip.

INDEX

CHERYL R. GANZ is Chief Curator of Philately at the Smithsonian National Postal Museum. She was the curator and designer of the "Pots of Promise" exhibition for the Jane Addams Hull-House Museum, Chicago, and is coeditor, with Margaret Strobel, of *Pots of Promise: Mexicans and Pottery at Hull-House, 1920–30.*

The University of Illinois Press
is a founding member of the
Association of American University Presses.

———————————————————————

Composed in 10/14 Trump Mediaeval
with Twentieth Century display
by Jim Proefrock
at the University of Illinois Press
Designed by Dennis Roberts
Manufactured by Four Colour Imports, Ltd.

University of Illinois Press
1325 South Oak Street
Champaign, IL 61820-6903
www.press.uillinois.edu